Technology and Events

How to create engaging events

Dedication

To our family and to all who believed
and helped in the project of this book

Vanessa Martin and Luiz Cazarré

Technology and Events

How to create engaging events

Vanessa Martin and Luiz Cazarré

 Goodfellow Publishers Ltd

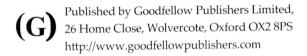

Published by Goodfellow Publishers Limited,
26 Home Close, Wolvercote, Oxford OX2 8PS
http://www.goodfellowpublishers.com

British Library Cataloguing in Publication Data: a catalogue record for this title is available from the British Library.

Library of Congress Catalog Card Number: on file.

ISBN: 978-1-910158-25-8

 Design and typesetting by P.K. McBride, www.macbride.org.uk

Cover design by Cylinder

Printed by Marston Book Services, www.marston.co.uk

Contents

Figures

Tables

Graphs

Foreword

The rapid rise of the technological revolution in the events industry has led to disruption as well as to enormous opportunities for new growth and greater attendee engagement. No one knows this better that Vanessa Martin and Luiz Cazarré, whose new book carefully analyses this massive shift from the world of 'or' to the world of 'and'.

Prior to the introduction of the internet, face-to-face meetings and events were often used as the primary communications tool for associations, corporations and other sectors. However, because of the development of the ubiquity of the Internet and greater WiFi and mobile accessibility, meetings and events today are often coupled with the virtual experience before, during and after the face-to-face experience.

According to Martin and Cazarré, this has led to the greatest opportunity in human history for deeper engagement and connection through events. This excellent new book literally takes you on a journey along the infobahn of high tech and high touch knowledge. The book begins with a careful definition and explanation of the importance of live events and then introduces the emerging role of technology and this is quickly followed by examples of the types of technologies that will enhance engagement for your event.

The book carefully describes how your event may benefit from incorporating various technologies before, during and after the face-to-face experience in order to enrich the experience of the attendee. This book is a treasure trove of knowledge, new techniques and easy to use ideas that will greatly improve the overall outcomes for your events in the future. By using this book to extend the reach of your event, you will be providing your organisation and your attendees with the opportunity to enter a new world of communications that I have described as "events without end."

The event without end is one that begins online as a virtual experience and as the connection deepens among the users, they feel a pull to become face-to-face participants. During the face-to-face participation, your attendees may then utilize technology to expand and deepen their experience through active engagement with the speakers and others at your event. Finally, following the face-to-face encounter, the relationship with fellow participants and others may continue ad infinitum, as the event truly has no end.

This extremely important and valuable new book is a prime example of how you may create events without end to improve the overall outcomes of your event and benefit your event-producing organisation. I commend

Vanessa Martin and Luiz Cazarré for researching and writing this profoundly important new book and encourage you to keep it within arm's reach as you accelerate and navigate upon the infobahn without speed limits that represents twenty-first century events without end. By using this most valuable new driver's manual, you will not only arrive safely but also reach a successful destination far ahead of your competitors.

Professor Joe Goldblatt, FRSA, EdD
Queen Margaret University
Edinburgh, Scotland

Preface

"For the first time in human evolution, the individual life is long enough, and the cultural transformation swift enough, that the individual mind is now a constituent player In the global transformation of human culture".

William Irwin Thompson.

We are proud and delighted to have Professor Joe Goldblatt write the foreword of our book. He has lectured in over 50 countries on five continents and is the author, co-author or editor of more than 20 books and hundreds of scholarly and trade publication articles. He was among the first inducted into the Events Industry Hall of Fame and received several others awards for his lifetime career achievements.

We wrote this book in order to support all those working in events organizations at any levelo, from the students to the most experienced professionals. Its challenge begins with its subject. We do not expect it to be a definitive work. The scale of the events industry, with hundreds of types and applications used by all economic sectors, as well as the scope of the application of technology in daily life and its constant and rapid evolution, make this task into one of the biggest challenges we have ever had as authors and professionals in the area.

All of our studies and research highlight the fact that technology has simplified mechanical activities as well as exponentially increased the potential for relationship and engagement, coupled with the targeted supply of quality content. The ability to capture, store, manage, study and extract intelligence from behavioral data from stakeholders has also increased in the same proportion.

That intelligence generates gains in the attractiveness, assertiveness and profitability of future events, making a continuous cycle of benefits to all involved, in which actions are controlled by the knowledge of the effect of their responses. As well as permeating all the phases of the event, it also extends of the residual value of the event and allows better tactical actions that support strategic decisions. It reiterates that the organization of events is not linear: it is cyclical and continuous.

By writing the book, our goal was to help you understand the key concepts and uses of communication technology in events and, for those readers who work directly or indirectly with events, to apply the content in their daily activities.

The notes at the end of each chapter list the websites and publications which served as a research base for the development of its contents. Those references can (and should) be explored by readers in order to become aware of the latest developments of each aspect covered in the book.

When we refer to online tools, apps, social media or software, we are referring to those which at the time of writing, in early 2016, were in greater use. We have put additional materials on the publisher's website for periodical update, enabling you to keep up to date with the evolution of tools to support event organizers.

This outlook for the future points strongly to the growth of demand for greater professionalization of events and gives greater relevance to the activities of meeting planners. We hope *Technology and Events* can help you transform your next event into a huge success!

Vanessa Martin & Luiz Cazarré

Section I

Concepts: Understanding Events and Technology

This section covers the most important concepts about the types of events and communication technology.

Chapter 1 – Events, what they are and why use them

- The concept of event
- Face-to-face, remote, online and hybrid events
- The stages: before, during and after
- The importance of technology in events.

Chapter 2 - Technology and events

- The concept of technology
- Social media and your event
- The key social media, apps and on-line tools for events
- Important resources and references
- How technology can help your event
- Where to start

Understanding Events

"Meetings provide a vastly richer, more targeted, and more focused learning experience than nearly any virtual meeting."

Corbin Ball

Introduction

As an efficient corporate tool, events can engage, involve and entice consumers like no other marketing tool can. Moreover, events accurately depict the scene, habits, consumption and trends of the historical moment in which they take place.

Technology has become an indispensable partner for meetings planners. This chapter presents the key concepts and benchmarks of the events segment and provides a brief introduction to the strengths that mark the firm relationship between events and technology.

Learning objectives

- To understand the concept and relevance of events today

- To learn about their main features and the concerns that organizers must have when working in the sector

- To highlight the most relevant connections that technology has imposed on events.

Events are present daily in all phases of life of a person and in all aspects, both personal and professional ones. Therefore, events are used for a multitude of reasons and goals by people and businesses in every industry and activity, of every size or purpose (social, commercial, economic, political, and so on). Every one of us has already commemorated or celebrated, more than once, some important events in life, such as weddings, births and anniversaries. Every company needs to advertise their products and / or services, or to participate in business events (meetings, conferences, trade fairs, and so on). Thus, events are part of society's daily life everywhere in the world and all the time.

In this feature lies the first major similarities between events and technology: their size and scope of usage. Both are intensely used by individuals and companies in all economic sectors all the time and for each and every purpose. In short, they involve everyone and everything, in every moment of daily activities, to the point of not being perceived in their entirety.

What is an event?

The vast coverage in its use makes it difficult to find a definition of events that satisfies everyone and brings together all the goals. The existing concepts usually incorporate the needs of an economic s ector, profession or even specific business areas. Due to the comprehensive nature of this book, the definition of events that will be used is as follows:

> *"The gathering or assembly of two or more individuals at the same place, in the same timeline, with common interests and specific goals, such as providing entertainment or leisure, purchasing products or hiring services; updating or divulging information; seeking improvement, harmonization or motivation in order to achieve or exceed targets; increasing participants' technical capacity; purchase of goods and ancillary equipment for the development of their professional activity, and so on."*[1]

In order to facilitate the understanding of the contents of this book and the reader's knowledge on the subject, there are two important concepts: typology and classification. The former can be defined in several ways. An easy analogy is to think of them as a math set, where everything that is contained in the set is typology and the line joining the typologies, forming and outlining a set, is the classification. Among sports events (classification), for example, various typologies can be found, such as Formula 1, the Olympics, championships, competitions and rallies. Thus, when a company says it holds social events (another classification), it means that it can perform both weddings and parties.

Each classification is related to the grouping of several typologies having a synergy between them, such as:

- By size, dimension or magnitude.
- By competition
- By show or exhibition
- By date or frequency
- By geographical coverage
- By category or a strategic role
- By the profile of the participants
- By goals or areas of interest
- By type of attendance

A single event can be classified into several categories at the same time. For example, Formula 1 is a championship (in terms of competition and also of objective or area of interest), worldwide (in terms of coverage), macro event (in terms of size, dimension or magnitude), with fixed dates and is held annually (in terms of date or frequency). It is an official event of the Formula 1 World Championship, which is the organization responsible for the category. The audience that sees the race is diverse (in terms of participant profile) and is not restricted in terms of admission, where it is only necessary to buy tickets in order to watch the races (in terms of type of attendees).

Events are true pictures of the historical moment in which they take place: the needs, demands and characteristics of all the stakeholders involved, the materials used, the venue, the typologies and formats of events and market dynamics clearly demonstrate the requirements and wishes of all parties involved. The market for events is also directly impacted upon by technology and consumer behaviour changes. Experts and research point to the continued evolution of this market, with an increase of digital solutions for events in all their phases. Further, as social media and applications for mobile devices (mobile apps) became more widely used, their incorporation in events is increasingly demanded. The growth of their use in events is one of the strongest trends for the sector. Other trends worth mentioning are the expectations of interacting participants, sharing opinions and having more complete information about other participants and the event content itself.

The dynamism and speed with which changes occur stimulate the disappearance or transformation of some typologies, while new ones are created. However, these transformations transcend this fact. As information is no longer the privilege of a few, the main value of technical and scientific events in now in relationship and networking, as well as in content, which is not provided as it used to be in the last century: in a rigid and ready to use format. Today, it is co-created by everyone involved in the events, thus

1

responding to the needs and desires of the different participating public. Therefore, the immediate demands of the market dictate and adapt the level of detail and depth, giving to all stakeholders a greater feeling of appropriateness and belonging. If in some circles people say that "content is king", in terms of events it can be said that "participants are the kings of content."

The typology of events is shown in Table 1.1.

Typologies		
Assembly	Course	Party
Auction	Debate	Performance
Autograph night	Dinner party	Premiere
Award	Election rally	Press conference
Barbecue	Exposition	Product launch
Bazaar	Fashion week	Promotion
Book launch	Festival	Raffle
Brainstorming	Forum	Rally
Breakfast	Gathering	Rave
Brunch	Graduation	Regatta
Business round	Gymkhana	Retrospective
Campaign	Happy hour	Road show
Carnival	Inauguration	Rodeo
Celebration	Journey	Round table discussion
Ceremony	Lecture	Seminar
Championship	Lunch	Show
Chorus	March	Show casing
Cocktail party	Mass	Soirée
Coffee break	Media conference	Tea party
Colloquium	Meeting	Teleconference
Competition	'Micareta'	Title granting
Concert	Motor show	Tour
Conclave	Olympics	Tournament
Conference	Open day	Trade fair
Congress	Open discussion	Video conference
Contest	Opening ceremony	Visit
Convention	Opera	Wedding
Cornerstone ceremony	Panel	Workshop
Council	Parade	

Table 1.1 : Types of events

Source: Martin, Vanessa. *Manual Prático de Eventos*. São Paulo: Elsevier. 2014. Page 47

Technology has brought profound changes to the daily life of individuals and corporations today. The events market has also adapted and renewed itself, creating new typologies and formats, taking advantage of the possibilities that technology can offer for performance improvement, commitment and results. Research conducted in 2015[2] showed the most commonly held events – see in Graph 1.1. This highlights the association events (performed by organizations and professional associations) and corporate (held by companies).

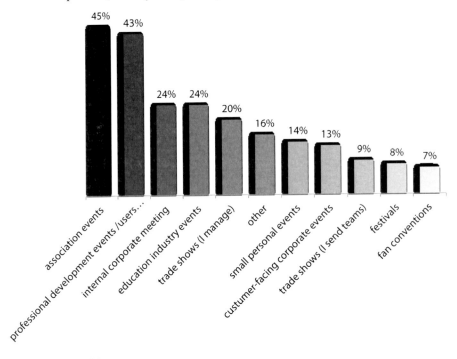

Graph 1.1: Events held
Source: www.eventinsight.com/document/the-state-of-mobile-event-technology-2015-uk/

Some changes that have taken place in new events are simple and particular, such as the PechaKucha®. It is a Japanese term (ペ チ ャ ク チ ャ) which means "chat"[3], designed in 2003 by Astrid Klein and Mark Dytham, from Tokyo Klein Dytham Architecture - kDa, for a presentation format in which the content is displayed automatically in 20 images lasting 20 seconds each, totalling six minutes and forty seconds. The PechaKucha Nights® is an informal and entertaining gathering, where people exchange ideas and experiences of leisure, study or work using that format.

TED (acronym for Technology, Entertainment and Design) is a non-profit foundation, established in the US in 1984[4]. It has become best known for its events, created for spreading ideas widely. Held since 1990, TEDx are local events programs, organized independently, with their performances recorded and limited to 16 minutes of duration. Publishing the videos via the Internet has ensured wide distribution and it is one of the reasons for its success (see Chapters 2 and 6). It is held in more than 130 countries[5], and is marked by a clean set design that highlights the figure of the speaker, and covers creative and different topics across all aspects of culture and science. Chapter 5 explains and exemplifies the visual web, a concept that contextualizes the use of images (photos and videos) to increase sharing, and to highlight information to consumers. That is a mega-trend that, once observed, is bound to help an event engage more participants, among various other advantages.

Events and corporate strategy

Events are essential strategic corporate tools for corporate communication, interaction, rapport, recognition, information, motivation, management, training and integration of consumers, employees, partners and suppliers, and also a product marketing and services channel. Research conducted by IMEX in 2015 shows that half of meeting planners surveyed believe the events have become much more strategic (Figure 1.1)

McDermott[6], CEO from SAP, contextualizes well such relevance in his testimony:

I've long believed in the power of pageantry to inform and inspire. Even in our digital age, bringing people together, in person, is essential to building great organizations. (…) There is no doubt that great things happen to companies and to economies when people come together face-to-face. From a dinner for 10 to a conference for 10,000, meetings are the places where brands are built and relationships are forged; where hearts are won and minds are opened; and where deals close and new opportunities emerge. I firmly believe the winners of tomorrow will be leaders who understand the power of pageantry and invest in that power today.

Figure 1.1 shows a survey conducted by IMEX 2015 on the opinion of meeting planners about events becoming more strategic. Almost all of them – 96% of respondents – believe that it represents the reality. That means that, as the prerequisite to make them more strategic lies in the greater professionalism of the players involved, customer demand for better results tends to become increasingly strong.

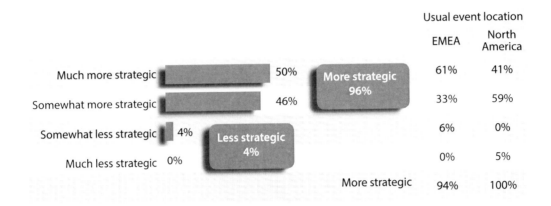

Figure 1.1: Events and corporate strategy

Source: Research *Event Planning & Mobile Technology*, IMEX. April/2015

Attendees now expect – and demand – a tailored, very interactive and all-inclusive experience at the event, an easy and fast way to find out and get additional content, real time updates, and tools to confirm meetings and to find exhibitors' stands.

As a result of a greater involvement of all stakeholders in the design of events, from its planning phase, throughout the execution and steps during and after the event, events have been increasingly viewed by the market as strategic tools. When one has the means to study, assess and respond directly to the demands of the public, in a specific way for each event, it is possible to act more strategically, focusing energy on what really is expected from the event in terms of presentation and delivery. This is reflected in events being increasingly customized to their audience, from the identification of the most suitable type and format, going through the many and different forms of communication, to the construction of the content that will be presented.

On the other hand, this increasing customization of events, which makes them naturally more strategic, means that ever-increasing levels of expertise in the various stages of their implementation are demanded from organizers. Thus, we see more and more specialized companies in certain types or categories of events. If before there was a higher frequency of events organized by the companies who own those events, now there is a growing increase in the use of outsourced agencies and / or specialized third parties. This also translates into greater speed and lower cost in terms of planning and production, generating economies of scale for the contractor. And, of course, more strategically aligned results, given the specific technological tools used by these specialized providers, which would otherwise be too expensive and complex to be used by the contracting companies, should they continue organizing their events internally.

For Caroline Carr[7] from WIRED Events, "

> *The challenge I see taking precedence in 2015 in the events industry is the*
> *need for more content marketing within our campaigns. I think marketers*
> *will need to be focused on three things – how to create better content, how*
> *to share greater content and how to better engage with their audience*
> *through this content."*

Her observations clearly reflect the greatest challenge of the event organizers today: how to use all the marketing and technological tools in order to create content that generates engagement among all stakeholders in events. It is a gigantic challenge that, when achieved, generates powerful results for the companies involved.

Currently, on the one hand people increasingly claim to have their individuality observed, respected and met; on the other hand, they constantly seek to interact with their peers, create and disseminate engaging content, which is the ultimate goal of any event. When organizers achieve this goal, they see their event not only achieve better immediate results, but also have a much higher survival rate, reaching sometimes to a "continuous life", where interaction among the participants does not come to an end between each edition. It is on the contrary strengthened in the intervals between them. Communication technology also plays an important role in this result.

Networking is more than a buzzword, as it is an objective, a desire and a result in itself. Networking, as well as the event itself, must be understood and implemented as an ongoing activity, which generates short, medium and long term results. Events must meet this market dictum, offering maximum opportunities to their participants. Technological tools enable networking to begin long before an event even takes place and to develop with maximum force during the event, at the stage where face-to-face meetings among participants happen and extend after the event comes to its end. There is no room for chance or fortuitous encounters. Professionalism of the sector and hence the search for better and better ratios of ROI and ROE (Return Over Engagement, which measures earnings, financial and/or strategic, earned by the generation of engagement between the participants in a given event), also boosts the ones related to networking, as shown in the testimony by Coutinho[8], co-founder of Meethub: *"According to studies, the 'Quality of Networking' is and will be the biggest factor that encourages delegates to attend events."*

After all, generating business events depends heavily on connecting with the right people, and it starts a long lasting relationship with advantages for all parts involved. At all event steps, organizers must ensure that they create as many networking opportunities as possible, and – most important of all – look for strategic networking. This means having profound knowledge of their public, understanding their needs and desires, and meeting them assertively, directly and dynamically. Currently the public looks to events much more in order to create networking and networking opportunities, besides differentiated and specific content on the topic discussed. If events had a role of disseminating information and specific culture in the past, today they have the obligation to facilitate the convergence of people with similar interests, generating better business and outstanding results.

One of the most significant changes in the typology of events, and also the most representative one in the Age of Knowledge, is the *hybrid meeting*, detailed in this chapter.

Regardless of the type chosen, one of the most efficient and productive ways to develop an event project is to define its backbone, to which the entire project will be subject: a clear identification of goals, needs and results desired by the customer, followed by detailed profiles of the direct participants (face-to-face) and indirect (virtual). When the project is established in this sequence, its preparation tends to be much more creative and efficient, enabling the meeting planner to find different possibilities from other components, such as types of events, format, schedule, venue and so on. Thus, the chances of the project being balanced and able to produce results perfectly aligned with the needs of customers and participants are increased. The choice of date, time and estimates of revenue complement the basic components in this first phase. At the end of this chapter, the *Practical Guide of the Chapter* shows a summary of the initial steps of an event project and the guidelines of goals and nee ds, which should not only be followed, but also harmonious among themselves.

Event Track 2015, the fourth annual edition of the Event Marketing Institute and Mosaic EventTrack, conducted a brand and consumer survey among Fortune 1000 companies. The key findings and insights are shown in Table 1.2. Since 2012, the top goals and strategies for experiential marketing have been to 'increase brand awareness' and 'drive sales'. Although 'Reduce price sensibility' got only 14% interest, this represented a rise of 250% from the previous year. Two other goals and strategies increased over 63% from 2014: 'Identify and develop influential consumer brand ambassadors' (B2C and B2B). The goal 'Conduct research, learn' rose almost 37%.

So far, this study shows that companies' most important strategies are focused on understanding consumer behavior and how to engage with them: 65% state that their event and experiential programs are correlated to sales, an increase of 10.2% from 2014.

The explanation might be on another insight: 'inclination to purchase as a result of attending'. 98% of respondents said participating at the event or experience made them more inclined to purchase. It is also relevant that

74% said that events and experiences positively improve brand perception. Additionally, 65% confirm the purchase of the product or service promoted at the event (35% increase from 2014), and 87% said they purchased it after the event at a later date. (59% more than the year before)

Event and Experiential Marketing Goals and Strategies	Years			
	2012	2013	2014	2015
Increase / create brand awareness	73%	79%	78%	81%
Increase sales	83%	77%	79%	79%
Enhance product knowledge and understanding	53%	58%	52%	62%
Influence deeper customer involvement	48%	52%	51%	57%
Launch new products	48%	50%	59%	55%
Gather leads	48%	58%	49%	50%
General media impressions / press coverage	38%	34%	39%	45%
Build prospect database	45%	44%	38%	41%
Increase website traffic or Facebook 'Likes', social media activity	34%	36%	31%	40%
Conduct research, learn	23%	22%	17%	26%
Identify, develop influential consumer-based brand ambassadors	22%	18%	23%	24%
Identify, develop influential B2B brand ambassadors	17%	22%	12%	20%
Increase effectiveness of other media	16%	19%	11%	18%
Reduce price sensitivity	10%	8%	4%	14%

Table 1.2: Event and experimental marketing goals and strategies
Source: Event track 2015 Report. http://www.eventmarketer.com/wp-content/uploads/2015/05/2015 EventTrackExecSummary.pdf

To get free samples or other giveaways (81%) and to get a discount or special offer (54%) both motivate event participation. However, 'to learn about the product or service being promoted' (49%) showed an increase of 12% from the previous year.

Other answers also reinforce the importance of the event as corporate strategy:

■ When asked what most influenced the purchase decision: 80% said they 'sampled, used and saw a demonstration of the product/service and liked it'; and 57% answered that they 'had a better understanding of the product/service from the event'.

■ Most consumers (87%) consider that live events are more effective than commercials in helping to understand a product and service.

The importance of communication technology

The growth of the virtual world and use of apps, affects almost all aspects of personal and professional tasks. The rapid development of social media and mobile technologies are leading to a significant change in the habits of consumers. The rise of digital companies and the constant launch of new products are causing deep changes in how people interact with one another and how they use the technology. Regardless of the use, all offer personalized experiences and great facilities for their users.

The increasing use of mobile devices, such as smartphones and tablets, encourages greater interaction between the stakeholders of an event, allowing a better experience, easy access to content, and much more interactivity (see Chapter 2). Users require applications that provide easy usability and functionality to match their needs. As devices become even more essential for consumers, mobility is having a profound impact in all phases of events, as shown throughout this book. One aspect worth mentioning is the growing importance of digital over traditional marketing, as digital marketing is customized, structured and targeted, based on recent purchasing habits, geomarketing and interests, among other factors (see Chapters 5 and 6).

Meetings Program Categories	From				
	North America	Europe	Central/South America	Asia	Global Hoteliers
Budget Challenges	3.4% ▲	3.1% ▲	1.7% ▲	3.8% ▲	2.6% ▲
Safety & security	1.8% ▲	2.2% ▲	2.4% ▲	2.6% ▲	2.3% ▲
Local Meetings	2.7% ▲	4.1% ▲	4.2% ▲	0.0% ▶	2.8% ▲
Destination driven meetings	0.9% ▲	0.6% ▲	2.0% ▲	0.8% ▲	1.4% ▲
Family friendly meetings	1.3% ▼	2.2% ▼	2.5% ▼	1.5% ▼	0.0% ▶
Adding meeting content to incentive trips	1,30% ▲	1.2% ▲	2.3% ▲	2.4% ▲	2.3% ▲
CSR / Charitable activities	2.0% ▲	0.0% ▶	0,90% ▲	1.4% ▲	1.3% ▶
Green paperless meetings	2.4% ▲	0.0% ▶	0,00% ▶	1.5% ▶	1.8% ▶
Use of social media	4.0% ▲	2.5% ▲	1.3% ▲	3.2% ▲	5.6% ▲
Use of mobile apps / meeting specific apps	4.9% ▲	3.2% ▲	2.6% ▲	4.0% ▲	6.1% ▲

Table 1.3: Global trends in events

Source: 2014 report from American Express Meetings & Events, 2014.

The report *2014 Meetings Forecast by American Express Meetings & Events* pointed to the main trends of the events sector (Table 1.3). Besides the strong growth in local events, the report also highlights the triumph of technology, with increased global interest in the use of social media and mobile apps with specific use for events. The interest in learning how to better use them at events is growing more and more.

The demand from customers for events that have a platform to integrate registration, reporting, event surveys, payment gateways, social meetings, speakers and abstract submissions, floor plans and so on, is also getting increasingly high.

This revolution is mainly led by the demands of the Millennials, the new generation of consumers (those born between 1980 and 2000), who have specific demands. As Harrington (one of the Millennials) says, *"To be of value to me, a meeting should include leading-edge technology. I would describe my ideal meeting or event as a mixture of entertainment and education, motivation and meaning."*[9] Their requests:

1   They need to engage.

2   They want to know that organizers are listening to them.

3   They want to be part of the conversation about what they are learning

4   They need to have variety in session format in order to keep their attention

5   They prefer games that have the goal of collective accomplishment rather than personal competition

6   They have a distinct preference for experiences over tangible items.

7   They expect recognition and rewards customized to their preferences and in short time frames.

■ Event apps

The key takeaway of the State of Mobile Event Technology 2015[10], a survey among 500 event professionals, confirms that most of them (91%) had a positive ROI when implementing an event app and that attendees demand or expect a tailored and interactive experience at all events they attend. Figures 1.2 to 1.5 shows that attendee satisfaction is a top priority for most organizers. Most of them, 86%, think an event app had a positive effect. For them, event apps are cost effective and environmentally friendly, add extensive value to the attendee experience and can be integrated into the registration process; as they operate in real-time, updates and notifications can be easily delivered before, during, and after an event. This facilitates and encourages communication, one of the strongest demands from the Millennials, and allows event organizers to learn a lot about an individual attendee's needs and preferences. According to the report, event organizers interviewed think the following about apps:

- They create an outstanding experience and measure attendee satisfaction.

- They inspire and allow new opportunities for sponsors.

- They offer real-time updates, customization and relevant data capture.

- They represent only 1.2% of the budget for each attendee (paper printing is twice as expensive).

- Almost 1/3 of organizers said they spent more money on apps because it is on top of latest trends and they can get more sponsorships and partnerships.

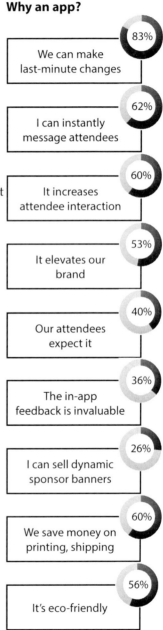

Why an app?

83% We can make last-minute changes

62% I can instantly message attendees

60% It increases attendee interaction

53% It elevates our brand

40% Our attendees expect it

36% The in-app feedback is invaluable

26% I can sell dynamic sponsor banners

60% We save money on printing, shipping

56% It's eco-friendly

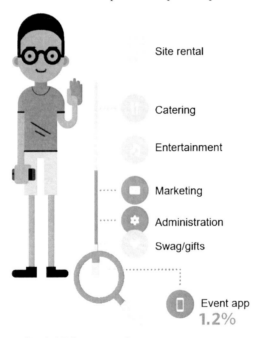

Site rental

Catering

Entertainment

Marketing

Administration

Swag/gifts

Event app
1.2%

Figure 1.2: (Right) Why an app?

Figure 1.3: (Above) How much does an event app cost?

Source: The State of Mobile Event Technology 2015 – UK. Guidebook. Layout adapted by authors

1

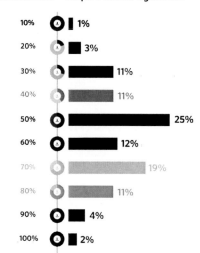

Download rate   Require this for a good ROI

10% 1%
20% 3%
30% 11%
40% 11%
50% 25%
60% 12%
70% 19%
80% 11%
90% 4%
100% 2%

Figure 1.4: (Right) How many downloads do you need in order for an app to be a good investment?

Figure 1.5: (Below) What makes a successful event?

Source: The State of Mobile Event Technology 2015 – UK. Guidebook. Layout adapted by authors

What makes a successful event?

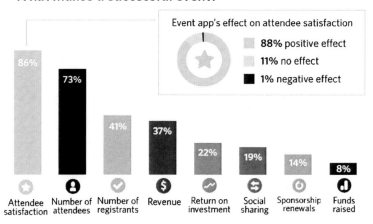

Event app's effect on attendee satisfaction

■ **88%** positive effect
■ **11%** no effect
■ **1%** negative effect

| 86% | 73% | 41% | 37% | 22% | 19% | 14% | 8% |

| Attendee satisfaction | Number of attendees | Number of registrants | Revenue | Return on investment | Social sharing | Sponsorship renewals | Funds raised |

For Gabriel[11], when technology is used, it allows the reorganization of society and in this new degree of organization new possibilities, new solutions emerge. In her opinion[12], the current education moved from the Information Age to the Age of Innovation: as the main changes provided by technologies were fragmentation and decentralization, more and more people talk directly with one another.

This model greatly accelerated the speed of changes, which now take place much faster than in the past. Thus, education and content spread require other skills, such as creativity, critical thinking, connection and reflection. Taking ideas and tips from the event industry, we get interesting concepts and applications:

■ Organizers must always be aware of the new emerging Technologies, the extent they can help and the opportunities they can bring to the industry.

■ Think of a wider business, one that includes people at the event and/ or anywhere in the world. Such a model can be paid, free or mixed, later on enticing more participants into the event. The event should provide an environment of trading and collaboration, to reflect on how it can favour the dynamics of the event and the environment outside it.

■ When the learning process changes, it changes everything around. The event needs to restructure itself and find its place in this new ecosystem.

■ Younger people master technology much more thoroughly than most speakers, who may only master a part of it. It is suggested that you embrace the new things that the young know, that you learn from this and reflect upon it, to coordinate information, and connect with different types of subjects.

■ The venue is no longer just physical and is giving way to hybrid events (virtual to physical). The more you open the range of con-nection and collaboration possibilities inside and outside the event environment, facilitating the training and monitoring groups of interest related to the topic of the event, the more the dynamics of belonging will be facilitated. To achieve that you should think about the event structure and use technologies that can integrate the online and offline environments.

Hybrid events

A hybrid event is the combination of face-to-face and virtual. For Vanneste[13]

A hybrid meeting is a meeting where a group of people in a face to face meeting in one location are connected to / joined by individuals or groups in different locations. They help to get people more or less together with limited accommodation cost, travel cost and travel time. It enables meetings that otherwise would be impossible to organize due to time restraints, calendars or cost. Like a hybrid car combines a fuel engine and an electric engine, a hybrid meeting combines a real with a virtual meeting, a face to face meeting with remote participants.

The main advantages of using it, are the increase in the life cycle of the event and the possibility of reaching an audience that would not be possible to contact by another format, thus exponentially enhancing the number of people reached.

For Pfeilsticker[14] from Hybrid Events Authority, a hybrid meeting is not appropriate for networking, sensitive issues, celebrations and collaborative team building. However, it can be better used for:

- Company updates

- New product launches/updates

- Internal meetings

- Sales updates

- Staff/project meeting

Box 1.1 shows a hybrid event held in England and three other countries. See Chapter 8 for more information on hybrid events.

To improve a hybrid event, she suggests that:

- The event design should start by working with a regular agenda and reconstructing it.

- After that, virtual providers/partners (streaming, platform and production or an A V company) should be chosen.

- The majority of your hybrid meeting budget (89%) it will be on streaming, platform and A/V.

- In order to promote, choose demo videos, emails, social media, website and reminders before the event.

- For virtual engagement, do not give the virtual audience an opportunity to get distracted and leave the event: offer additional and useful extra content or information during the breaks: private chats, social media activities, etc.

- After that maintain communication between virtual providers/ partners (streaming, platform and production or an A/V).

Like Pfeilsticker, the traditional view of hybrid events is that they are more appropriate to certain types of events than others, but the fact is that, rather than choosing the shape of the face to face or virtual event, the ideal is to always think of a combination of both, through the so- called 'hybrid events'. The most common uses of hybrid events nowadays are in educational, medical conferences, class and business associations. This is possible because it is easy for hybrid events to welcome participants from all over the world, who can relate virtually with what is happening in the physical environment, both to extract information and knowledge, and to mobilize them.

Box 1.1: The Global Medical Experts Meeting

By Maarten Vanneste

The case

The medical world of oncology gathers experts in three countries, plus another one where the Chairman and a technical team conducted the event.

The time set aside for this meeting was two hours and the time difference was up to 12 hours, providing great opportunities for unique content, involvement, sharing and connection. Each city (London, Buenos Aires, Hong Kong and Seoul) had its own appropriate meeting room called a hub, and the objectives of this hybrid meeting were: to make each location learn from the other; to increase connections among individuals and to create collaboration in a research project.

The program

The two hours were split over three interactive presentations (one for each country). Each was planned to be 30 minutes plus some extra time for the introduction and the closing moments.

Every presentation was done live and by a speaker present in each location. It included 'plenary' discussion time, some voting and time for questions. Besides the plenary activity, a discussion system on laptops was used for parallel discussions, in break-out groups.

The chair

The chairman was a top and very busy surgeon who works in London. We worked alone, on the fourth location, but connected to three groups 6 hours before and 6 hours after him in time.

The connections

To have a good connection between all the groups in the different countries and to engage participants, the use of all possible channels is needed. Interaction is a challenge in a normal conference or meeting, but with participants spread over four countries this needs some extra care.

Video

The highest emotional bandwidth (see Banzwidth in https://prezi.com/jutuwu8pi0lb/ma-in-8-chapters/) after face to face contacts is good video contact. The ABBIT team provided a multi-camera setup connected in a zero delay environment with the possibility to share the presentation from any location. During discussions, everyone could see the person that was speaking. For cost reasons, every location had only robot cameras so no cameramen are needed.

The chair in London starts and moderates discussions, interrupts speakers for clarification, concludes and introduces the next speaker.

Discussion

Sound is extremely important and having a lip-synch video and zero delay in the sound makes discussions and conversations possible. For presentations, a delay is not an issue, but as soon as a discussion starts, sound delay can be a project killer. All speakers had a wireless microphone for presenting and all participants a push to talk conference microphone. Anyone who speaks in any location at any time is heard in all other locations. Just as if all people were in the same room.

Buenos Aires – 6 hrs

London control centre at 0 hrs

Hong Kong at + 5hrs

SEOUL AT +6hrs

Voting / ARS

A well-known technique to get interaction among participants and to create valuable output from a group is a voting system or Audience Response System (A.R.S.). In this case, every participant in every location had a keypad.

As soon as the question appeared on the screen, everyone could start to vote and the number of votes (from all countries) was visible so anyone could see it go up. After about ten seconds, the Chair decided to close the vote.

Immediately the results of all votes from all countries would become visible to any participants in any country. Very fast and with immediate demographic split per discipline or per country if needed.

Text discussion system

To create virtual break out rooms to discuss several topics, the Discussion system was installed. This linked a number of laptops and an on-line system, and covered several topics. At a given moment all the surgeons from all the countries could 'meet' in one room and have a discussion about a specific topic. At another time in the session, multi-disciplinary teams with participants from different countries could discuss about a case they would choose out of a list.

The control centre

The control centre in this case was in London. The figure on the right (Box1g.jpg) show a view from the fourth location in London showing the conference chair, the client, the chief technician and the chair assistant / facilitator with the discussion system. In the background, at a fifth location the voting technician was working from the ABBIT offices.

The headquarters were in a constant parallel communication with all technicians to get them ready for the next cue in the script. In the headquarters, the chair had his own camera and microphone so he could interrupt a speaker, ask a question or start a discussion. The chair had a countdown system and the facilitator helped counting down every presentation, communicating with the chair via cards. The back-up presentations were available in London just in case. The discussion sessions were started by the chair and the facilitator. The sound levels were controlled, presenter rights given to the country that needed them, cues given to switch etc. by the chair and facilitator.

Conclusions

■ As everything worked well, this hybrid event really gave to all participants a great feeling of engagement: real discussions happened, great ideas were shared, voting was fast and complete, the text-based discussion delivered good output. In many ways this was a more dynamic meeting than a traditional meetings (one location/ expert).

- Roughly calculated, this hybrid format saved about €100k in travel and accommodation. Maybe, even more important is the fact that about 150 professionals didn´t have to leave hospital for days, plus several dozens of operations and other cancer treatments did not have to be postponed.

- The format fulfilled its objectives by learning from presentations, discussions and networking.

- Sound was extremely important and having a lip-synch video and zero delay allowed good discussions and conversations.

- For presentations, a delay is not an issue, but as soon as a discussion starts, sound delay can be a project killer. All speakers had wireless microphones and all participants a push-to-talk conference microphone. Anyone who spoke in any location, at any time, was heard by all other locations, just as if everyone was in the same room.

For Cross[15], hybrid events will be one of the biggest event trends, but a great hybrid event demands hard work to engage and involve virtual attendees. She describes extra elements that you should bear in mind and 10 important aspects of a hybrid event:

1 **Be prepared** - Test in advance slides, video and background information and ensure the speakers will understand how important it is to respect deadlines and to know well the system that will be used.

2 **Rehearse** – Ensure that cameras are well located and positioned and the speakers are well briefed, comfortable and familiar with the technology used

3 **Strong facilitation** – a well briefed facilitator can be crucial and a great link between live and virtual delegates. Although, for Cross the best option is to have two dedicated roles, if you can. Then, ensure it is clear for both the agree signals and protocol for timing, feedback, questions and comments for all delegates.

4 **Acknowledge on the online audience** – during introduction, welcome the virtual attendees, as well as the live ones. Involve them. Let them know they are part of the event too: share details about the online participants (how many are watching, from which countries they are from, etc) and mix questions from attendees online and live.

5 **Think specifically about the online perspective** – Think carefully for continuous content even when the conference is on a break: She suggests that you "schedule in interviews, feedback and additional behind the scenes content; never leave your online participants looking to an empty conference room."

6 **Use social media** – Ensure you have a great strategy to get your live and virtual attendees involved and encourage them to do plenty

of activities. Twitter is the best platform to connect and facilitate conversations and feedback

7 **Keep to time** – When providing a live stream is even more vital to keep it to schedule.

8 **Engagement and interaction** - Remember that the online viewer may be watching alone and not able to discuss the content with another colleague, as live attendees can. Include them on discussion by polls, voting, submitting questions and ask them to respond via a comments tab or social media. Give them feedback of the highlights from each table or subject.

9 **Dress code** – Avoid heavily patterned or striped clothing.

10 **Capture the spirit of the event** – Have in mind to give to online participants a valuable insight of the event. Physical attendees enjoy more real benefits and value than online participants, like networking opportunities and personal connections. But a hybrid event "can broaden your audience and exposure, offer an international perspective and provide a richer experience for everyone involved." She also points out that "there is some emerging evidence from a number of events of a high conversion rate from virtual attendees to actual loyal delegates at future events", since the online ones can be motivated to become live attendees.

The Association of Corporate Travel Executives (ACTE)[16] confirms this evidence among the members, who list education as the number one reason to attend their global conferences:

62% of attendees said this experience makes it more likely they will attend a future ACTE event face-to-face	**30%** of countries were represented at the virtual conference, creating a sense of a global community.	**60%** of virtual attendees were non-members, creating a new avenue for ACTE member generation.	**85%** of attendees rated the event as excellent or above average for experience and content.

However, as time restraints, lack of budget, and travel restrictions inhibit some delegates to attend live events, they decided to increase the face-to-face attendance and to expand their community, by offering content in live and complementary virtual conference attendance to members and non-members. They decided to start by offering a few sessions from the conference. Another smart step was to greet the members logged into the conference by a welcome video that gave them a quick acquaintance with the navigation.

If your event wants to embrace a difference-making mission in its efforts to break down the financial and physical barriers and to increase the number of members and to offer great quality sessions, hybrid events must be the best way.

Chapter summary

Richardson[17] clearly defines the relevance of technology for events:

> *Event technology is at the heart of our business, but when talking with customers we put it aside to get to the bottom of what their aims and objectives are, and then explore the best ways to achieve this. Technology should be a facilitator in the process, it can add novelty and interest, and slickness and sophistication, but to be really effective it should not be the 'thing' itself.*

Therefore, meeting planners should be familiar with new emerging technologies and their applications to participants anywhere in the world. By clearly identifying what they want to achieve and promote, as well as the physical and the virtual settings of the event, they will be able to find the best way to create environments that can meet and even exceed the desired goals.

In an increasingly global business environment, the ability of the participants to attend personally all events that interest them is more and more unfeasible, especially due to budget constraints. Therefore, as shown above, hybrid events appear as the best solution in these cases, to provide individuals who cannot – or do not wish – to move to the physical event, the ability to participate virtually in the event.

The broadcast of events via web platforms greatly amplifies the impact of the event, with an additional cost that is marginally quite low. On the other hand, it should be noted that the assembly of a hybrid event, although it is becoming easier, still presents some difficulties. As technological requirements are added, there is a need to plan the event strategically from the start in order to deliver outstanding content and networking opportunities. The participation of specialized suppliers in the creation and transmission of specific content for the web channel is necessary to achieve maximum results in this type of events.

When starting your operations in hybrid events, do it with just a few sessions. Evaluate and enhance the experience of the online participant in the next edition, and increase the number of sessions to be offered in a sustainable and progressive manner.

Practical guide to the chapter

Here is the roadmap of the essential steps described in the chapter, for practical application in your daily activities:

Item	Description
Objectives and customer needs (What)	Reasons for and/or results that are to be achieved with the event
Target audience (Who)	Clear identification of direct (in person) and indirect (virtual) public
Type, format and event schedule (How)	Event type and format that can obtain the best results and meet or exceed the goals set
Date and time (When)	Most propitious day and time for achieving the goals
Revenue (How much)	Estimates of revenue

For further reading, questions for reflection and additional materials please go to the book's page at the publisher's website:

www.goodfellowpublishers.com/technologyandevents

Notes

1   Martin, V. (2014) *Manual Prático de Eventos*. 2nd edn. São Paulo: Elsevier.

2   http://www.eventinsight.com/document/the-state-of-mobile-event-technology-2015-uk/ [19 Jun 2015]

3   http://www.pechakucha.org/ [06 Feb 2015]

4   http://pt.wikipedia.org/wiki/TED_(confer%C3%AAncia) [20 Apr 2015]

5   http://tedxtalks.ted.com/ [20 Apr 2015]

6   http://www.cnbc.com/id/102594122?utm_source=myQaa&utm_campaign=4cfeba91d9-Monthly_Picks_April_30_2015&utm_medium=email&utm_term=0_c03352e6c2-4cfeba91d9-76381877 [06 May 2015]

7   Research "30 experts predict the event trends that will shape your 2015". Eventbrite. 2015.

8   Research "30 experts predict the event trends that will shape your 2015". Eventbrite. 2015.

9   http://meetingsnet.com/site-files/meetingsnet.com/files/uploads/2014/10/MeetingsNetsMillennialSecrets_2014a.pdf [12 Dec 2015]

10 http://www.eventinsight.com/document/the-state-of-mobile-event-technology-2015-uk/ [19 Jun 2015]

11 Gabriel, M. TEDx FIAP. Tecnologias do Futuro, 2013. https://www.youtube.com/watch?v=E0PtC0IhLjw [20 Nov 2015]

12 Gabriel, M. (2013) *Educ@r: a revolução digital na educação.* São Paulo : Saraiva

13 Vanneste, M. Interview with authors.

14 www.prolibraries.com/player/?libname=virtualedge&sessionID=246# [23/06/15]

15 www.eventmanagerblog.com/tips-preparing-hybrid-event [28 Nov 2015]

16 reach.inxpo.com/rs/924-COQ-679/images/ACTE-Case-Study-Tips.pdf [19/11/15]

17 http://www.eventmagazine.co.uk/blog-technology-facilitator/event-technology/article/1374921?bulletin=event-the-weekend-edition-bulletin&utm_medium=EMAIL&utm_campaign=eNews%20Bulletin&utm_source=20151128&utm_content [19/11/15]

2 Communication Technology and Events

"the press is an army of 26 tin soldiers with which you can conquer the world."

Johannes Gutenberg,

Introduction

To fully understand the impact that technology currently has and will have on the organization of events is paramount to all involved in this segment. There have never been so many possibilities of integration for all players involved in events, be they organizers, suppliers or participants.

Learning objectives

- To name and detail the current uses of technology applied to events, as well as to infer the probable or possible future technological platforms.

- To allow readers to choose, apply and measure any relevant forms and technology platforms to their work, in all their stages.

What is technology?

Today's consumers care more about experiences than about material goods. As technology simplifies the lives of ordinary people and makes chores easier, when it comes to events, it must be used to manage and improve the experience of their participants, promote inclusion and integration, enable and encourage co-creation of content, continuous learning and sharing those experiences, as well as to manage and reduce costs and optimise revenues.

We are in the era of new connections, new behaviours and new opportunities. Among the 10 most important consumer trends identified by *Trend Watching*[1] for 2015 are the Internet of Things and the Economics of Sharing, which will stimulate the exchange of goods in more spontaneous, helpful, fun and profitable ways. Those trends, which are already happening, are related to the increasing number of objects that have become connected. When we speak of connected objects, we analyse the most common and prosaic ones (in today's environment), such as smartphones (which have become true pocket computers with the communication, management and sharing tools of PCs), household items such as television sets, video games and even refrigerators, means of transport such as cars (more and more connected), as well as 'wearables' (such as wristwatches, which also allow full Internet connection, from the most varied platforms and locations.)

This daily technology immersion scenario and all its possibilities of connectivity and interaction enable new ways of deriving value from those connectivity objects through shared access. The quest for well-being, new knowledge and skills becomes increasingly strong by consumers, who embrace rewards offered through devices that promote improvements in terms of relationship, such as turning the time of payment into a moment of pleasure.

Payment via smartphones is already a reality in some countries, and that is an increasingly accessible and common trend. In the near future, the vast majority of personal business transactions will be carried out through smartphones, which will take the place that today is occupied by physical, plastic credit cards. Also related to the above, another notable trend is the *Sympathetic Price*[2] or the price of sympathy – the price of caring for the fellow man, of the solidarity. It indicates creative ways of giving discounts that can help alleviate problems or difficult times for the fellow man.

Google's CEO Larry Page's phrase "We are no longer in a mobile-first world, we are in a mobile-only word"[3], describes well the profound social transformation that happens in the relationship between mankind and technology in all aspects and areas.

In many societies, especially among the poorest segments, mobile devices, mainly smartphones, are the gateway to the digital world. Content consumption, access to news and interactions among people via social media find in those little technological platforms a channel to flow needs and desires that gets swollen every day. Today it is already possible to perform almost all the commercial and social transactions that one wants using mobile devices and applications of several different types, from any location, easily and securely.

This revolution in communications, reported throughout this book, has completely changed the ways of conducting relationships, are including professional ones, affecting directly and strongly the events market.

When we look at the geographical distribution of Internet use around the world (Graph 2.1), we also notice a strong inequality. However, when it comes to Internet access for professional/commercial use, this current distribution does not represent a problem, since large cities, which are the centers of the vast majority of business events, have extensive broadband Internet coverage. It is worth saying that the Wi-Fi offer in venues for events is still of poor quality in some locations, given the growing demand of visitors to events. According to some experts, it is common that the technological structure of connection at events is still faulty, though it has been improving in terms of quality at an exponential rate.

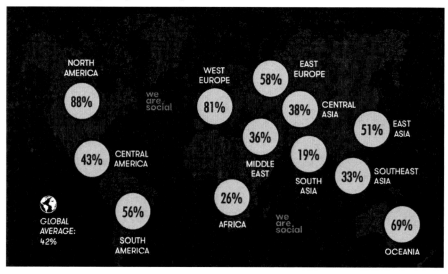

Graph 2.1: Internet use, geographical distribution
Source: http://wearesocial.net/blog/2015/01/digital-social-mobile-worldwide-2015/ 21 Dec 2015

Time spent online worldwide is rapidly growing, which clearly demonstrates the growth in terms of importance of access to communication and interaction platforms among people. It is noteworthy that among working age people, the time spent online is higher, a clear sign of the importance of using technology in all environments and times of work (Graph 2.2).

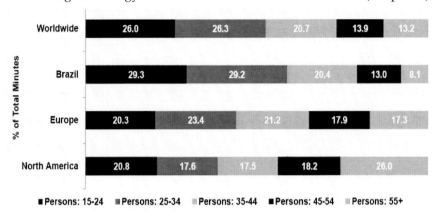

Worldwide	26.0	26.3	20.7	13.9	13.2
Brazil	29.3	29.2	20.4	13.0	8.1
Europe	20.3	23.4	21.2	17.9	17.3
North America	20.8	17.6	17.5	18.2	26.0

■ Persons: 15-24   ■ Persons: 25-34   ■ Persons: 35-44   ■ Persons: 45-54   ■ Persons: 55+

Graph 2.2: Time spent online by age group
Source: Research 2014 Brazil Digital Future in Focus. comScore. May/2014

On its 2015 *US Digital Future in Focus Report*[4], ComScore found huge growth in mobile media consumption: "More than 3/4 of all digital consumers (age 18+) are now using both desktop and mobile platforms to access the Internet, up from 68% a year ago. (...) Meanwhile, the 55+ consumer segment is actually the fastest growing faction of mobile users, increasing its combined multi-platform and mobile-only share of audience from 60% to 74% in the past year." Among the Millennials, 21% are no longer using desktop computers to go online: it seems they will be a mobile-only Internet usage generation.

At events, this is not different. People of working age increasingly demand access to the Internet, and this fact can in no way be disregarded by event organizers. It is no longer a mere wish of the people, not even a need to be met: access to technology is now expected by all.

Another factor to be considered very carefully is the time spent by people on social media. Here lies a huge business opportunity, which is neither well understood, nor well worked on by most companies. Although social media were devised as social interaction platforms, they are becoming more and more important as business channels. We are still watching the first moves of the corporate world in terms of social media, in a stage where social media are still (erroneously) used as dissemination vehicles, like other pre-existing mass media.

The proper use of social media by companies should be the exploration of the possibilities of interaction, dialogue and information exchange between brands and their consumers, current and potential. In the context of events, the use of social media is still largely confined. Here the possibilities are much greater, as are the benefits to be drawn from these communication platforms. To use social media as a channel where relationships between brands and their stakeholders begin (and are kept) and also among the stakeholders themselves should be the goal pursued by companies. The possibilities of communication, relationship and extraction of market intelligence are immense and have barely begun to be explored.

The event industry has in social media a tool that can lengthen the survival rate of events on an ongoing basis, so that they can remain indefinitely relevant to their audiences. Moreover, the behavioural study of the public involved in events, through observation via social media, allows tailoring events, their form and content more and more to meet the needs and desires of their specific audiences.

Finally, more active participation of the public at events through the use of social media allows the next big step in this segment: co-creation. Co-creation occurs when the content of an event is built upon the needs and desires of each and every party involved, expressed by their interaction with the dynamics, organization, execution and content of events.

The importance of technology as an essential tool in the success of events in the Age of Experience can be found in the quotation by Holub[5], which clearly defines the changes of event participants:

The dynamics of events will continue to change, from passive reception to active engagement. Participants will be more participatory; event organizers will offer events with technological tools that encourage this active participation. As a result, participants will be co-creators of their own experiences at events.

This change in consumer behavior has helped to make events valuable as corporate strategy, since it is the only marketing tool that provides interactivity and physical, live and real closeness between consumers and businesses.

Thanks to technology, the physical presence of participants is no longer mandatory, but rather optional, as seen in hybrid events, which was discussed in depth in Chapter 1. It is necessary to pay close attention to this factor because it affects directly and strongly the event industry before, during and after the event, in all its phases. If before networking happened much more on face to face terms (by the proximity created by events), today's professional interactions can take place among people who are geographically distant from one another, but still in a personal way and in real time.

According to Pinchera[6], technology will soon enable people to watch an event remotely, as if they were physically present through the virtual reality devices such as Rift glasses. It will be possible to control technological devices th at can move around within locations at events, so that users feel as if they were personally involved in the event, which opens business possibilities that are only in the field of imagination. However, one can imagine, for example, that a person can participate in various events around the world in one day, without having to move physically to those places. Nowadays, when time is an asset increasingly scarce and valuable, such technology multiplies the possibilities for events to generate results exponentially.

In addition to helping events become increasingly engaging and effective, technology should also be used to guarantee the privacy of personal data of participants. The importance of applications for mobile phones and tablets gains strength in corporate events, among other factors, for their use in place of printed material, easy immediate access to large amounts of data and event information, and ease of updates and/or critical information corrections. All research bets on the increasing use of social media to leverage connections that create and add value to participants, in all phases of events.

The growing importance of mobile phones and tablets for events

The use of mobile platform is becoming increasingly widespread throughout the world, and in developing countries that trend is even stronger. For economic reasons, especially among the disadvantaged strata of society, the smartphone often assumes the role of sole instrument of Internet access.

Statistics from the 2014 Global Digital study, *We Are Social*, show that the penetration of mobile phones in the overall population is currently above 93%, whereas the penetration of the Internet itself is in the range of 35%, with 26% actively using social networks.

According to GSMA Intelligence, by the end of 2013, under half of the global population had subscribed to a mobile service. Their *2014 Mobile Economy Report* predicted growth in all indexes evaluated (Figure 2.1). All this clearly indicates that, regardless of type, size or focus of an event, the use of platforms for mobile phones is simply indispensable. Besides the obvious communication activities of the event itself, from its advertising to the disclosure of its results, every phase of an event (before, during and after) can and should benefit from the use of mobile platforms. Just to name a few examples, in the pre-event phase mobile devices can be used in the relationship between organizers of the event and their suppliers and exhibitors. In the trans-phase, visitors to an event can make their registrations via mobile phone, as well as access all kinds of information about the event itself and its exhibitors. In the post-event phase, mobile platforms may be used to conduct satisfaction research and for construction and maintenance of networking among the various people addressed by the event.

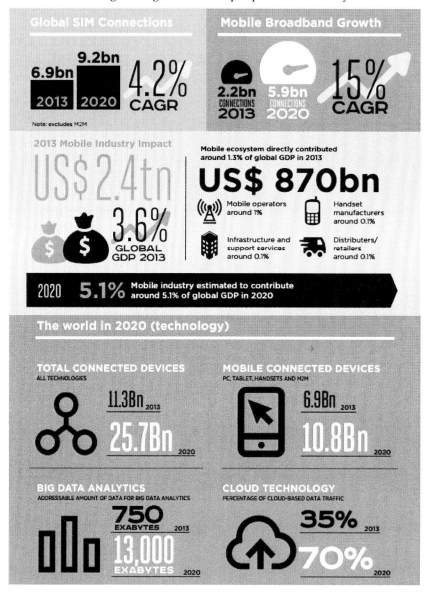

Figure 2.1: The digital future

Source: GSMA Report_2014

Corroborating what had been said earlier about the importance of mobile platforms, we see that the use of mobile platforms (smartphones and tablets) has been growing over time, and the use of PCs has been falling gradually.

It is inevitable that at some point in the near future, the number of users accessing the Internet on mobile devices will exceed those who access on PCs. Therefore, event organizers should consider this information as of now, in order to gradually adapt their communication platforms to this changing reality. Just to give an example, observe how many website events, some of great global importance, are not yet ready for access by mobile devices. Having a responsive website (one that automatically adapts to the type of device that accesses it) is no longer a differentiator, but rather a requirement all websites must meet, otherwise they may be rendered inaccessible to a growing number of Internet users, relegating its contents to a significantly lower number of users.

The following graph (2.3) show the importance of responsive websites, given the different platforms accessing them.

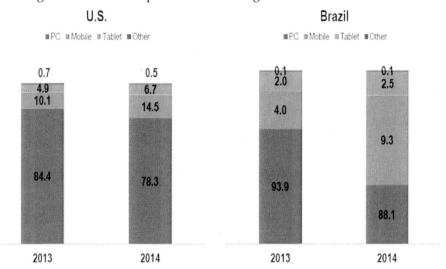

Graph 2.3: Platform access for page hits
Source: Research 2014 Brazil Digital Future in Focus. comScore. May/2014

Another factor to be considered with utmost care is the increasing use of mobile apps. They allow you to build a specific interaction platform that meets the needs and goals of the parties involved in a particular relationship. For example, instead of event organizers publishing on their website a map of the layout of the exhibitors in a particular fair, they can create a mobile app that allows users to not only to get the physical location of a stand, but also to see information about the exhibitors, contact them directly through the app, download information and technical and promotional materials, interact with other attendees of the event, and so on.

The possibilities of apps are numerous and their boundaries are practically dependent on features that their designers are willing to offer to end users. To build specific apps is becoming easier and cheaper, and event organizers can still count on readily available apps, customizable to meet their needs. The 'white label' market in apps, those that can be customized in terms of their appearance or their functionality, is already large, and likely to grow strongly in the coming years, precisely because of their increasing application in various types of businesses.

The following graphics show the way mobile and mobile apps are more used in terms of time spent (Graph 2.4), the increasingly adoption of mobile devices (Graph 2.5) and the time spent over mobile devices is fast growing (Graph 2.6). The massive growth of mobile usage has doubled digital engagement in the past three years (Graph 2.6). As can be seen on Graph 2.7, web searches are rising very fast on mobile devices too. Graph 2.9 show types of content and their impact on time spent.

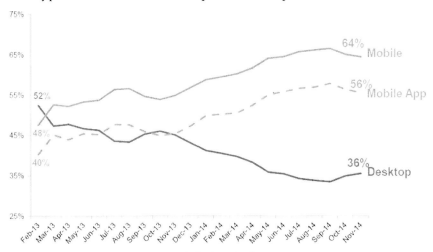

Graph 2.4: US digital media time spent shifts by platform
Source: Fulgoni, G. A Digital Update, By The Numbers. www.comScore.com . 2015.

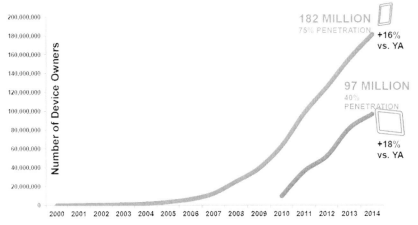

Graph 2.5: Number of U.S. smartphone and tablet owners
Source: Fulgoni, G. A Digital Update, By The Numbers. www.comScore.com . 2015.

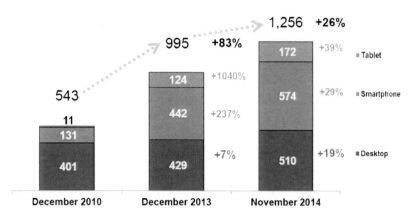

Graph 2.6: Total US Internet usage in minutes (billions) by platform
Source: Fulgoni, G. A Digital Update, By The numbers. www.comScore.com . 2015.

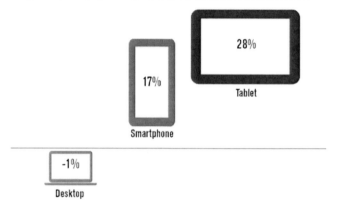

Graph 2.7: Y/Y growth in total searches by platform
Source: Report U.S. Digital Future in Focus. comScore, 2015. Page 17

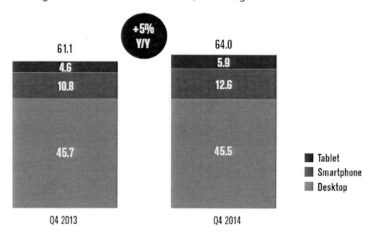

Graph 2.8: Total multi-platform web searches (billions) by platform
Source: Report U.S. Digital Future in Focus. comScore, 2015, page 16

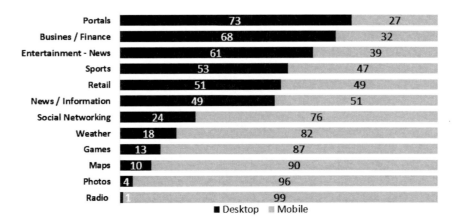

Graph 2.9: Share of content category time spent by platform (in %)
Source: Fulgoni, G. A Digital Update, By The Numbers. www.comScore.com. 2015.

In the Brazilian edition of Lollapalooza 2015[7], all major sponsors invested in brand activations involving entertainment options, tied to social networks. Skol, the official beer of the event, created differentiated space, inspired by old amusement parks overlooking the Skol Stage and set up a vinyl record factory where visitors could record the hits of the bands that have played at the event. It generated numerous posts on social networks. At the same event, the Chevrolet space, brought in a roller coaster, and also a key test (which granted access to the VIP area near the stage if the key turned on the engine of a car), set up studios for makeup and tattoo, as well as space to charge the phone and free access to Internet; all those activations generated many selfies and a multitude of posts on social networks.

Mobile marketing in events is here to stay. And it gains increasing importance year after year to enhance the results of actions of the brands before, during and after events. As demonstrated, all research confirms and strengthens this scenario.

How technology can help your event

As already described in Chapter 1, events are historical pictures of the needs of stakeholders involved and the environment and physical, economic, social and political moment in which they are performed. Thus, the events market has been strongly affected by the technological revolutions that have been happening over the years. Today, technology permeates the entire event and it is neither restricted to the environment of the event rooms, nor even to the point in time during which the event takes place. Demanding modern consumers ask for more and more functionality, speed, accessibility, innovation, involvement and engagement – and this last one is directly dependent on increasing participation and interaction of the public with one another and with the event itself.

There are several ways already available to promote this interaction inside and outside the venue and among all stakeholders. According to Buckhurst[8], two aspects affects the use of technology in events: budget and deadlines. He says that, organizers should always refer to the objectives of the event, and answer at least four major questions that will define the choices that can be made. For him, the choice of the most appropriate technologies in this scope can only be decided after answering them:

- **Why is the event going to be held?** Why will the audience get together? Is the purpose business, fun, a regular meeting or any other purpose?

- **Who are the participants?** Are they employees, customers or consumers? What are the demographic data for this group? What are their expectations? Are they regular users of technological resources?

- **What are the messages the event intends to convey?** What is the main information that the event wants to convey? What are the participants expected to learn?

- **What results are you expecting?** What information do you expect to obtain from the participants? Are they going to participate in a poll or send messages? Will there be information retrieval for exhibitors?

By automating time-consuming activities, managers can streamline customer service and increase their free time to dedicate to essential tasks that improve profitability and agility in the decision-making processes of events. This automation is already growing inexorably in all sectors, and the demand now is for the use of integrated platforms that increase the impact of events, with fewer resources and expenses and – very importantly – with less environmental impact through the less intensive use of printed materials. Experts suggest a few simple steps to choose the applications or software that can automate time-consuming activities in event management:

- They should be directed to create real value for participants and generate profitability for the event in a clear and concise way.

- Make sure they can grow with your business; scalability is strategically very important.

- Online event registration procedures should be customizable, as the first experience with the event should be clearly identified with it.

- Customer database access tools should enable optimal segmentation in order to increase the success rates and ensure that the event meets the needs of the target audience.

- Should offer optimal functionality in sending invitations, confirmations, pre-determined e-mails, news; that is, they should help you monitor and meet deadlines and tasks efficiently.

- They must be flexible and have a user-friendly interface and excellent navigability.

- They must have a receipt and payment system which includes cancellations and refunds.

Above all, search for simplicity, seek technology that makes your life easier, ones which have user-friendly interfaces and offer direct and simple control of all available resources. Choose suppliers that offer support and appropriate technical assistance to meet your needs.

Buckhurst[9] considers it fundamental to engage as soon as possible with the technology partner, who becomes a 'sounding board' of organizing ideas, gaining the status of consultant rather than just a supplier, suggesting services and solutions tailored to the needs and objectives of the event. The earlier the hiring takes place, the easier it will be to bypass the restrictive aspects mentioned above: budget and deadlines.

The winning format to stimulate the use of technology in events is to motivate users by giving them benefits from doing so. Organizers must also be careful to avoid bombarding users with large amounts of unnecessary information as maintaining the relevance of the information is essential to avoid being intrusive.

Moreover, one should consider how information will be shared among the organizers and participants, and vice-versa. Will the promised interactivity of some apps for mobile devices be effective and relevant to all parties involved? Is the type of information being generated aligned with the objectives of the event? Is data security being carried out?

There is already an abundance of software and applications for fixed and mobile devices for specific use in all kinds of events. New options pop up every day. This scenario, coupled with increasingly demanding consumers, turns the selection of management software into something vital. Moreover, this urgent need is difficult to be met, as there is no such thing as a single cake recipe. Several factors should be taken into consideration in this analysis, such as the size of the event, customer demands, the specificity of the event, the degree of customization of software and so on.

One of the first options is the possibility of developing your own event management software. However, due to development and maintenance costs as well as the growing range of products, more and more companies, particularly the medium-sized and small ones, choose from the variety of products already available on the market.

The main social media and your event

According to Kaplan and Haenlein[10] in their fundamental and world-renowned 2010 article *Users of the World unite! The challenges and opportunities of social media*, social media is "a group of Internet applications, built upon the basis of Web 2.0 ideological and technology foundations that allow the creation and exchange of User-Generated Content (UGC)." Following, updating and deconstructing this reasoning, it can be said that at the beginning of the Internet, website-based forums and even e-mail groups within companies could at that time be classified as social media and, nowadays, from Pinterest, which basically contains only images, and even WhatsApp, with its user groups, should be regarded as social media.

The definition of social media adopted in this book is any communication platform, used by Internet-based technologies and for any hardware platforms that enable their users to exchange information at any given time and place, according to their convenience or needs.

Social networks are an important part of the current scenario, conceptualized by Gabriel[11] as:

> *"Social structures that have been around since ancient times and are becoming more comprehensive and complex due to evolving technologies of communication and information. However, it is important to emphasize that social networking is about people, relationships among people, not with technology and computers. It has to do with 'how to use technology' for the benefit of social relationship. The essence of social networking is communication and technologies are catalysts that facilitate the interactions and communication sharing."*

Therefore, social networks are groups of people, brought closer by any common interest among them, and social media are the digital platforms where social networks can happen in the virtual world. However, there is a consensus that has been built on the differences between social networks and social media. This consensus is strong globally, where the vast majority of digital players today refer to social media and not to social networks. Thus, in line with the market, the terms 'social media' and 'social network' will be adopted in this book to cover the concept of social networking.

The *2014 Report Meeting Forecast of the American Express* for the event industry pointed out, among the major trends, the use of social media and applications for mobile devices, now just called apps, as shown in Table 2.1. Among the main items identified in the Report[12] is the growing concern and desire of organizers to know how to choose and use the best apps and the specific advantages of each one of them to their events, especially for medium-sized and large events.

Meetings Program Categories	From				
	North America	Europe	Central/South America	Asia	Global Hoteliers
CSR/Charitable Activities	2.0% ▲	0.0% ▶	0.9% ▲	1.4% ▲	1.3% ▲
Grem/paperless meetings	2.4% ▲	0.0% ▶	0.0% ▶	1.5% ▲	1.8% ▲
Use of socialmedia	4.0% ▲	2.5% ▲	1.3% ▲	3.2% ▲	5.6% ▲
Use of mobile app / meeting-specific apps	4.9% ▲	3.2% ▲	2.6% ▲	4.0% ▲	6.1% ▲

Table 2.1: Main global trends for events
Source: 2014 Meetings Forecast of the American Express Meeting & Events. Page 20

Participants are becoming more and more familiar with the apps for mobile devices for personal use, which will facilitate their adoption for event applications:

> *"According to a recent research conducted by the IDC, in 2013 the number of smartphones grew by 110% over the previous year – and consequently the applications are gaining increasing importance in people's lives. Mobile apps are good for people and they can be decisive for companies. The market for corporate apps provides power solutions, capable of managing thousands of data streams. With different functions, each application can be developed or adapted to the needs of a particular industry. More than sending reminders and connecting people, corporate apps can work in logistics, organization of teams, or registration of salespeople and consumers, for example. The truth is that there is no limit: for every problem it is possible to develop a solution.* [13]

Among the options used, social media is a strong and unique reference. The Report 2015 also pointed out the first step to be taken by organizers, namely to identify existing internal policies for the use of social media by customers. It noted that only 29% of customers in Central and South America had their own internal policies, against almost double that figure in North America (50%). It is an important point, as it gives the direction to follow in preserving the confidentiality of information, besides protecting and guiding the use of the brand and the actions to be taken via social media

The Report 2014 from American Express[14] suggests some best practices to be followed when developing a social media policy for companies:

- Review the current policy; to clearly identify which employees should use company social media, clustering them into groups by type of permitted interactions;

- Analyze the best practices of social media policies of their peers in the market to determinate the social media risk level for their industry;

- Align the policy with the company's values; identify potential scenarios to avoid possible mishaps;

- Develop a screening plan to prevent disasters; win the trust of employees and differentiate internal and external use of social media and, of utmost importance, set up a crisis management plan.

Since the company will be open for interactive communication in social media, therefore, it should have a plan to tackle crises and/or negative contingencies. The report also suggests consulting the website www. socialmediagovernance.com in order to develop or improve this document, whether the communication demands an audience response and the degree of involvement with the event.

Social media will continue to evolve. Among the trends for 2016[15] stand out:

1 **Real-time engagement** – 70% of Twitter users expect a response from brands; and 53% expect it in less than an hour.

2 **Live streaming video** – live stream is a step further in social media marketing.

3 **Social commerce** – more commerce-focused features are constantly created for marketers and advertiser, and these can be integrated to your content and social media strategies.

4 **SEO (Search Engine Optimization)** – As content is still king and advertising costs rises, social content is at its highest demand.

5 **Mobile first** – for most social media user, mobiles have become the primary screen.

6 **Data-driven decisions** – social media offer amazing data about consumer preferences. Marketers can dig deeper into specific social media strategy to craft personalized experiences to customers.

As rules and laws governing the use of the web vary widely from country to country, it is essential to study the specific local web legislation where the event will take place.

Online social networks are web-based networking platforms, where their users create personal and/or business profiles and seek to relate to their peers (people or companies with the same personal or professional interests), creating and exploring a network of contacts. It is estimated that there are over 300 different types of social networks, with different themes: photos, videos, music, friendship, dating, blogging community, social addresses and professional relationship, search for known or specific interests, among many other options[16]. In general, all of them request the same steps and conditions.

The challenge for event organizers and marketing departments is the same for all social apps and media: how to achieve the maximum number of downloads of your app; how to entice users to use the different social media and how to ensure their access throughout the event. Figure 2.2 shows some relevant data about some of the most important social media. More details are described below.

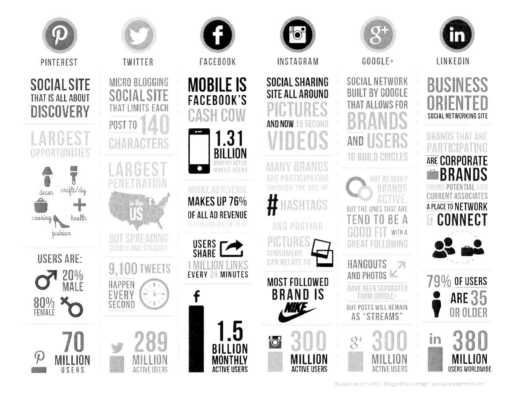

Figure 2. 2: Social media comparison infographic - 2015
Source: https://leveragenewagemedia.com/blog/social-media-infographic/ 20 Mar 2016

■ LinkedIn

This a social network was launched in 2003, exclusively for professional relationships, aimed at business and focused on people and their achievements. The registration stage resembles a professional resume, highlighting academic and professional background, with separate entries for previous and current jobs.

LinkedIn is the world largest professional network. In 2015, most of its 227 million users worldwide were aged between 35 and 54[17]. In the same year, they announced that the milestone of 20 million Brazilian users had been reached, with the city of São Paulo (the largest and one of the most important cities in Brazil) being home to one quarter of that total. In addition, women's participation has been showing significant growth (31% in 2010 to 45% in 4 years[18]). The most basic and passive relationship is made up of people who want to keep in touch with their colleagues and former colleagues. The active one comprises those who seek and offer jobs and those who search for business opportunities.

1 **Registration** – Users are asked to register on the site, with the creation of a profile (providing some personal and/or corporate data). There can be several sequential steps in which more detailed information is requested.

2 **Initial contact network** – Users are asked to add contacts, making their network through their own contacts in other social media, their emails or by LinkedIn suggesting people with similar profiles.

3 **Differentiated plans** – Like some social networks. LinkedIn offers a paid package, besides the basic and free one, containing additional benefits and broader facilities.

4 **Improved contact network** – This is the goal of every social network and of those who are part of it. The more economic returns or satisfaction it offers, the greater its use. They provide and facilitate the most for users in order to create and / or join various interest groups (co-workers, friends, family, profession, and so on) and also for integration and constant interaction among their members.

5 **Tools** – In order to foster relationships, social networks offer several free and paid tools, such as job search engine by LinkedIn, sending messages, additional applications such as SlideShare.

As a business model, by 2014 LinkedIn had no corporate sponsor or advertising. It charges users for certain services, such as LinkedIn Corporate Solutions (a powerful enhanced search tool and management software for recruiters and corporate headhunters), with payment of annual subscription fees. From 2015, it began to commercialize ads on specific locations on its pages, offering precise segmentation to sponsors, allowing brands to convey ads with different messages in specific locations of the site. For example, when accessing pages with prices, the message is different from that received by those accessing the site for the first time.

To get an idea of the potential of connectivity, a LinkedIn user with 41 connections can have more than 200,000 members in his or her network, formed by about three levels of his or her relationship[19].

LinkedIn applications in events are numerous, depending much more on organizers' creativity than the event characteristics. Some of the possibilities include:

- Identification of groups that address the same issue of the event, in order to study the behavior and interests of its participants.

- Pinpointing possible opinion makers, who may become collaborators or promoters of the event.

- Research contents of similar events, on either the targeted segment, geographic location or target audience, in order to observe best practices in terms of organization, marketing, communication, etc.

■ Facebook

This was created in 2004 with the name thefacebook.com, in order to put Harvard students in touch with one another to share photos and meet people. A year later, it had reached 800 university networks, having 5 million active users, and changed its name to Facebook. It maintained the objective of providing users with an easy and fun way to chat with friends, share messages, links, videos and photos. Among other purposes, its applications allow users to create events, make lists of videos, and integrate publications on other sites, such as YouTube and Twitter.

While LinkedIn is focused on professional and academic achievements of people, Facebook (a.k.a. FB) has the emphasis on relationships and social groups, sorting its users according to their personal interests, friendships circles, geographic location, institution where they studied and so on. Facebook is increasingly used as a paid media channel, precisely because of its high reach with the public and its wide capacity of segmentation. There are variations of preference according to the nationality. Brazilians spend more time on FB than Argentines and Mexicans spend online together[20].

On September 2015, Facebook had 1.49 billion monthly active users. Here are some other figures:

- An average Facebook user has 130 friends[21]

- Facebook users are 53% female and 47% male.

- 56% of online seniors aged 65+ are on Facebook and 63% are aged between 50 and 64.

- 80% of online users aged 18-29 are on Facebook[22].

- 74% of college graduates are on Facebook[23].

- 72% of online users with income more than $75K are on Facebook[24].

- Facebook's annual revenue amounted to US$ 12,47 billion in 2014, an increase of 58% year-over-year[25].

- Facebook's stock-market valuation tops US$245 billion and has now passed Wal-Mart.[26]

■ Twitter

This social network allows its registered users to send and receive updates from other contacts, in texts of up to 140 characters (known as tweets or micro blogs), received in real time. Its use in business is more strongly based on giving publicity to more extensive content, its users' own content or third parties' content present in other social media or mass communication channels. You will find more about the psychology of Twitter in Chapter 5.

■ YouTube

Created in 2005, its name derives from two words in English: you + tube (pipe or channel, and also slang for 'television'). It is a site that allows uploading and sharing videos in digital format. To have an idea of its popularity, every minute over 100 hours of new videos are posted worldwide. For events, YouTube is mainly used for the disclosure of event content in order to generate greater attraction to it, and the publication of UGC (user-generated content) from the very visitors to the event, who greatly contribute to its promotion.

■ Instagram

This is a network for posting pictures, identified by hashtags that allow indexing and searching by topics, it also allows people to place texts accompanying their photos, and comments from third parties.

As Instagram posts generate traffic to the link that is connected to the profile, it is used to promote and strengthen brands. In 2015, 29 million out of the 400 million global users are Brazilians, the largest market outside the US[27].

■ Pinterest and other social media for images

There are numerous social media to share images (photos or short videos), such as Pinterest, Flickr, Picasa, Vimeo, etc. Those channels are very useful to publish images of the event during its development, and later serve as a repository of image information, presenting a kind of memory of past events from the same organizer.

In USA, 15% of Internet users are on Pinterest. It grew at an exponential rate from 700,000 at the start of 2011 to more than 20 million users by the end of 2012. Its users (well educated, young people with high-income), who have clicked in order to make purchases, comprise 59% of the total and spent around US$ 80 per purchase (twice as much as Facebook buyers). 35% of items pinned were related to entertaining and 83% of users are female.

Important resources and references

■ Sites and the landing page

In order to gain enormous reach in SEO (Search Engine Optimization) and the Millennial worlds, you must incorporate mobile-friendliness and responsive design within the event website.

When performing research on the web (banners, social media, website, etc.), or access parts of an email marketing, some links refer to a specific page on that desired information, called the landing page, and not the home page of that particular company. It has the following functions[28].

- ■ To take consumers to the desired service or product through the least possible effort.

- ■ To avoid distractions by keeping users focused on the product or service.

- ■ To offer the most specific information.

- ■ To ensure maximum conversion of that offered commercial proposal into actual sales

The advantages of working with landing pages are that individuals are taken directly to the page with the most important information to convert the visit into action. Disclosure of landing pages in marketing emails, for example, always has a call to action, a call to the target of that communication to take an action: sign up for an event, get for more information, or take other actions of interest. When those individuals are taken to the landing page, the entire communication environment that they see is prepared to lead them to the action determined by the event organizers.

It is absolutely essential that the landing page be constructed properly in order to ensure the best results. To this end, the information placed there, and the order it is presented are of utmost importance. A common mistake in landing pages is that they do not contain all the information that the individual needs in order to make his or her decision. Therefore, make sure all information about your event is present on the landing page in a clear and concise way. As well as text, use images to convey information in a fast way, so that it can be quickly understood and, most important of all, have a call to action absolutely clear and visible. If you want a person to sign up, have a button where it is written: Sign up now! If you want the person to register, have a button: Join now! Whatever the intention of your landing page, have a compelling call to action, visible and easy to click on.

Remember that a landing page is not always well indexed by search engines, so it is essential that it be publicized through marketing emails, posts on social media, advertisements in online and offline media, and so on. Regard your landing page as part of a promotion, and feature it prominently in timely (and not perennial) marketing.

The following tips can ensure that your landing page will increase profitability and produce better results:

- Have a short and clear title on the page, indicating what one should do, and why

- Place your call to action preferably on the top right position.

- Use pictures of your previous events, their staff and equipment, so that the visitor feels confident about you and your event.

- Place all the contacts of your company in a visible area.

- Write the text as bullet points, as that greatly facilitates quick reading.

- Include some testimonials from people who have already bought what you offer and attest to its quality.

■ Interactivity on the site

This is one of the key demands of event consumers, valid for all forms of communication before, during and after an event. Follow the same steps as for choosing social media for your event, to reconcile their needs before identifying and selecting from the possibilities.

The tool developed for the Rock in Rio 2016 Edition site offered online interactive experience through an interactive map that brought together happenings from past editions of the event in three countries: Brazil, Portugal and Spain. By creating their own avatars, users became players and their own storytellers on those editions, placing fans as the protagonists of the event and recreating the experience with the affective memory of the event.

■ Hashtag (#)

This is the keyword preceded by "#" mark, used to categorize an issue, some information, a topic or some content published on social networks. The hashtag turns into a hyperlink, that can be indexed by web search engines. Thus, by clicking on it or performing search, the user has access to all who participated in the specific discussion and can share, comment or enjoy the content, i.e., "hashtags are used to categorize content published on social networks, that is, they create a dynamic interaction of content with other members of the social network, who are interested in the subject matter published"[29]

Some useful and relevant information about hashtag[30]:

■ Hashtags can be a great way to engage with followers on the platform, to introduce new products or services, and gain traction for an event.

■ Hashtags make it easier for people to find and follow discussions about brands, events, and promotions.

■ They started out on Twitter but have spread to Facebook, Google+, Instagram, Google search and other platforms.

■ A good hashtag is memorable, unique and relevant to your campaign. It should be distinctive and simple for followers to remember. A generic hashtag, like #food, is too broad and too hard to track.

■ Create an easy-to-understand message: craft a hashtag around one particular message; keep it short; make the call-to-action clear, consistent and easy; steer clear of slang.

■ The effect of hashtags on retweets - on Twitter, tweets with hashtags get two times more engagement than tweets without (but those with one or two hashtags have 21% higher engagement then those with three or more). On Instagram, posts with 11 or more hashtags have the highest interaction, but note that on Facebook, posts without hashtags outperform those with hashtags.

When creating a hashtag some precautions should be taken[31]:

■ Find information: you cannot just be promoted through a hashtag; it can be used as a search tool with specific content. For example, in case you are interested in "Social Media", write #SocialMedia in the search engine and find all kinds of content.

■ Avoid using **too long hashtags** on **Facebook**, because they end up being incomprehensible to view #examplethatwilltaketoolong toberead.

■ Type a capitalized letter after every word, that is, #SocialMedia will always read better than #socialmedia.

■ Remember that #hashtags may be included in the middle of your sentences, not only at the end.

■ Watch out! #Do #not #fill #your #phrases #with #hashtags. Do not publish them in your responses to others: both actions are regarded as SPAM."

The use of hashtags in social media can increase engagement of participants by 50% to 100%, making this the fundamental marketing tool in social media platforms. Despite this importance, many still do not know what they are or how to use them. Chapter 4 has further discussion of that hash mark.

■ Blogs

Using a blog as a promotional channel for your event is a relatively low-cost strategy, but it is effective. This is a channel where you can disclose information in advance on the main points and highlights of your event, generating interest among your target audience. Another advantage is that if you allow comments on your blog, you will have an important source of information about the needs and desires of your audience, and when appropriate, upon receiving criticism, you will know in advance about negatives aspects regarding some points in the organization of your event, allowing you to take corrective actions quickly.

In the pre-event phase, use the following tips:

■ Set up a planning for posts considering your preparation schedule and assembly of the event. With this, you can program each type of content to be posted, respecting the phases of the organization of the event.

■ Start posting on the blog weeks or even months before the event. This allows you to realize what kind of subjects or information interest your audience most, which will enable you to make adjustments in strategy or communication of your event.

■ Interview speakers or prominent figures that will participate in your event. As a result, you can take advantage of the scope and impact of those personalities on your target audience as an advertising tactic for your own event.

During the event, use the blog as a news channel, showing the daily life of the event, its highlights, happenings, important visitors, achievements, etc. Remember that this is *your* communication channel, where you can direct the information the way you find most relevant and productive.

In the post-phase of the event, the importance and use of blogs change. At this stage, the published posts will serve not only to show a balance of the results achieved, but they can lead your audience to establish a long-term relationship with you. This is very important as a marketing tool, especially in events that take place in series, continuously through time. In the blog you should post in the interval between events, information useful to your audience in order to keep this communication channel open. Here are some tips for using blogs in the post-event phase:

■ Make presentations conducted in the lectures of your event available.

- Consider linking an external tool of content, such as SlideShare, Instagram, YouTube or other ones, where you will have a repository of imagery and event information available to your audience.

- You probably used one or more hashtags about your event. Use the blog to publish third-party posts that have used those hashtags, adding the scope and relevance of these other people to your event.

- Post testimonials of important people who attended your event.

- Post content co-created with your sponsors and supporters; use the blog as a networking tool also with the circle of businesses of your interest.

Finally, think about your blog not only as a communication channel, but also as a data capture and intelligence tool. Observing the reaction of the public to posts at each event phase will provide you with important lessons about their interests and needs.

■ Crowdshaping

This seeks to use data generated in real time by participants in order to enhance their experience at an event, causing participants to end up influencing the construction, development, formatting and execution of the event. That is:

"it is the use of data generated by people within a defined space to adjust and customize an event or experience, often in real time. While Crowdsourcing refers to people intentionally and actively sharing their opinions, preferences or ideas, Crowdshaping is relatively passive, usually using technology that detects preferences and interests of people based on their actions." [32]

Pepsi made a spectacular Crowdshaping experience at SXSW Festival in Austin, Texas, in 2014. It equipped the entire audience with bracelets that measured physiological metrics such as body movements, heart rate, electrical responses of the skin and other information. With the only instruction that participants do not remove their bracelets, software recorded the biological data of all participants and created an environment with music and light that reacted to the average 'emotional tone' of the public. The experimental event became known as 'Pepsi Bioreactive Concert' and was a huge success, demonstrating the possibilities of Crowdshaping taken to extremes.[33]

■ Gamification

First of all, we must understand that the use of gamification in organizing events is greatly facilitated by the fact that events, in their vast majority, combine business, socializing, and fun. How many 'games' have been used at events in the past, as a way to break the ice and foster socialization among participants? However, the techniques usually applied to encourage socialization among the participants of an event cannot be properly regarded as gamification. Gamification involves applying elements and principles of electronic games in a 'non-game' context. Among others, those elements can be:

- Accomplishing tasks,
- Challenges,
- Creation of narratives, or
- Distribution of points or badges.

Gamification strategies in organizing events work because everybody likes to accomplish tasks, collect points and badges, and best of all, to feel recognized within their communities, especially in business. Therefore, gamification techniques exploit the natural tendency for people to socialize, collaborate, learn, compete and win a status or position of prominence among their peers.

The idea behind gamification is to generate greater engagement of the public, reaching higher levels of interaction with them, thereby increasing the effectiveness of the event that uses gamification.

Early in the use of gamification at events, it was common to distribute prizes among participants who stood out in certain tasks, but this often led to somewhat unethical behavior, little cooperation and collaboration between the parties, due to the excessive sense of competition generated by the practice. That is why today there is an attempt to try to 'reward' people engaged in gamification in a more subjective way, giving them the satisfaction of having actively participated in a collective process that generated a positive result for the group and, in more advanced gamification processes, for the group to which they belong to or even to society. Rewards through badges or rankings are also used and, to a lesser extent, distribution of products and gifts.

According to Dr Cathy Key of the Event Manager Blog[34]:

"Events are a perfect arena to practice gamification because they typically put together a group of people for a short period of time to connect, learn and have fun. For the meeting planner, the goal is not to turn events into a game, but rather to use principles that work in games so that we are

more effective at engaging our attendees, staff, exhibitors, vendors and sponsors so that we create better, more satisfying events. Engagement is the antidote to passive participation. It allows the attendee to become part of the experience, to actively generate their participation in the event. Engagement can be challenging, risky, exciting, social, and it is ultimately highly rewarding for everyone".

According to the same blog, the gamification of goals in organizing events is important because:

"Games and game-playing are highly effective in creating active participation. Using game-thinking, we can apply those compulsive, exciting and rewarding elements of games to our events to stimulate active participation by the attendees.

So, how do we do that? The first step is to get clear on what you would like to achieve. Possible objectives are:

- *Better attendance at sessions, especially during low periods, such as early mornings or at the end of the day*

- *Increased engagement with exhibitors,*

- *Improved networking, increasing the number of connections made at the event,*

- *Social media impact, increasing the number of tweets and social media hits during the event,*

- *More fun and a better attendee experience overall.*

Dr Key concludes that *"Games are compelling, engaging and the overwhelming majority of people play them to socialize".*

Finally, keep in mind that in order to create an effective gamification strategy, you need to clearly determine what behaviors you want to encourage in your audience, and choose the games that will be applied to make the audience do what you expect from them. Consider the motivations of those who go to an event: to learn, to build relationships, to demonstrate their knowledge and see what is new in their industry. Therefore, if your gamification strategy rewards the participation of the people involved with more learning, broader or deeper relationships, more information on their sectors of activity or the acknowledgement of their individual abilities, you are bound to get the best results.

■   ## Audiovisual – AV

A successful event is obtained as a result of many factors, the combination of which must generate engaging experiences for all participants. AV is not just a checklist item, for its importance grows in proportion to the needs for involvement and engagement required by the demanding consumer of today.

Human senses are largely responsible for this perception, and require rich environments involving the brain to produce the sensory experiences desired by participants. Thanks to neuroscience, we can better understand how the brain interprets and records the stimuli, and use that information in the context of meeting design in order to maximize learning, expanding experiences of participants and significantly helping to achieve and exceed the goals of the event.

The more the brain is activated, the more associations are made by it and the stronger, broader and more effective the learning. Thus, at events, targeted activation of the brain will enable participants to have deeper and more inspiring experiences. As human experience is multi-sensory, it requires constant and varied stimulation from different fronts, helping participants to better understand and retain information. AV allows the audience to filter and better retain relevant information.

The use of AV at events has been around for quite some time, since the use of overhead projectors, to modern day PowerPoint, slides, videos, lighting and music, which help and facilitate the experience and learning of the participants[35]. Chapters 3, 4 and 5 contain details of the various options and their advantages and applications.

Where to start

Before you decide on one technology, it is necessary to stop and identify what improvements in terms of services and products are needed and desired. There are many options available or under development which deserve to be considered.

Among the main concerns and difficulties faced by organizers are: the definition of what social networks you may need to use to maximize the impact of the event and how to use it within the event planning.

Before becoming increasingly confused and anxious about where to start looking and what to do, stop and take a simple review (but also a very powerful and efficient one) of your event, by following the steps below. Because of event budget restraints, such a review can only be made by your company or through specialized agencies:

1 What I want

Start by listing and synthesizing (using dashes or bullet points) within the global scenario, your needs and also the needs of the customers, highlighting the objectives to be achieved, the target public and the budget of the event, and choose the most appropriate type of event in this scenario. Define clearly and directly what goals you want to achieve.

2 What help I need to have

Specify what kind of help you need to get from technology tools (without specifying the tools themselves at this point)

3 Information on the main digital platforms

Research them, with as many details as possible, identifying the differences among the platforms and seeking to understand them to help you in the decision-making process.

4 What I desire and need to measure

Professionalization of events, combined with demanding consumers and the growing demand from sponsors for results, turn measurement into a mandatory item for event planning. Therefore:

- Identify the aspects need to be measured

- For each, specify the data that can be used for the measurement.

- Each platform used must contain parameters and tools for measurement that enable data gathering and analysis of the data and other aspects that were selected.

5 How to plan, implement, execute and monitor

If the budget of your event permits, consider the development of apps for mobile devices that meets your specific needs. Follow this model:

- In the planning phase, make sure to define all the needs that the app should cover, the minimum technical parameters required, and determine metrics to measure its success.

- In the implementation phase, thoroughly test the stability and accessibility of the app, including testing it on multiple platforms and different operating systems.

- When running it, be sure to make your app known, disseminating it in all event communications. The more people use the app, the more results you will obtain.

Monitor the use of the app by all those targeted, at all stages of the event, measuring the metrics set in the planning phase.

Fifty editions were held in the 19 years of existence of Campus Party. Aimed to the geek world, the festival is a great technology experience. Brazil's 8th edition (held in São Paulo in 2016) had 8,000 Campus-goers coming from 21 countries and every state in the country (see Box 2.1).

Box 2.1: Campus Party Brazil!

Since the first edition in Spain in 1997, 50 other editions of Campus Party have been held in 13 countries. It is considered one of the largest events in the world for innovation entrepreneurship , science, creativity and entertainment.

To boost young talent and entrepreneurs to create or deploy their projects, Campus Party Brazil 2016 #CPBR9 was held in São Paulo. We had four main areas: Innovation (development, security, networking and free software); science (astronomy and space, modding, electronics and robotics); Creativity (social media, design, photo, video and music); and Digital Entertainment (games and simulations). Each had a organizer and staff responsible for organizing activities (lectures, debates, competitions, etc.) .

Nearly two-thirds of the 82,000 visitors to the 2016 edition were men (66%) and 64% were 18-29 years old. There were 8,000 campus goers and 600 speakers, and 600 hours of activities.

Campus Party in numbers

8,000 campus goers

6,500 tents

80,000m optical fibre

40GB of network speed

+3,000 people in the organization

60,000m of network cables

2,280 articles online

187 printed articles

32 radio articles

+60 million spontaneous social media outputs

16,000 new campus goers in social media

66,000 followers on Twitter

120,000 likes on Facebook

2

The event brought in project Startup 360 for the 2nd consecutive year. In this, programs like Startup and Makers Camp selected 200 startups as exhibitors to publicize and test market products for 4 days. As well as the exhibition area, there were workshops, challenges, networking, hackathons and special activities, and lectures covering seven content areas, with national and international names sharing their successes, relevant cases and innovative ideas .

Dozens of small stands were hosted by several companies. Future entrepreneurs received training and could develop their ideas through mentoring with professionals from various fields of knowledge in Business Marathons.

'Like a Boss' promoted meetings with investors and project presentation. The Future Campus gave visibility to the 64 most creative university projects and selected innovators, whose prototypes were exposed to the public to experience and enjoy.

Like a Boss: a presentation

Chapter summary

The relevance of the importance of applications for mobile phones and tablets gains strength in corporate events. Among other factors, key ones are their use in place of printed material, the easy immediate access to large amounts of event data and information, and ease of updates and/or critical information corrections.

On the one hand, technology and its different tools and platforms are creating new optimization possibilities for event organizers. On the other, it imposes upon organizers the need to choose which tools they will use, to begin relationships with new suppliers and partners, to train employees in their use and to find out how to measure the results. This creates a learning scenario and the constant monitoring of current and future technologies, which should be understood as essential for everyone who works in the events business segment.

The challenge for planners and event managers therefore lies in acquiring in-depth knowledge of all technological possibilities applicable to organizing events and utilizing this knowledge to gain the maximum profit from its possibilities.

The technology applied to events allows you to optimize processes, automate steps to increase the involvement of all stakeholders and ultimately monetize any business events market.

For Edward Poland, Co-Founder of Hire Space,

"The rapid growth of event industry websites, blogs and social media means that event bookers are better informed than ever. They have more choice, better access to supplier inventories and abundant curated feedback to inform them. As such, they take decisions more confidently.

This means two things: First, traditional events agencies need to stay ahead of the game. This means offering a service which goes beyond familiarity with the industry and its providers. Innovative thinking and bespoke solutions will be the key to staying relevant.

Second, venues need to think beyond traditional marketing channels and contribute to conversations online. If agencies stop providing leads, they'll need another source of business to survive. Venues are already engaging with social media platforms at a faster rate than ever before – expect this trend to continue in 2015, and a new industry to emerge to support it".

This text refers to the year 2015, but it is applicable for the following years in a business environment that is increasingly demanding regarding the use of new technologies.

Practical guide to the chapter

Here is the roadmap of the essential steps in the chapter for practical application in your daily activities:

Item	Description
Define your objectives facing the new technologies available in the market	Study and learn characteristics and features of as many technological tools you can, in order to discover which suits your needs better
Start relationship with new suppliers	Getting close to technological suppliers will give you not only a better knowledge of products and technology, but it will also give you an edge over your competitors
Apply your new technological tools to your business	Spread the knowledge over your entire crew, in order to fully explore the benefits of those new technologies
Think about your costumers	Keep in mind who is the final user of the new technologies – it has to be good for them to be good for you.

For further reading, questions for reflection and additional materials please go to the book's page at the publisher's website:

www.goodfellowpublishers.com/technologyandevents

Notes

1   http://trendwatching.com/trends/10-trends-for-2015/?utm_medium=email&utm_campaign=10TrendsUpdate-15SCA&utm_content=10TrendsUpdate-15SCA+Version+B+CID_3bab3ea13be179ba25a868594af9dba5&utm_source=Campaign%20Monitor&utm_term=Briefing%20Examples#slide-17. [15 Feb 2015]

2   10 Trends for 2015 – Global Trends. Trend Watching. Dec, 2014 to Jan, 2015 – available at www.trendwatching.com

3   http://www.proxxima.com.br/home/mobile/2015/04/17/3-tendencias-moveis-importantes-para-as-empresas-em-2015--.html?utm_source=newsletter&utm_medium=email&utm_campaign=newsletter-Proxxima-diaria&utm_content=noticias_diarias. [03 May 2015]

4   http://www.comscore.com/Insights/Presentations-and-Whitepapers/2015/2015-US-Digital-Future-in-Focus

5   http://www.brightbull.co.uk/hs-fs/hub/188124/file-2487573491-pdf/30-Experts-Predict-The-Event-Trends-That-Will-Shape-Your-2015-updated.pdf

6   Pinchera, Michael. Interview with authors. April, 2015.

7   http://www.proxxima.com.br/home/conectados/2015/04/27/Interacoes-sociais-musica-e-mobile-Por-Diana-Leiko.html?utm_source=newsletter&utm_

medium=email&utm_campaign=newsletter-Proxxima-diaria&utm_
content=noticias_diarias

8   Buckhurst, Joe. Choosing Technology for Corporate Events (parts 1 and 2)
    available at https://www.LinkedIn.com/pulse/choosing-technology-corporate-
    joe-buckhurst. [18 Feb 2015]

9   Buckhurst, Joe. Choosing Technology for Corporate Events (parts 1 and 2)
    available at https://www.LinkedIn.com/pulse/choosing-technology-corporate-
    joe-buckhurst. [18 Feb 2015]

10 http://en.wikipedia.org/wiki/Andreas_Kaplan 20 Jan 2016

11 Gabriel, Martha. *Marketing na Era Digital*. São Paulo: Novatec Editora, 2010, pp
    194, 196

12 2014 Meetings Forecast by American Express Meeting & Events, pages 20/21

13 http://www.administradores.com.br/artigos/tecnologia/
    apps-corporativos-para-alavancar-resultados/76274/

14 Report 2014 *Meeting Forecast* from *American Express* pp 43 to 45

15 Beese, Jennifer. 6 Social media trends that will take over 2016. http://sproutsocial.
    com/insights/social-media-trends/#infographic. [16 Jan 2016]

16 Research 2014 Brazil Digital Future in Focus. comScore. [05 May 2014]

17 http://www.businessinsider.com/infographic-who-really-uses-LinkedIn-2012-2.
    [30 Sep 2015]

18 http://www.proxxima.com.br/home/social/2015/02/10/LinkedIn-chega-
    a-20-milhoes-de-usuarios-no-Brasil.html?utm_source=newsletter&utm_
    medium=email&utm_campaign=newsletter-Proxxima-diaria&utm_
    content=noticias_diarias. [13/02/15]

19 http://tecnologia.hsw.uol.com.br/LinkedIn7.htm

20 Research 2014 Brazil Digital Future in Focus. comScore. [05 May 2014]

21 http://www.pewresearch.org/fact-tank/2014/02/03/6-new-facts-about-facebook/.
    [20 Dec 2015]

22 http://www.adweek.com/socialtimes/social-seniors/612256. [20 Jan 2016]

23 http://www.therainmakerblog.com/2015/09/articles/social-media-marketing-for-
    law-firms/how-to-determine-which-social-media-networks-work-best-for-your-
    firm/. [20 Jan 2016]

24 http://www.therainmakerblog.com/2015/09/articles/social-media-marketing-for-
    law-firms/how-to-determine-which-social-media-networks-work-best-for-your-
    firm/. [20 Jan 2016]

25 http://investor.fb.com/releasedetail.cfm?ReleaseID=893395. [20 Jan 2016]

26 http://www.omnicoreagency.com/facebook-statistics/

27 http://www.meioemensagem.com.br/home/midia/noticias/2015/11/09/Instagram-
    chega-a-29-milhoes-de-usuarios-no-Brasil.html#ixzz3rlqJ7hjl. [17 Nov 2015]

28 http://www.proxxima.com.br/home/negocios/2015/02/13/Infografico-descubra-como-como-otimizar-uma-landing-page-para-conquistar-leads.html?utm_source=newsletter&utm_medium=email&utm_campaign=newsletter-Proxxima-diaria&utm_content=noticias_diarias. [16 Feb 2015]

29 http://www.significados.com.br/hashtag/. [24 Feb 2015]

30 Hashing out the almighty #hashtag. Available at http://blog.surepayroll.com/hashing-out-the-almighty-hashtag/. [15 May 2015]

31 http://tecnologia.umcomo.com.br/articulo/como-usar-os-hashtags-no-facebook-11269.html#ixzz3S5apjQzq. [18 Feb 2015]

32 http://www.bizbash.com/why-crowdshaping-can-give-guests-the-event-they-want/new-york/story/29948#.VOUdAPnF-n8. [18 Feb 2015]

33 http://businesslife.ba.com/Ideas/Features/People-Power-crowdshaping.html | http://www.bizbash.com/cisco-global-sales-experience-cisco-global-sales-experience-meeting-august/gallery/157357. [15 Jan 2016]

34 http://www.eventmanagerblog.com/event-gamification#ia1taQ12C5KFMM33.99. [15 Aug 2014]

35 Audiovisual technologies and adult learning in meetings Report. Brains Strength System & PSAV Technology Meets Inspiration. 2011.

Section II

How to Choose and Apply Technology to Your Events

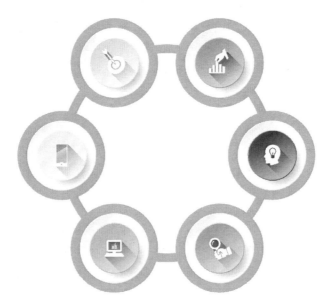

This section describes the main steps in the planning and managing of the event, pointing how to choose and plan the communication technology.

Chapter 3 - Organizing the Event

- Integrating technology and strategy: a general management perspective
- Modern tools for planning and organizing events
- How technology can improve the profitability, sales and communication of events
- How to use the mix of social media, apps and online tools in the planning phase.

Chapter 4 – Accomplishment

- How to choose the best technology suppliers and other third parties
- Best ways to use technology to communicate the relevance of the event;
- How technology helps to get subscriptions
- What to look for in the venue infrastructure to optimize the technology.

3 Planning and Organizing an Event

"The rapid rise of the technological revolution in the events industry has led to disruption as well as enormous opportunity for new growth and greater attendee engagement "

Joe Goldblatt

Introduction

The words above by Professor Goldblatt are part of the preface to this book. They were highlighted here to call the attention to the importance of technology in the events industry. They also portray one of the main motivations for the content of this book.

Regarding this commitment, this chapter shows changes in the event project design that will help you use the great tools that technology offers to meeting planners in a more efficient and productive way. All those changes not only highlight, but also reinforce the strategy and focus for the best results.

Learning objectives

■ To provide overall management perspective integrating technology and strategy.

■ To learn about the main current tools for planning and organizing events

■ To identify how technology can improve profitability, sales, and communication in events.

A survey conducted by Eventbrite in 2015 among industry experts pointed out several trends for the events market, including the enhancement of quality over quantity in corporate and educational events, valuing smaller, more intimate and effective events. "Participants are demanding new and unique perspectives and increasing their expectations regarding deliveries, as well as more interactive training to accelerate their results."[1]

It is becoming noticeable that participants of events demand more and more overall quality regarding their expectations on the subject, whatever it may be. The present focus is on accurately defining the needs and desires of the public, and the planning and execution that will be able to achieve the highest degree of accuracy in the delivery of the proposed events, adding value and generating returns for them. This will be further explored later.

Technology is crucial for achieving the results desired by organizers and demanded by the public. With all the possibilities for observation, research and interaction with various stakeholders, event organizers today can be much more specific in defining the scope of their events and consequently in delivering them.

Furthermore, throughout all stages of an event – from pre-event phase (organization), through the execution to the post-event phase (study of results and planning of upcoming events) – technology allows all sorts of possibilities in terms of results measurement. To set priorities, establish KPIs (key performance indicators), choose measurement tools and interpret the data generated are becoming more and more important parts of organizing events of all kinds and types.

The difficulty is to choose which technologies will be used in order to increase the effectiveness and profitability of modern events. Starting with research tools, free and paid, public and private ones, through the social media and P2P (peer to peer) interaction channels and ending with the communication and interaction tools represented by websites and applications (apps), the range of possibilities within the reach of organizers is gigantic.

Some of the key takeaways from KPCB's Mary Meeker's *Internet Trends Report 2015*[2] show these global Internet trends:

- Internet users have risen from 35 million in 1995 to more than 2.8 billion today and Internet engagement continues to rise.

- Digital mobile media time is significantly higher when compared to desktop.

- Consumers spend more time on their mobile devices, as they can be connected 24/7. Connectivity (via the Internet) rose from 9% of population in 1995 to 84% in 2014. Via mobile smartphone up from 18% of population in 2009 to 64% in 2014.

■ User-generated / curated / shared content continues to rise.

■ Demographic shifts are helping to accelerate technology changes. Millennials are now the largest generation in the workforce and their work / life expectations differ from previous generations (see Chapter 5 for more information about Millennials).

More details on those and other features can be found in Chapters 2 and 5.

> **64%**
>
> of corporate event planners said they have used, or are considering creating, a mobile app for their events in 2014

Mobile event apps

Research conducted by IMEX with the event organizers in their database on the mobile event apps (mobile deviceapplications for events), pointed out these key insights about their use globally in the past two years (Figure 3.1):

Mobile event apps are underutilized, but there is room for growth

Even though 60% of organizers have used mobile event apps, most of them have used them just for some events

There are variations in usage, when opting to use them.

40% of organizers use common platform, whereas 27% ask for a new application every event.

Facilitating communication is considered an important benefit for their use:

– Communication between organizers and participants and sharing (91%)
– Communication between participants and sharing (79%)
– Maintaining relationships after the event (78%)
– Starting the relationship prior to the event (75%)

Time and cost are the main barriers for use among those who have not used apps yet.

Budget (84%); Wi-Fi connection (83%) and time for programming (78%).

Figure 3.1: Highlights from IMEX research

Source: Event Planning & Mobile Technology Study - IMEX. May/2014

- 60% of events held have used those applications.

- Among the items that make first-time users reluctant are the variety of cost options and the time spent for development.

- Initiating a conversation with the participants before the event and prolonging the relationship after its end is relevant to more than 75% of respondents.

- User-friendly interface (91%), the use of statistics (84%), unique experience with the brand (81%), integration with social media (76%) and registration for the event (73%) are the main characteristics sought by organizers.

- They want the application to be integrated with the registration system (85%), social media (75%), CRM (75%), business Intelligence (75%), educational systems management (68%) and automation systems for marketing (66%).

- The choice of app is mainly based on the recommendations of peers and colleagues (84%) and by the use in another event (75%).

The research concluded that encouraging communication and increasing and improving the relationship are the primary motivations for their use. It also indicates that there is room for growth in use and that it is possible to increase perceived value, due to the growing awareness of other strategic benefits of that technology. It is important to point out that app producers should make their products user-friendly, with good usability and integration, and make sure their customer service teams are prepared to help their customers choose the best option to meet their needs. It is clear that one of the barriers to wider use of apps is still event organizers' low level of knowledge of the possibilities and applications of apps, as well as their implementation and integration with other systems and event management processes. As for the organizers who use apps in their events, the main concern should be the dissemination of their apps, so that a larger portion of the public use them appropriately, generating better ROI and intelligence gathering.

According to myQaa[3] and Quick Mobile[4], some of the main takeaways about mobile apps from event planners are:

- Improving communication, reducing carbon footprints and printing costs, enhancing networking opportunities and increasing exposure for sponsors.

- *Advice* – find out your delegates' needs, compare and choose apps suppliers that meet their needs and provide technical support.

- *Favorite thing* – having the ability to customize agendas

- *Dislike* – having too many unnecessary features; to download the app just for an on-off event; apps that are difficult to navigate.

- *Barriers* – having someone downloading the app and using it.

Successful event app – an app is successful when:

1   Attendees use it frequently and great feedback is provided after the event.

2   It is fully functional and has everything in a single solution (agenda, networking, social media feed, etc.).

3   It contains seamless tech, it provides useful attendee insights that can deliver ROI for future events.

4   Its features are relevant and they help the mc or event facilitator to guide the audience and to increase learning.

The most important features for a mobile app are being user-friendly in terms of Content Management System (CMS)[5] usage of analytics, branding, social media integration, user help request, ability to register for the event through the app, and year-round engagement.[6] The top two perceived benefits of mobile apps for Meeting Planners International – MPI are organizer-to-attendee communication and reduction or elimination of paper (Graph 3.1, below).

The role of social media and event apps extends far beyond those aspects: meeting planners can rally event attendees and increase affinity; stimulate engagement; sustain the event buzz long after the event has come to its end and ensures the event can reach a wider audience. Social media can be a phenomenal and valuable source of feedback, but it must be responsive.

Everything can be measured!!

More than ever, event organizers need to professionalize and equip their teams with both management and communication tools, aiming to extract maximum results from each event.

> *in* **digital**,
> absolutely **EVERYTHING** can be
> **measured!**

The C & IT's State of the Industry Report 2014[7] shows that the number of corporate event planners who are considering the creation of apps for mobiles at their events has more than doubled since 2010 to 64%. In 2010, it was 23%. 19% already plan to use some social media in all their events; 22% are investing in mobile event apps and 15% say they prefer management software.

In addition to offering significantly lower investments, in the digital world absolutely *everything* can (and should) be measured. It is in measurement and lower costs that organizers can find two unbeatable advantages in the relationship between digital and offline. However, obtaining data is only the first step of the process. It is necessary to transform data into knowledge, strategy, decisions, and effective actions that provide the desired return on investment made in the event. For Almeida[8], the measurement

> ... combined with a good strategy and supported in business intelligence (BI), with clear objective to bring the return on investments in communications, whether in branding campaigns or performance, can certainly generate satisfactory results to the expectations of companies. (...)

It is not only a matter of offering optimization of a website, development of apps, search campaign management or simply create a fan page. It is necessary to think strategically, combining intelligence, performance, and branding, so that they each one of them is connected to the others.

Graph 3.1 shows the most important features of event mobiles apps for MPI members. All of them have been described on previous pages of this chapter.

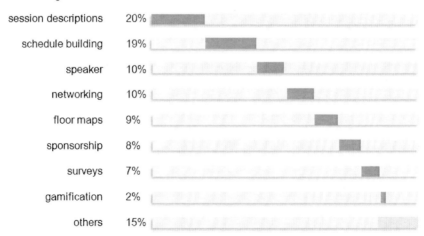

Graph 3.1: Most important features of event mobile apps – MPI respondents

Source: QuickMobile_Summer_Surveys_2014

Although this whole process can seem complicated or inaccessible for many organizers and too costly for the budget of an event, this is not the reality. On the one hand, complex solutions may need the hiring of specific providers, several simple and inexpensive actions can be used, but with excellent cost-benefit ratio for the event. Moreover, even the complex ones may be incorporated into the budget, since they provide the desired feedback. The key here is the proper planning for event organizers to be able to choose which among the numerous options available will add the highest returns to the lowest investments. The role of event planners becomes increasingly crucial for the perfect development of an event, in all its phases. There is no longer room for adaptations, makeshift or amateur solutions in the events market. Chapter 4 will show to you how to choose the best event app.

Apart from this, the Millennial generation features (as detailed in Chapter 5) the great importance of the smartphone[9] (87% say their smartphone is never out of sight), which makes imperative the use of digital tools in communication and interaction at events. Thus, understanding their functioning, applications, benefits and costs has become imperative for organizers.

■ Internet of Things

In the Internet of Things, or IoT, there is very intensive use of sensors in generating information to feed a system that operates and executes tasks automatically. Its purpose is to enhance and enrich people's lives, allowing dynamic interconnections between intelligent devices

> *Mobile has already redefined consumers' experiences in many aspects of their daily life, as well as created a range of new business opportunities and services. New technologies, imaginative use of cases and business models are likely to generate even more profound innovations, with mobile increasingly linking the digital and physical worlds. Rapid smartphone adoption allows the creation of new products and services, whether they based on apps or on the development of low power components that are the building blocks for new connected devices. Consumers are beginning to realise the transformative potential of the Internet of Things (IoT), with an increasing number of services and launches focused on, for example, wearables and the smart home.[10]*

IoT is expected to bring sharing and collaboration protocols, radical transparency and greater control by end users, transforming the corporate landscape and introducing new business models. For Kranenburg[11], "the Internet of Things will create a better balance between the end user, government and economic sectors. It will expose the deficiencies and provide people with greater control in mission-critical services."

The IoT deployments are targeted primarily for monitoring and tracking. It will be made by connecting billions of devices (sensors, tags, and activators). It is based on the acronym M-to-M or M2M, short for "machine to machine", which are "machines defining actions without direct interference of human beings by doing something that someone else needs.[12]" The most trivial example is ATM (automatic teller machines) that do not require intermediation of operations by bank clerks. Event organizers and attendees already use the IoT and intensify their use more and more. The most significant uses of IoT in event organization today are:

Automated onsite registration

The latest mobile devices now include connectivity such as BLE (Bluetooth Low Energy), NFC (Near Field Communication), GPS (Global Positioning System) and Wi-Fi. Those connections can be used to automate the registration for attendees at events. With BLE connectivity, attendees can use their mobile phones to communicate with onsite registration software to check-in when they are around the event venue. At the same time, a notification can be sent to their mobile phones and prompt them to proceed to a badge collection booth to collect their event badges. This cuts down on waiting time and manpower required to manage onsite registrations.

Heat map and movements

If we get attendees to connect to the event Wi-Fi or if we add BLE chips into the event badges, we can start to generate a heat map of the event floor plan where most attendees currently are. We can also start to see the common ways attendees navigate around the event venue when we track the routes they take. With this new data available, we are able to start improving the way organizers create event venue layouts. Organizers are also able to start selling 'hot' zones where most attendees are shown to always walk along. This creates new channels for marketing or price increases for booths in certain areas.

Interactive posters

Through the use of NFC, attendees can start to use their mobile devices to tap on posters or products that they are interested in to get more information. At the same time, these provide exhibitors with a list of potential customers who are interested in their product offerings. Those were just two cases of implementing sensors or devices around events to collect or provide information to the audiences. Having said that, the potential of IoT does not simply stop at making inanimate devices smart or connected. The true value of IoT is having data collected from every device. If an event organizer integrates or consolidates all event and attendee data together with the attendee and event data, it gives them a wealth of information they can use to create more personalized experiences with their audiences. This allows organizers to:

- Provide targeted recommendations to attendees

- Allow exhibitors to see a list of attendees who may be interested in their offerings

- Drive people to exhibitor booths or sessions that they are close to

- Spread out the crowd on exhibition floor when certain areas are overcrowded

Event project design

Until recently, the phases of an event could be considered as separate and well-defined stages. Demand for sponsors for better and better ROI has boosted the professionalization of events. One of the solutions found by meeting planners was to extend the residual effect of events. By widening their actions also before and after the event and with the help of event apps and social media, all steps began to interrelate and intertwine more intensely. This change can be observed in Figure 3.2, where colour shades smoothly from one phase to another. The title and content of Chapter 7 reinforces this concept by questioning: is it a post event or a new pre event?

Figure 3.2: Event steps and tools

By analysing the tools provided by event apps and how events use social media it is clear that they all come down to just three groups:

1 **Event management** – the administrative, operational and financial management of an event.

2 **Event marketing, ticketing and registration** – responsible for the marketing and strategic planning of an event, and/or the registration and commercialization of subscriptions or free or paid tickets.

3 **Event engagement** – responsible for the engagement of the participants and other stakeholders

Event organization experts are unanimous in affirming that technology providers must be involved in the planning process from the very beginning, in order to reduce the possibilities of error and maximize projected results. The taxonomy of *Meeting Architecture*[13] uses five categories of tools:

■ **Concept** – covers formats, types and event techniques

■ **Human resources** – organizers, technicians, photographers, facilitators, and other suppliers

■ **Art** – brings together music, dance, video theme, etc.

- **Technical support** – involves audiovisual, furniture, uniforms, set design, etc.

- **Technology** – includes apps, webcast, social media, online events, hybrid events, etc.

The preparation of an event project can be made by using several methodologies. The most efficient ones start by defining the objectives of the event. Graph 3.2 shows meeting planners have expectation of growth for most of types of corporate events, especially for road shows, and for dealers and distributors meeting.

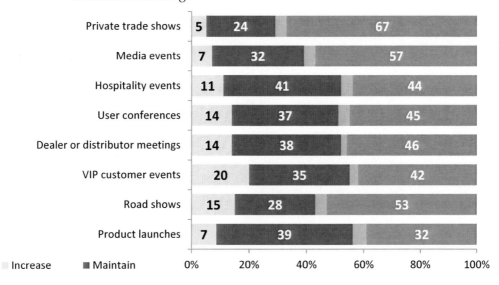

	Increase	Maintain	

Graph 3.2: Will your organization increase, decrease or maintain spending in 2015 on the following types of corporate events (in percentage)?

Source: http://www.statista.com/statistics/257280/planned-change-in-spending-on-corporate-events-in-the-us-by-type-of-event/ 23 Dec 2015

During the event the *Fresh Conference 2013* (see Boxes 3.1 and 6.1), in just 10 minutes the co-creation activities using Spotme (mobile app) generated 150 ideas to define blocks that helped with the formatting of events sessions. They were grouped into seven categories:

- **Participants**: includes group size, classification and decision of mixing it or breaking it up into smaller groups.

- **Time**: is related to the duration, shortening or lengthening sections, the script, the dynamics of the set design.

- **Tools**: what tools (non-conceptual) will be used: People (facilitators, keynote), Art (Music), Technical (materials, AV, demo, toys) or Technology (ICT, apps).

- **Dynamics**: which ones will be necessary (separating people who know one another, joining peers, free consultants, and so on)

- **Objectives / Output**: The specific goals to lead the session and shape it: learning, motivation, and so on.

- **Movement**: will attendees be sitting or moving around?

- **Interaction**: setting time to talk, listen, discuss, question, read, etc.

- **Change**: defining the change interval of the planned activities

- **Event space**: identify its best advantages in terms of dimensions, surface, colour, ceiling height, etc.

■ Content

By facilitating unrestricted and easy access to information, technology also brings a great challenge to event organizers, namely how to create better content, how to share it and how to best involve the public through it (see the section on Content Marketing in this chapter and in Chapter 6).

The FRESH Conference is an annual conference on meeting design that gathers meeting professionals (including meeting planners, meeting designers, facilitators, and so on.) It provides presentations and room for discussions around all possible meeting design topics and offers a large number of experiences that enhance the learning and application in future events. It also allows and encourages experimenting and testing of tools, techniques and formats. In Box 1.1 (Chapter 1), Maarten Vanneste presents FRESH, which has been a hybrid event from its conception.

Maarten proposes that, with all the complexities and ways, meetings must adapt to rapidly evolving technologies and their demands. The industry needs a new generation of planners who understand the strategic importance of meetings and can execute a holistic approach to the success of meetings.

Improving education is the key. One of Maarten's key arguments is that universities must recognize the importance of this growing field and offer Masters programs dedicated to training this next generation of meeting planners. In Box 6.1 (in Chapter 6), Maarten underscores the impact of the meetings industry once again with contextual statistics on how meetings are affecting numerous other industries in the hospitality and media fields.

Box 3.1: Engagement, creativity and innovation

The online participants

They have evolved from passive and silent, sometimes a little grumpy viewers to happier and engaged participants. Since FRESH's first edition, the online moderator remains the same person that also managed the social messages (mainly from Twitter). As we grew, more attention was given to the online participant. In 2014 and 2015, two people were full-time watching and interacting with the online participants. As the cost of bringing the content online can drop below 10 cents per viewer, it is much cheaper than bringing your teams or clients to one location. The more people see it, the better, especially if you have the potential to reach tens of thousands more than on-site.

FRESH offers a different channel for its online participant every year. However, a regular conference needs to evolve, to grow as much in terms of consistency as possible. I recommend you to improve the attendee experience year by year, but stick to the same technology base whenever possible, so participants can get used to it. Keep in mind that you have to take into consideration different public and points of view.

■ Corporate: The online participant is an additional participant (client) learning about the new services (from the company).

■ Association: The online participant either is a paying participant or will be one in the future by becoming a paying on-site participant.

The online participant creates value, even if it is sub-optimal or limited value, often at limited cost, but with potentially great ROI.

The engaged online participant

If you are only interested in more viewers, you may not be looking to engage the participants. Nevertheless, an engaged viewer who feels himself or herself as part of a community will become a loyal viewer. If you are looking for more paying participants, you need to look at the online audience as future on-site participants.

Social media and social media monitoring

Creating a hashtag and inviting people to tweet. This can be supported by on screen reminders for online participants or by an invitation to post from the online moderator. More impact comes from showing to online participants you are actually listening and often responding to the chat.

What seems to work well is to select a remark or question from the online participants and ask the speaker to respond to this "question for the online audience". This brings the remote participants closer to the on-site event.

Voting

Voting with keypads is the best guarantee to get all votes. When you are in control of the AV on every HUB, you can give everyone a keypad for fast and easy way of voting with the best possible participation rates. All votes done in several countries by hundreds of people immediately appear on the screen on all hubs. These can even be split by demographic criterion.

An alternative is to use mobile apps for interaction. It allows people to use their smartphones to vote, to tweet and even to place a direct question.

Interactive mobile conference apps

Another good and affordable solution for interaction may be a conference app. Most conference apps have one or more ways to get your participants engaged: by voting, texting or even an elaborate co-creation system to get the right people together around a table for discussing a topic of mutual interest. If you still need to select a conference app, make sure you check it out on its audience engagement systems for both on-site and online participants.

Discussion brainstorm tools

The most powerful tools around are discussion or brainstorm tools. They allow all participants to go to a web page and type their ideas which anyone can react to or comment on. Later, all ideas can be analysed and categories will be synthesized. Those categories become folders with category names and anyone can sort out their own ideas in the appropriate folders. Those folders now become a 'space' for both online and on-site participants to have deeper and ongoing discussions.

Main lessons so far

Attendees

Create a hashtag and invite people to tweet. More impact comes from showing to online participants you are actually listening and often responding to the chat.

The tools

Tools will get more inexpensive, better and faster: software, app, social media and new robotics will help us design better hybrid meetings and choose the right tools (depending on the objectives from either corporate or association meetings).

The production

One thing is clear: the online participants entail a separate production: sound, video and most of all a specific moderator or facilitator. The attention given to online audience should be 100% and the will to connect them must be absolute.

Maarten Vanneste is CEO of ABBIT Meeting Innovators, author of Meeting Architecture and founder of the Meeting Design Institute and the FRESH conference

In corporate events, participants increasingly demand new and unique perspectives, and increase their expectations regarding what is presented, which requires training and more interactive capabilities that accelerate results. They want to be recognized as individuals, be involved and inspired. In fact, nowadays content is everywhere! For Holub[14], "Content is less about knowledge building *per se* these days. It is more about engaging participants and triggering interaction among them." To leverage content throughout the event life cycle and increase ROI for attendees, he suggests two steps during pre-event phase:

- **Leveraging the power of a crowd** – Stimulate your event community to co-create your event by enabling them to submit, review and vote on their favourite speakers and topics proposals (by themselves or by the event planner). In order to vote, use simple polls using services (as SurveyMonkey or sli.do)

- **Promoting and giving out content snippets** – as the date of your event draws closer, start sharing content samples using, for example, a Twitter contest with prizes related to the event, such as free tickets, free exhibiting space, etc. that encourage them to tweet and spread the word about the event. Publish on the event blog sneak-peaks of your speaker's presentation and/or short video teasers produced by them, giving reasons to attend their sessions. It will give more visibility to speakers and facilitate tweets to online communities.

The challenge is even greater when the event's target audience is comprised of CEOs or executives in management positions. Among the key components that can entice them, we can mention relevance to content (exclusive study results, valuable information for future possibilities, and so on), high quality of attendees and other possibilities of networking.

■ Hybrid events

The essence of a hybrid event is to have attendees and virtual participants (those coming through the web) simultaneously. Although the hiring and operation of this format represents an increase in fixed costs of the event, there is no comparison as to the geographical coverage that is enabled by a hybrid event. With it, anyone anywhere on the planet can participate in the event by registering and accessing the platform. Moreover, precisely because of the possibility of attracting more attendants by virtual means, the use of hybrid events may lead to a better ROI, even if the initial cost may be increased.

Hybrid events also allow meeting planners to increase revenues of events substantially, even when they choose to offer a free registration and admission option for online participants. In this case, access to lectures is restricted, without covering the speeches of keynotes, for example.

Some of the key takeaways from MPI report[15] among their members about hybrid events are that although 50% hadn't organized and other 25% have never attended or organized a hybrid event, most of them (75%) believe it will an important issue. They are still beginning to understand its concept, and believe that hybrid elements are a "way to overcome challenges in existing live events". The respondents think they are expensive and "require new ways of content delivery and engagement".

The report points out that "there is no such one-size-fits-all for hybrid events" and indicates four main formats for hybrid events: a) broadcasting to remote delegates; b) connecting remote locations in relation to the venue of the event; c) connecting remote speakers and d) connecting multiple site to a broadcast studio.

MPI report pointed out the different needs of live and remote audiences. It suggests meeting planners take special care about the content, since not all of them suit online audiences and need to be adapted to remote audience needs, such as shorter sessions (not longer than 20 minutes). Content must be relevant to avoid distractions and it may be necessary to provide exclusive content for virtual attendees: "Content is what gets people through the door, engagement is what keeps them there and makes them come back for more." New tools to design and deliver content (must be shorter) will be needed; as for engagement, "the use of man-on-the street interviews and talk show and news-desk formats as more engaging ways to deliver hybrid content than speaker-behind-the-podium".

MPI says the following about the importance of special preparation and training the speakers for hybrid events: "Because the attention span of remote delegates is shorter, speakers must be more engaging. They must acknowledge remote attendees and look at the camera. The loss of physical connection requires speakers to develop new skills to engage." According to the report, "meeting professionals are still trying to figure out the right revenue model of hybrid events" and they "need more information around hybrid events sponsorship opportunities."

In fact, the difficulties mentioned above are great opportunities for organizers who want to make their companies and their events different from their competitors' ones.

■ Speakers

In technical and scientific events, speaker performance is critical to the success of the event for the content that is conveyed in the lectures. For that purpose many precautions should be taken when selecting, hiring and making arrangements. In many countries (particularly in the US), there are several associations that group speakers and are great sources of reference, such as the National Speaker Association.[16]

Macedo[17] suggests some precautions:

- **Test drive** – the way knowledge is transmitted makes all the difference to engage and hold the audience's attention. Before hiring, watch videos or lectures by the chosen speakers, as well as check references or testimonials by former clients and listeners, online or face-to-face.

- **On demand** – nothing is more de-motivating than going a long way to attend a lecture you have already seen or that is outside the context of the event. Make sure that the speaker will customize his or her lecture by providing him or her with accurate and abundant information on the event, such as the public, market, business, goals, and other lectures already confirmed.

- **Co-branding** – in open events (those paid or free events to which the public is invited) negotiate with speakers, so that they support the dissemination to the audience through their websites, blogs and any other media that they use. Take the opportunity to negotiate with them courses / books / software / products that can be sold during the event at discounted prices as well.

■ Promotion

Planning for the promotion and dissemination of your event must be anchored and directed according to the audience (socio-demographic profile, preferences, most used channels, both digital and face-to-face) and the message to be conveyed, which is built according to the differentiation and positioning of the event. Such information is vital for the preparation of planning and schedule that integrates all selected options. See more details in section on *Digital Strategic Planning for Events* in this chapter. Among the digital instruments that can be used by meeting planners, we can include:

- **Email marketing** – it can be very effective if the messages and their frequency are well thought out.

- **Speakers** – short videos and hangouts help engage the interest of the public for their participation in the event. See also Co-branding in the previous item (Speakers).

- **Contests or competitions** – running one on Facebook with a prize is an easy way to gather data and promote social sharing.

- **Photo campaigns** – they also get people's attention, promote the event and they can be displayed on a social media wall in the event area.

Graph 3.3 shows the most used mobile advertising by Millennials.

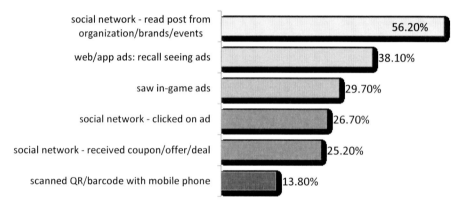

Graph 3.3: Mobile advertising activities performed by Millennial smartphone users (18 to 24) in the United Kingdom (UK) as of March 2013.

Source: http://www.statista.com/statistics/286342/mobile-advertising-activities-among-uk-millenial-smartphone-users/

Commercialization

When the event is a paid one, the price is a key component of the attendance of participants. In addition to the payment method and the ways that will be used, other options should be considered when making the financial planning of the event, as they may stimulate the rapid adhesion and the formation of groups. The most used are:

- **Batches** – groups of tickets or registrations with specific period for sales. Each batch also has different prices from the others and becomes more expensive as the date of the event draws closer.

- **Promotions and giveaways** – offering discounts conditional on presentation of coupons or granting gifts or advantages for participants.

Sponsorship is a key factor for the financial survival of events of any size, purpose, and scope. However, the seduction and conquest of sponsors depend on numerous factors, such as project adherence to the corporate strategy, potential consumers or the public, cost and items that make up the sponsorship quotas, the time when the event is held, offered brand activations or the brands allowed in relation to the editions, etc. Previous favourable results, as well as the information and results expected in the edition are also important factors in the decision-making process. Social media, event apps and event management software can provide insights and great tools and possibilities to help meeting planners to win prospective sponsors and keep them engaged.

Event apps offer great possibilities to add value to sponsorship. Macedo[18] describes seven ways to unlock potential sponsorship features in event apps, at much lower costs:

1 **Banners:** Sponsor banners are highly visible and a constant presence in an event app. If you have multiple sponsor banners, you will also get the added movement of the banners rotating, drawing your users' eyes to the ad.

    Banners are more traditional, but they can easily capture engagement metrics and allow sponsors the flexibility of linking to a wide variety of content. In addition, thanks to its ubiquitous visibility, you can charge a premium for it.

2 **Sponsor icons:** For a particularly high-level sponsor, you might feel it appropriate to give them their own menu item with a sponsored icon. The content is up to them – but it certainly offers the sponsor great visibility and, again, the ability to measure engagement easily.

    Custom menu items stand out, get many taps, and allow sponsors to get creative with what type of content they are linked to.

3 **Multi-sponsor module**: You can give props to all your sponsors with a module dedicated solely to your benefactors. A user perusing this list can see thumbnail logos, then dig deep to find links and information.

    Organizers can even rank the list based on sponsorship level, allowing premium levels to be displayed first or have a special designation that demands more attention.

4 **Sponsored event sessions:** Offering to allow sponsorship of your keynote or lunches gives yet another chance for branding. Incorporate the sponsor's name into the session title or include their logo in the session's listing. You can reinforce it with branding in the session itself – perhaps as part of a pre-session slide on the presentation screen.

5 **Sponsored tweets:** Event apps are ideal for encouraging conversation on social media. Imagine the added value provided to your

sponsors if they were a part of your social conversation surrounding your event.

Within the event app Twitter module, you can load a sponsor-related hashtag to be included with each tweet. Sponsors will appreciate the chatter and the social data generated.

6 **Sponsored polls:** You can really take advantage of an event app's ability to generate data by creating a sponsored poll. Work with the particular sponsor to find out what types of insight they would like to gain from your audience, and then include that in an organic poll that can eventually help you create a better event and added awareness for your sponsor.

7 **Scavenger hunt:** If you and your sponsors are looking for an interactive way to engage the audience, consider gamification. A scavenger hunt can influence attendees to engage multiple times with one brand over the course of an event, or encourage app users to interact with many sponsors by checking off booths on a list. Either way, encouraging your attendees to move through your event space to engage with the sponsors will add significant visibility and value.

■ Satisfaction surveys and certificates

It is more than advisable to get feedback from key stakeholders (participants, sponsors, speakers, partners and suppliers) on the event. Set the relevant aspects that need to be addressed, but make sure they are only few questions, formulated in an objective and short form. They can be obtained during or after the event or right after the end of the event. In this case, the return of the responses tends to be more significant if it is sent within four days after the event. In addition to traditional printed questionnaire, there are several free and paid digital tools that can be used for this assessment research.

28%
Bump in retweets on
post with video

35%
Bump in retweets on
post with images

Whether to prove attendance or to be valid documents for academic curricula, multiple event types require the issuance of certificates after their termination. Delivery of printed certificates is becoming increasingly rare, as certificates are being issued digitally and sent online to participants. As well as in research, which sometimes is required as a prerequisite for the delivery of the certificate, there are several applications and management software options for it.

■ #hashtag

As shown in Chapter 2, you can create a hashtag of your event, but also another one to make it easy for attendees to find all the broadcasts from your event on Twitter. After you have plugged the event hashtag, release videos, photos and encourage attendees to share them with their friends and followers.

■ Emoticons

Emoticon comes from the words emotion and icon. An emotion icon, or emoticon is used to express feelings in an on-line communication. It is defined as "a meta-communicative pictorial representation of a facial expression that, in the absence of body language and prosody, serves to draw a receiver's attention to the tenor or temper of a sender's nominal verbal communication, changing and improving its interpretation. It expresses a person's feelings or mood. (…) As social media has become widespread, emoticons have played a significant role in communication through technology[19]".

The first recorded use of text characters to represent a facial expression occurred on March 10, 1953 in the New York Herald Tribune on a film advertisement for Lili, starring Leslie Caron. It read "Today You'll laugh :-) You'll cry :-(You'll love <3 'Lili'". The smiley ":-)" in electronic media such as e-mails and social networks was first used in 1982 by Scott Fahlman, assistant professor of computer science research at Carnegie Mellon University.[20] The first emojis were designed by Shigetaka Kurita in the 90s. The term comes from the Japanese expressions of "e" (picture) and "moji" (character). The first set had 176 pictures with 12x12 pixel resolution, and sought to express human emotions and were a success in Japan. Their use was expanded worldwide after the launch of iOS 4 from Apple and later in Android and Windows devices.[21]

In 2011, the little faces were included in the iOS keyboards and two years later came to Android. From there they have gained more and more space in the preference of users, such as in Instagram, where half of comments, captions and hashtags use them in their posts. The growth of their use shows the importance of graphic display for users of social media and should be taken into consideration by event planners, since emoticons may have a major role in enhancing the perception of the message by the public of several languages. The brands have woken up to the power of emoticons. Nowadays, emoticons are here to stay and to take over the world. And what about your event?

3

■ Sharing photos/videos

The importance of graphic display in communication with consumers emphasizes the need to use photos and videos and to have adequate visual layout to meet their tastes and preferences. According to Shutterstock's 2015 Creative Trends[22], posts with videos (+28%) or photos (+35%) are more likely to get re-tweeted. Technology continues to make everything evolve. As the so-called 'selfie' is the most important cultural trend (+2,166%) today, communications and promotions must consider this option.

■ Live streaming

Even before the event starts, it can help build excitement on attendees: live streaming interviews with speakers and participants, with tweet questions live, a film of rehearsals in progress, or the crew setting up.

Hybrid events are booming since they allow people to attend digitally, as some could not otherwise attend. Since going hybrid in 2012, the Convening Leaders event held by Professional Convention Management Association (PMCA) has had record-breaking attendance for online and offline attendees each year since then. In 2014, 17% of the total audience (877 people) attended remotely, while 76 attended both remotely and face-to-face over the duration of the event.[23]

■ Email marketing

Today's consumers want to be valued and respected in terms of their desires and individuality. Thus, it is important that e-mail communications marketing offer the option to unsubscribe from the contact list. By the way, in many countries local laws require the possibility to opt-out (when one chooses not to receive messages from a company) to be clearly visible and enforceable.

■ Online registration system

In addition to the efficiency and convenience offered to consumers by enrolling online for an event, this allows organizers to replace a manual process with a simplified, automated and efficient process. According to research by IMEX in 2014, 85% of organizers consider that use important or very important.

Besides the choice of the most appropriate software for your needs, it is necessary to define marketing strategies that increase the profitability of the event. The first is to encourage advance purchase: the greater the advance, the greater the discount obtained. In cultural events such as concerts, it is common to release batches of tickets to each predetermined period. The closer the date of the event, the more expensive they will be.

■ Payments

The use of mobile devices such as smartphones and tablets (see Chapter 2), allows participants to interact better and more deeply with one another and with the sponsors and organizers of events. With those devices, users have richer and more interactive experiences, besides access to more diverse and detailed content and at all stages of the event, much more than in the past. The prediction of the evolution of the total of sales and e-commerce globally shows that, despite the increment of the absolute number, the growth rate in percent is slowing down. This is a clear indication that professional experience in online sales is increasingly necessary. Payment methods have also adapted to this new scenario. Graph 3.4 shows the global evolution of e-commerce and Graph 3.5 shows the evolution of e-commerce in the US considering Desktop and Mobile platforms.

(US$ billions)

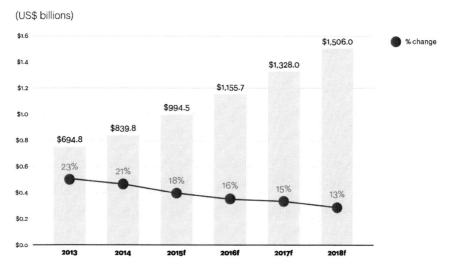

Graph 3.4: Global e-commerce sales in US$ billions – 2013-2018 (forecast)

Source: www.atkearney.com/consumer-products-retail/e-commerce-index/full-report/-/asset_publisher/87xbENNHPZ3D/content/global-retail-e-commerce-keeps-on-clicking/10192.

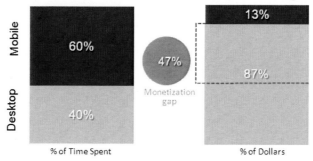

Graph 3.5: Percentage of time spent vs. percentage of retail dollars spent by platform

Fonte: Relatório U.S. Digital Future in Focus. comScore, 2015. Page 19

Strategy and focus

Today, the increased length of the residual value of an event, engagement, networking, identifying and generating business and relationship with and between participants, among other numerous benefits, all arise through the adoption of good practices in social media.

Each event and company will create a specific strategy that makes sense in terms of its objectives. To increase positives outcomes, you must have an online and offline marketing plan and a social media strategy for your event. Before starting your path, you should start by understanding how they relate to the event's needs and evaluate each of the most used social platforms: their purpose, target audience, what differentiates one from another, key metrics, estimated time needed to reach expectations, etc. You will also need to guarantee a great client experience at all times.

Therefore, the commitment to provide unforgettable experiences to participants is also directly related to the understanding of their needs and how they relate to social media. The answer to the meteoric rise of YouTube and other platforms like Instagram may be in the way our brain reads, processes information, and establishes relations of trusts. According to Shter[24], videos are the best way to create links:

> *About 90% of the information captured by our brains is visual and we process images 60,000 times faster than we can process texts. Therefore, videos allow us to select visual elements and explain complex ideas to any number of people, anywhere. (...) Videos involve us on a visceral level. They help us connect ideas and products through visual narrative. The emotional connection turns videos into highly efficient communication tools. Videos are even more effective and important when we try to engage with the public on a personal level. If you want people to understand your message in a profound way, videos are the way. (...) Our brains are built to establish trust through face-to-face contact.*

■ Overview of available technologies

Due to the wide variety of platforms and apps for events, Bruno listed on Table 3.1 some solutions and marketing software products to help organizers identify gaps and overlaps, to visualize interdependencies and relationships, to promote synergies and to better allocate resources.

By Department	By Event Cycle	By Stakeholder
Marketing	Budget preparation	Attendee/delegate
Marketing automation platform	Accounting/financial reporting software	Registration system
Website software	Strategic meetings management platform	Check-in app
SEO app	Venue Selection	Coat-check app
Advertisement distribution solution	e-RFP tool	Event-mobile app
Social media and public relations platform	Contractor management platform	Appointment-setting platform
Content development and distribution app	Exhibitor/sponsor sales	Peer-to-peer networking software
Operations	CRM solution	Social wall
Event management platform	Online floor plan app	Gamification platform
Check-in app	Lead generation software	CEU tracking system
Registration system	Conference program development	RFID/NFC/beacons
Audio-visual planning tool	Speaker management platform	Exhibitor/sponsor
Project management software	Call for paper or presentations software	Website software
e-RFP tool (venues, hotels, contractors)	Session picker app	CRM solution
Event-mobile app	Audience promotion/ exhibitor marketing	Marketing automation platform
Attendee networking app	Marketing automation platform	Lead generation software
Volunteer management tool	Website software	Online floor plan/booth allocation platform
Social wall	SEO app	Proposal software
Room block management tool	Advertisement distribution solution	Contractor/hotel/venue
Accounting/financials	Social media and public relations platform	e-RFP tool
Forecasting/budgeting software	Content development and distribution app	Room block management software
Cash flow analysis tool	Registration	Contractor management platform
General ledger, P/L, payables, receivables system	Registration software	Speaker
Invoicing software	Room block management platform	Speaker management platform
Strategic meetings management platform	Travel management solution	Abstract management software

3

Exhibit/sponsorship sales	On-site event management	Media
CRM solution	Event management platform	Online press room
Online floor plan app	Check-in app	Marketing automation platform
Lead generation software	Project management software	Content development and distribution app
Customer service	Event-mobile app	
Telephone/email/messaging system	Attendee networking app	
Call center solution	Appointment-setting solution	
Conference program	Volunteer management tool	
Speaker management platform	Surveys/data collection	
– Call for papers or presentations software	Session evaluation tool	
– Session picker app	– Audience response systems	
– Attendance monitoring app	– Attendance tracking app	
– CEU tracking system	– RFID/NFC/beacons	
	– Event-mobile app	

Table 3.1: Collection of technologies on event industry

Source: Bruno, Michelle. The Best Way to Wrap Your Head Around Event Technology at http://www. eventmanagerblog.com/wrap-your-head-around-eventtech. Author's layout.

Digital strategic planning for events

To speak of digital strategic planning it is also essential to address digital marketing (its relevant aspects are detailed in Chapter 6). When one hears about it:

> Or any other creative combinations that can be made with those words, we are talking about using the Internet effectively as a marketing tool, involving communication, publicity, advertising and all the arsenal of strategies and concepts already used in the theory of marketing.[25]

Digital marketing with a focus on digital consumer behaviour structures the activities to perform and the way they will be implemented for effectiveness and coverage in the digital strategic planning. Chapter 6 describes the digital marketing model that meeting planners and suppliers must follow in order to achieve or exceed the objectives of the event.

■ Content marketing or inbound marketing

With the Internet having increasingly collaborative information, consumers started to refer to it in the search for the most useful, relevant and diversified content.

Inbound marketing, also called content marketing or branded content, is one of the digital marketing tools. It can be defined as "a strategic approach focused on creating and distributing content that is relevant, consistent and valuable, in order to attract, retain and convert prospects, leads and customers of your company."[26]

It is used in a variety of formats and tools, such as news, blog posts, articles, e-books / white paper, social media, instructional videos, pictures, newsletter, infographics, etc. See details in Chapter 6.

Using social media to boost events

How to define the best social media strategy for your event? This is one of the most common questions for organizers. Experts suggest the best place to start is to understand the most widely used social platforms thoroughly, as well as the purposes and attributes related to your event and stakeholders' needs. Always remember that 'social' is the keyword in social media. That means that all platforms are a two-way communication: your event must interact with them, not only post photos, videos and articles.

The infographics from Eventility[27] (an event management platform) highlight the best practice to use social media in four easy steps (Figures 3.3 to 3.6): 84% of meeting planners use Facebook, 61% Twitter and 42% YouTube to promote their events. In addition, 78% of them plan to increase their use in the future. However, social media can be used far beyond than just to promote events. Eventility advise us:

> With the right strategy and tools in place, event organizers can harness social media to attract more attendees, cultivate engagement and extend the lifetime value of their events. (...) Whether organizing a conference, seminar, fundraiser, concert or a club or group event, social media can play an important role before, during and after an event. (...) Social networks provide a remarkably easy way to collect RSVPs and generally have a higher response rate than paper invitations.

> Social media also offers the opportunity to involve attendees in the actual organization process. By asking your audience to vote for their favourite speakers, bands or activities, you can create an event program that you know people will enjoy. What is more, by giving attendees a voice and making them feel involved, you are also likely to increase the affinity they feel towards the event.

> Once you have plugged the hashtag, released some promotional videos, and encouraged your attendees to share the event with their friends and followers, you ought to have a respectable turnout. (...) Some simple ways of doing that include live streaming, check-ins, Twitter walls and offering prizes to the most engaged attendees, but it is important to consider the role

3

of social costumer service as well. Users are increasingly turning to social media for customer care issues, so Event Organizers will need to identify and respond to enquiries quickly. (…)

Lastly, do not forget that social media is a valuable source of feedback. By using a social media-monitoring tool to analyse the conversation during and after the event, you can ascertain what was popular and what could be improved.

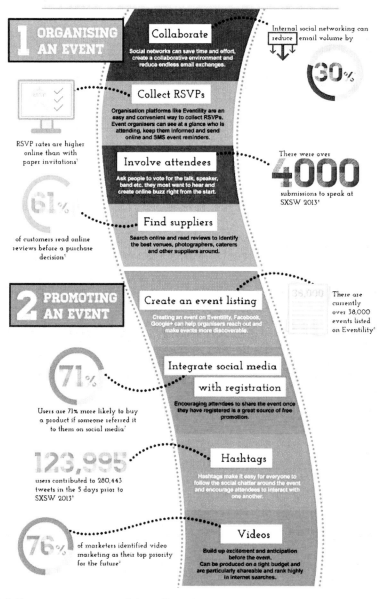

Figure 3.3(a): Four ways to use social media to boost events

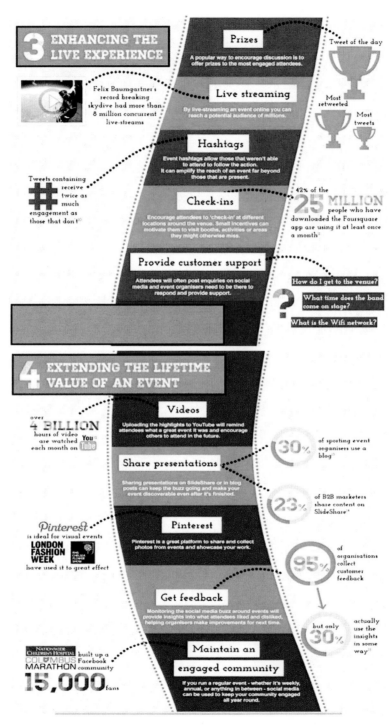

Figure 3.3(b) : Four ways to use social media to boost events

Source: http://oursocialtimes.com/using-social-media-to-make-your-event-a-dazzling-success-infographic. [21/09/15

Figure 3.4: Key steps for planning social media.

Figure 3.4 shows a summary of the steps to follow that can help you maximize the use of social media in events, which are detailed below:

1   Determine your target market and the reason why companies would want to be sponsors or stakeholders to subscribe to your event.

2   Make sure your event objectives are aligned with your target customers.

3   Establish your social media policy and determine which social media are most suitable for your needs.

4   Set clear criteria about which apps should be used, when, and how, as well as about the advertising campaigns that will be carried out in social media.

5   Centralize all the information from social networks into a single tool, which allows greater speed in the message shots, as well as greater control over the actions already taken.

6   Create strategic and specific actions for each of the chosen social media, aiming to value participants (Check Table 3.2 to understand the advantages and disadvantages among the most known social media. Table 3.3 show some of those differences.)

7   Increase participation and stakeholder engagement, feeding them regularly with relevant information about the event, such as news and what will be found at the event and/or in the next edition.

8 Centralize information and answers because social media users require agility and practicality.

9 Monitor. Follow all that is said about the event and the brands involved (what, who, when, where and how). Do not forget to define KPIs and metrics using the tools of social media to evaluate whether your efforts are generating the best results.

10 Prepare management of the comments, from the feedback obtained.

	Facebook	Twitter	Pinterest
Purpose	Builds brand loyalty and reputation. Establishes your business as an authority through interesting content and informational posts.	Shares breaking news and quick updates, promotes new products, content, or brand contests, collects instant feedback from your audience.	Acts as an online scrapbook, displays products and brand essence through inspiration boards.
Unique attributes	Reaches a variety of segments of an audience with one post	Serves people looking for quick info, company news, and immediate response to questions about products or events	Generates leads and drives traffic to other content (or back to your website)
	Offers opportunity to create ads to drive traffic to your website/blog	Focuses on dialogue creation and starting conversations with customers	Visually promotes and highlights products/services through images
	Encourages dialogue and depth with a customer base	Known for its hashtag (#) communication functionality	Provokes immediate or future Call-To-Action (CTA) responses
	Ideal for sharing personal stories, testimonials, detailed information about your business	Best platform for PR/publicity purposes when traditional media does not respond	Allows you to micro-target your search with clearly defined categories
Commitment of time: how often you should post	1-2 times per day or 6 times a week	3-4 times per day or 20 times a week	2-3 times per day or 10 times a week

Table 3.2: Social media purpose and attributes

Sources: http://www.verticalresponse.com/ http://www.verticalresponse.com/blog/social-media-your-business-choosing-the-best-platform/ | http://www.omnicoreagency.com/author/sam/

> **Businesses should use social media as a source of '2-way communication' with their audience, regardless of the platform. You need to interact with them!**

Social Network	Advantages	Disadvantages	Suitability
Facebook Ads	Campaigns can be targeted taking into account age, gender, language, interests, demographics, and other target audience details.	A lot of competition and need for investment to boost publications.	Companies that wish to widely advertise goods and services.
Google AdWords	Campaigns appear just when users make a related search on Google – portal used by about 90% of Brazilians.	The cost per keyword is high	Ideal for all sectors and companies working with content marketing.
YouTube	Possibility of posting ads in three different places: in-stream (before the video), in-display (next to the audiovisual content) or on top of a search on the page.	The cost varies by segment and requires planning. In addition, campaigns need to be audiovisual to ensure good return on this social network.	Companies that use strategic marketing and have products and services that generate engagement.
Twitter	Possibility of real-time interaction with customers, avoiding future problems and brand wear-out.	The promotion of products and services is not recommended, as information on Twitter is real-time.	Suitable for companies that want to interact more with the target audience, offering complementary information to customers.
Spotify	Allows various types of ads, from jingles during music programming to display of videos, banners and brand playlists.	The public that uses this media is younger and may be totally different from the customers of your company.	Companies with bold marketing strategy, with viral and irreverent content.

Table 3.3: How to choose the most suitable social networks

Source: Thiago Regis. http://www.proxxima.com.br/ Adapted by authors.

Involving and engaging attendees are among the most important issues of every event. As each platform has its own average age and gender and its best approach, you have to bear in mind your target audience, needs and specific content, before choosing the best options for your event.

The growth in the use of mobile devices, shown in Chapter 2, demands from companies and meeting planners a special care for the campaigns via mobiles, whose users handle their devices differently from other electronic devices. Among the issues suggested by Djoulizibaritch[28] is the integration of the campaign for the mobile digital planning, allowing continuity between all devices, thus creating a cross channel communication. However, the same information needs to be adapted to the format and specific profile of each media, directing or customizing appropriate messages for each audience.

He warns that it is essential to offer practicality and to get higher conversion rates, as consumers require a simple interface, with easy to read campaigns and mechanisms to facilitate and speed up purchases. Moreover, creating responsive websites and streamlining purchasing processes are other important items, avoiding giant forms and identifying those who have real interests in a particular product or service. He points out the importance of accuracy and better results, the creation of unique campaigns with objective and direct messages, and neat focussed design (a clean look and one that offers users a clear message of what the brand wants to communicate).

In 2014, Deluxe[29] conducted a study with small business owners about their digital marketing practices. Their conclusion was that the digital footprint of the owners (Figure 3.5) is not a very active one. 20% spent 2-3 hours per week updating their web presence and 10% spent 4+ hours. 70% of those small business owners spend less than one hour a week on website maintenance. Check it out and compare it to your company and/or event.

■ Monitoring social media

The use of social media has significantly affected the way participants interact with one another and with brands, and how they build and develop relationships. All sources consulted estimate growth in their use in events in coming years. As already pointed out in this chapter and in others, performance in social media is a key advantage sought by organizers with the use of mobile event apps. Besides these and many other benefits, their use can also cause difficulties and bring risks to organizers. Social media is here to stay.

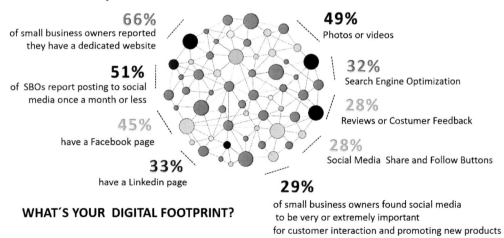

66%
of small business owners reported they have a dedicated website

51%
of SBOs report posting to social media once a month or less

45%
have a Facebook page

33%
have a Linkedin page

WHAT´S YOUR DIGITAL FOOTPRINT?

49%
Photos or videos

32%
Search Engine Optimization

28%
Reviews or Costumer Feedback

28%
Social Media Share and Follow Buttons

29%
of small business owners found social media to be very or extremely important for customer interaction and promoting new products

Figure 3.5: Digital Footprint

Source: http://www.verticalresponse.com/blog/small-business-owners-time-digital-game-infographic/

Figure 3.6 highlights some of the main characteristics and where care is needed in its use and in the digital marketing in events. First, it shows that each social media has a specific type of user and the best day and time for engagement. Know your target audience preferences. Content is king: you will gain the most attention through relevant content that reflects your event culture. As well as written content, include photo and video posts which increase interaction on most social media. Be prepared to handle negative comments. Someone may not agree with everything you post, but social media can be used as a search engine and a great source of ideas.

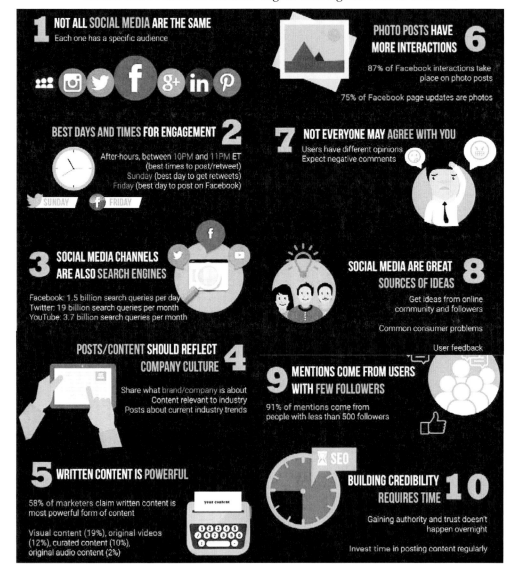

Figure 3.6: Ten things you might not know about social media

Source: Infographic courtesy of Kryptonite Digital Media http://KryptoniteDigital.com

Monitoring is the act of keeping track of and evaluating something for a certain period. Regarding the web for the corporate world, monitoring social media refers to observing and evaluating what is said, written and/or filmed about what is being studied (company, brand, product, service or person) in the virtual world. Torres[30] conceptualizes monitoring as:

> *Strategic action that integrates the results of all other strategic, tactical and operational actions, allowing one to check the results and take action to correct course or improve actions. It occurs in various ways, including monitoring of access to sites and blogs, emails and SMS messages, videos and widgets in viral actions and visualization and clicks on banners. (...) Unlike other types of monitoring, where we measure actions created in digital marketing, social media monitoring measures not only those results, but also the image of the brands, the opinion of consumers, product and service problems and other miscellaneous information about a company.*

To Laine and Fruhwirth[31], they are tools for monitoring social media. They are (mostly) software services over the Internet:

> *to filter and analyse the textual content produced by and in social media. The tools find content based on keywords defined by users. The tools incorporate multiple functionalities, with analyses of volume, source, author, keyword, region, and feeling, and report those analyses conveniently in graphic mode.*

Monitoring social media allows the identification of the best options to follow regarding the event. According to Silva[32], it applies before, during and after the communication and the factors that are shaping the digital nature of information and data flows, and formation and the construction of virtual social networks. For him:

> *the digital data are reflexes and trails of behaviour, actions and physical and symbolic actual events. It has been a long time that it does not make sense to draw a line separating what is real from what is virtual. The term social media monitoring encompasses a market sphere that aggregates services, tools, media, professionals and conceptions of essential resources for understanding and performing digital communication.*

■ The monitoring strategy: why to do it and how?

Known as the monitoring and evaluation of brand image in social media, monitoring is more than just that. This strategy is what will guide your content and product actions, as well as online relationships, which will provide relevant information to understand how the company's performance is being conducted and received by the audience. Thus, monitoring of social networks makes it possible to identify the best ways that the event should follow. Other reasons for focusing on monitoring strategy:

- Detecting market opportunities, identifying the improvement of products and services.

- Creating new ways of engagement.

- Identifying influencers of the brand, those who can serve as spontaneous media and disseminators of content.

- Analysing the competition. Thus, you can prepare for dealing with the novelties from the competition and detect what changes can be made in your company.

- Avoiding crises[33].

Always keep in mind that although monitoring is a process of data analysis, it deals with the perceptions and reactions of people to information or messages. Remember, first and foremost, that monitoring is about people.

Monitoring and content strategy

More and more customers and event sponsors demand results that offer measurable, actionable, and more effective insights. Muniz[34] lists ways to deliver online content on social media:

> The **first** one is based on what we determine to be relevant to a type of audience, based on what engages that public. That is, a content curation, a search, a mapping of what we want to show. The **second** possibility would be to understand what people say about their brands in different environments, to understand the strengths and weaknesses, turning them into content. This is one of the classic ways of monitoring, which involves the search for brands and what is said about them. The **third** is the one where we go beyond relevant content, beyond what directly involves the brand name, it is the one where we investigate behaviours and desires, where we offer what people want, long before they discover that need.

This content comes from the knowledge gained from and supported by data and measured information, as explained in this chapter.

■ The monitoring process

The timeline of the monitoring process (Figure 3.7) goes through the following points:

1 **Observe**: in an unstructured way, look for references to your object of interest in social media. This will give you a general idea about the public perception about your brand, as well as on which social media there is greater occurrence.

2 **Plan**: with the information obtained in the previous step, you can make a detailed planning of the questions to ask and the answers to seek.

3 **Select tool**: it is time to choose a monitoring tool that best fits the objectives of monitoring.

4 **Classify**: at that time read all captured mentions (or a sample, depending on the volume), and classify by polarization: positive, neutral or negative.

5 **Categorize**: through tags, which identify the important variables, information is sorted out.

6 **Consolidate**: here the processed data are observed from the viewpoint of the focus of the monitoring, and prepared for the next phase.

7 **Analyse and interpret**: here come the more subjective aspects of monitoring, when the data are looked at by people with full knowledge of the reality and customer needs, in order to extract as much intelligence from the processed data.

8 **Present results**: make reports submitting from raw data, through the processed data and the perceived information, to the extracted intelligence, reaching insights and suggestions for actions, based on the overall results of the monitoring in question.

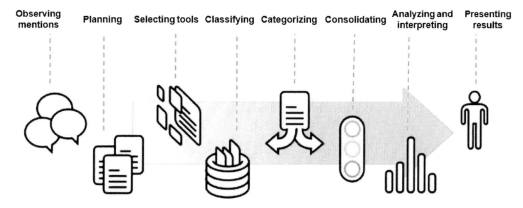

Figure 3.7: Monitoring steps

Source: Dourado, Danila. Software pleno de monitoramento: a análise que faz a diferença. In Silva, T. *Para entender o monitoramento de mídias sociais.* Available on http://misterkanu.com.br/wp-content/uploads/2012/11/Para-Entender-o-Monitoramento-de-Midias-Sociais.pdf.

When thinking about social media monitoring, the first step is to define the purposes of the monitoring clearly. Of course, there is an expectation regarding the results, but one should always think from the point of view of the public that is being monitored, which will be the object of observation. Therefore, before you think about getting good answers, focus on defining clearly what questions should be asked. All monitoring is born from a need for information (question), the captured data (information), which undergoes analysis to generate results (answers). Figure 6.3 in Chapter 6 shows the most used metrics by CMOs to measure social media.

■ Types of monitoring

There are basically three types of monitoring:

1 The first can be called **snapshot**, which 'takes a picture' of the presence of the monitoring object in social media. This is a time-limited process; it takes place at a certain time, in environments where the occurrence of mentions of the subject matter is more frequent. It is also a situational monitoring process, which checks the positioning of the brand, product or service in your market or segment.

2 Another type of time-limited monitoring is what we call **landscape**, which analyses the monitoring object, as well as some of its competitors. This allows a comparison between different positions among companies operating within the same market or segment.

3 Continued monitoring, which we call **panoramic**, is the one applied to the object monitored over time, observing the public's reactions to its actions and the market scenario as a whole.

Snapshot and landscape monitoring are usually made by companies in action planning stages for new products, or repositioning, so that they observe their results and build planning in order to respond to the strengths and weaknesses uncovered by monitoring. The continued monitoring (panoramic) is used more strategically, usually by brands and companies already established longer in the market, which seek to encourage, establish and operate relationships closer to their public and extract competitive advantages of knowledge in terms of behaviour of their target audience, including being able to discover and interact in different ways, from their main disseminators and detractors.

There is also another type of monitoring, the so-called netnography, that instead of observing public behaviour in social media regarding a brand, product or service, aims to explore a theme. For example, a telecommunications company can conduct netnography on smartphones usage habits among young people in preschool, rather than trying to investigate if this target audience comments on the product on social media. Therefore, it is considered a much more strategic type of monitoring, and its role is much more focused on capturing intelligence and extracting behavioural insights about a particular topic than investigating social media in market terms.

The choice of the most appropriate type of monitoring to meet your needs will be a bit subjective. However, in basic terms think of the following:

- Is your goal tactical? Use a time-limited monitoring to see how your brand, product or service is perceived at that time and in that digital environment, allowing you to create quick responses.

- Is your goal to gain insight to a plan or product launch? Use a time-limited monitoring as above, as you will have a view of your market position at that moment.

- Is your goal to reposition the brand? Use netnography, which allows you to find out what the public thinks about the market segment in which your product is inserted

- Is your goal strategic? Use netnography and/or continuous monitoring in order to get a view of the interests and desires of your audience about your area of expertise (netnography), or follow the reactions of this same audience regarding the development of your brand, product or service over time (continuous monitoring).

Classification

The classification happens "when monitoring is no longer a mass of data and it acquires a great value for the brand"[35]. For quality monitoring, it is paramount to have a classification scheme before starting it, since the speed of the virtual world prevents subsequent reclassifications.

Experts consider it essential that the monitoring starts with the correct configuration, so that the classifications can bring the expected information, and avoid rework or even worse, the loss of information from that period.

It is important to note that while many monitoring tools optionally make automatic classifications, human classification (made by people who know the business environment and objectives of the monitoring object) always achieve more satisfactory results, due to the subtleties present in any kind of human communication.

The difference between the monitoring of small and medium-sized enterprises and large companies is that as a rule, the monitoring of small and medium-sized ones seek results that are tactical, momentary and closer, whereas that of large companies tends to be strategic, for use in the medium to long term. The classification process takes place following the steps below:

1 **Observations of mentions and monitoring planning**. It is the initial phase, which begins with a free exploration of social media, watching what people communicate or share about the monitoring object.

2 **Selection of the tool**. The selection of the most appropriate tool will depend on the needs of the monitoring. Try to choose one that enables the integration of monitoring with customer service and CRM actions, which can be very useful over time, allowing systematization of interactions with your audience through social media.

3 **Categorization and classification**. At this stage, the data obtained and compiled are grouped according to their relevance and pertinence, and then classified as positive, neutral or negative. Applying tags that categorize the information in the captured references allows all sorts of applying filters, enabling a wide range of information crossings, which in turn allows different extractions of data set intelligence.

4 **Consolidation**. Here the processed data is studied analytically, to extract intelligence – answers to the questions that led the monitoring. It is the most strategic and critical phase of monitoring, requiring a professional with a thorough knowledge of customer reality and its market environment, as well as the goals in relation to monitoring.

5 **Analysis, interpretation and presentation of results**. The graphic display of results will depend, among other things, on information that the meeting planner needs, on which social media are part of the database, the data filter options of the tools available and on the crossing of data chosen to measure results.

Geolocation

Geolocation can be understood as the use of the geographical location of people for the systematic application of resources to make your life easier.

Geolocation describes a set of technologies that enable automatic determination of the location of a user or device. Thus, from devices installed mainly in mobile phones and tablets, or even through the IP of the machine used, it is possible for sites equipped with geolocation mechanisms to "know" where we are. (...) The location itself is nothing more than an abstract set of numbers. Geographical coordinates are codes devoid of emotions, history and identity. Moreover, the use of geolocation-based social networking provides a way to attach meaning to numeric expressions representing the scanned space. It builds this hybrid bond between man and objects, a relationship to trace historical permanence and mobility.[36]

Geolocation can be used from initial enrolment of people in events, allowing them to provide specific information as their location (providing differentiated registration fees, transportation options and lodging, etc.). Then, through the trans phase, when you can know exactly where the person is showing you the options of nearest events, to the post-event phase, allowing you to create groups of people depending on the location where they live or work and thus facilitating networking.

Chapter summary

The quality of the events is increasingly more important than the quantity. To get to the "bull's-eye" is paramount, which means: focus on interaction and engagement. After all, just throwing huge amounts of content does not assure great results.

Many marketers have chosen a lazy approach to social media. It is all about scheduling huge quantities of posts. Importing an Excel file with one month's worth of posts at once; republishing content; ignoring people who interact with you. There are much better ways to approach social media.

Quality will win over quantity. Marketers will realize that posting fewer but greater posts is the way to go. Interacting with the audience will bring better results than posting many mediocre posts. It is "A more human approach to social media marketing", if you will.[37]

Quality is translated as "events that fulfil my needs and desires" by attendees, and "use of data and intelligence to make better financial results" by organizers.

Technology is the key to reach best results on events organization and there is a vast range of tools to look, understand and to choose from. The use of specific event apps is growing fast, for all steps of the organization of events, and to process automation that impact on costs and revenue and data capture, which allows for measurement.

IoT (Internet of Things) is becoming a major factor, as it allows attendees to act by themselves in many activities, and gives organizers a lot of useful information regarding public behaviour.

Technology suppliers must be involved with the event organization from its planning through its whole lifetime.

Hybrid events are gaining a huge overall importance in the industry as you can have both face-to-face and remote attendees, all contributing to the success of your events. The future points to hybrid events having an even bigger impact on event business.

Social media is vital not only for communication, but as a business tool, as the engagement of all parties is more and more of capital importance. All event organizers have to master social media content and monitoring in order to explore their possibilities in full and get the best results.

Practical guide to the chapter

Here is the roadmap of the essential steps described in the chapter, for practical application in your daily activities:

Steps	Description
Clearly define your goals and KPIs	Determine your target market and why companies would want to be sponsors or participants to subscribe to your event. Use this to set your KPIs so you can evaluate the evolution of your results through time.
Get to the point	Chose quality over quantity in all aspects, as every single attendee demands to be fully understood regarding his/her needs and desires.
Strategy and focus	Create specific strategy that makes sense regarding objectives. Increase positives outcomes, by having an online and offline marketing plan and a social media strategy for your event.
	Start by understanding how they relate to the event's needs and evaluate each of the most used social platforms: their purpose, target audience, what differentiates one from the others, key metrics, time needed to reach expectations, etc.
Technology is the key	Study and learn as much as you can about technology possibilities, to stay on the upper side of the industry.
Apps became essential	Their importance goes way over simply communicating, as they play a role in all processes in events. You need to have a clear understanding of how you will use them, as that affects all of your planning.
Everyone on the same page	Suppliers have to be part of the planning from the beginning.
Hybrid events are for real	Treat attendees well face-to-face or on other locations, too.
Choose best social media platform.	**Use social media to boost your event** – Engagement is everything, so include everyone involved in an event to get the best results.
	Organize – Collect RSVP, involve attendees and find suppliers.
Create your social media campaign and define types of content for each one	**Promote** – Create an event list. Integrate social media with registration. Create and promote videos.
	Enhance the live experience - Offer prizes. Check on about live streaming. Hashtags can amplify the reach of your event. Provide customer support.
	Extending the lifetime value - Upload the highlights to YouTube and Pinterest. Share presentations. Get feedback. Keep in touch.
Hashtag	Create a hashtag of your event, but also another one to make it easy for attendees to find all the broadcasts from your event on Twitter or other social media that suits your needs.

Monitor results and correct your campaign, if needed	Define the evaluation tools to measure the KPIs and prepare to answer the feedbacks. Keep monitoring all the time to collect intelligence. It will help you evaluate the results and change what is not working properly.
Research satisfaction	Set the relevant aspects that need to be addressed, but make sure the questions are few and formulated in an objective and short form.

For further reading, questions for reflection and additional materials please go to the book's page at the publisher's website:

www.goodfellowpublishers.com/technologyandevents

Notes

1   Stephanie May. "30 experts predict the event trends that will shape our 2015". Eventbrite, 2015

2   www.kpcb.com/internet-trends. [31 May 2015]

3   MPI. Technology Adoption Report_v2

4   blog.myqaa.com/post/116544679891/takeaways-from-the-latest-eventplannerstalk-about?utm_source=myQaa&utm_campaign=02d4601bb6-Monthly_Picks_May_2015&utm_medium=email&utm_term=0_c03352e6c2-02d4601bb6-76381877. [28 May 2015]

5   www.cimunity.com/fileadmin/uploads/startseite_en/QuickMobile_Summer_Surveys_2014.pdf. [20 Dec 2015]

6   en.wikipedia.org/wiki/Web_content_management_system. [26 Dec 2015]

7   QuickMobile_Summer_Surveys_2014

8   C&IT's State of the Industry Report 2014

9   Almeida, Gustavo. Publicidade digital, crise e oportunidades para sua marca. http://www.adnews.com.br/artigos/publicidade-digital-crise-e-oportunidades-para-sua-marca. [30 May 2015]

10 GSMA Report 2015. The Mobile Economy. http://www.gsmamobileeconomy.com/GSMA_Global_Mobile_Economy_Report_2015.pdf. [27 Jan 2016]

11 www.kpcb.com/internet-trends. [20 May 2015]

12 www.youblisher.com/p/840119-Internet-das-Coisas. [08 Oct 2015]

13 www.proxxima.com.br/home/conectados/2015/10/Como-inovar-no-mundo-da-internet-das-coisas.html?utm_source=newsletter&utm_medium=email&utm_campaign=newsletter-Proxxima-diaria&utm_content=noticias_diarias. [08/10/15]

14 www.meetingsupport.org/

15 www.mpiweb.org/docs/default-source/Research-and-Reports/HYBRID-Executive_Summary.pdf. [12 Jan 2016]

16 blog.socialtables.com/2015/03/24/how-to-use-content-to-maximize-roi-for-attendees-at-your-event/. [09 May 2015]

17 www.nsaspeaker.org/. [28 Dec 2015]

18 www.dicaevento.com/artigos/como-definir-um-bom-palestrante-para-seu-evento. [15 Jul 2015]

19 guidebook.com/mobile-guides/event-app-sponsorship. [11 Sep 2015]

20 www.pt.wikipedia.org/wiki/Emoticon [03 Jan 2016]

21 blogs.windows.com/devices/2015/05/23/emoji_history. [28 Dec 2015]

22 en.wikipedia.org/wiki/Emoticon. [16 Nov 2015]

23 www.shutterstock.com/blog/shutterstock-2015-creative-design-trends-infographic-report. [18 Jun 2015]

24 www.eventbrite.co.uk/blog/guide-to-meerkat-app-for-events-ds00/#sthash.2YBYfkgg.dpu. [31 May 2015]

25 www.mundodomarketing.com.br/artigos/vitaly-shter/35069/por-que-preferimos-videos-a-textos.html?utm_source=akna&utm_medium=email&utm_campaign=news+01.12. [02 Dec 2015]

26 Torres, Claudio. (2009 : 45) *A bíblia do marketing digital*. São Paulo : Novatec.

27 Tendências do Marketing de Conteúdo 2015. Rock Content. http://materiais.rockcontent.com/. [20 Nov 2015]

28 oursocialtimes.com/using-social-media-to-make-your-event-a-dazzling-success-infographic/. [21 Sep 2015]

29 www.adnews.com.br/artigos/os-erros-e-acertos-das-empresas-ao-adotar-o-marketing-mobile. [16 Nov 2015]

30 www.verticalresponse.com/blog/small-business-owners-time-digital-game-infographic/. [09 Oct 2015]

31 Torres, Claudio. (2009 : 79) *A bíblia do marketing digital*. São Paulo : Novatec.

32 Laine, Mikko; Fruhwirth, Christian. Monitoring social media: Tools, characteristics and implications. (2010: 193-198) In:Tyrväinen, P; Jansen, S; Cusumano, M.A. (Eds.): *Lecture Notes in Business Information Processing*, **51**(2, 7)

33 seekr.com.br/blog/a-estrategia-do-monitoramento-porque-e-como-fazer/. [19 Dec 2015].

34 Muniz, Priscila. O monitoramento na estratégia de conteúdo in Silva, T. *Para entender o monitoramento de mídias sociais*. Available at misterkanu.com.br/wp-content/uploads/2012/11/Para-Entender-o-Monitoramento-de-Midias-Sociais.pdf. [14 Dec 2015]

35 Diego, M E Aazarite, R. Classificação in Silva, T. *Para entender o monitoramento de mídias sociais*. Available at misterkanu.com.br/wp-content/uploads/2012/11/Para-Entender-o-Monitoramento-de-Midias-Sociais.pdf. [14 Dec 2015]

36 Spuza, V. Geolocalização: como compreender o cenário. In Silva, T. *Para entender o monitoramento de mídias sociais*. http://misterkanu.com.br/wp-content/uploads/2012/11/Para-Entender-o-Monitoramento-de-Midias-Sociais.pdf. [10/01/16]

37 Saric, Marko. 10 key social media trends to Watch in the year 2016, locowise.com/blog/10-key-social-media-trends-to-watch-in-2016. [03 Jan 2016]

3

4 Execution

"As events become more immersive experiences, technology has inevitably heightened the expectation of event attendees"

Gareth McTiffin

Introduction

The technology of communication greatly impacts events and offers numerous advantages such as the engagement of participants (between them and sponsors), networking, ease of selection and monitoring of suppliers, defining metrics, measurement and follow up of results, etc.

It is a great facilitator for increasing the residual effect of the event, but can also have real impact before and immediately after the event. However, it is used mostly while the event is being carried out.

Event app plays a key role in getting all these advantages and they must be chosen strategically.

Learning objectives

This chapter examines the use of technology in events, covering:

- The need of keeping track of your event in real-time
- How gamification and engagement tools can enhance your event
- The key to acquiring actionable data to inform future events
- How to plan and choose the best technology suppliers and other third parties;
- The best ways to use technology to communicate and increase the reach of the event;
- How technology helps to get subscriptions;
- What to look for in the venue infrastructure to optimize technology.

■ The need for keeping track of your event in real-time

To act quickly and have a rapid response to the actions that should be designed and implemented in the event, it is essential to understand the behaviour and the needs of consumers (see more on this in Chapter 5). By adding real-time monitoring of data to support and maximize the potential opportunities that may appear on several fronts, such as generating specific content, marketing activities, corrective actions and prevention of crises and bottlenecks, you will have some of the key components for a successful event.

Thus, by quickly and consistently collecting and analyzing real time data, you can predict the patterns of behaviour of potential participants or prospects, creating a solid basis for decision-making with quality and speed. This way, you will be able to do what is needed to ensure that the event reaches the right people.

The role of technology has changed the way of communication between people and it is critical in events. For Gareth McTiffin[1]

Technology has always played a part in the industry by shaping how guests understand and network through events. Today, this technology plays an even bigger role, helping to streamline admission and operational processes, as well as helping event organizers market and interact with attendees before and after the event.

Technology has (and it will continue to have) without any doubt, the largest impact on events. Changes in the use of technology in the organization of events have been accelerating more and more in recent years. Less than ten years ago fax, telephone and email were still essential in the implementation phase of events; nowadays the quantity and diversity of communication tools available is enormous.

This greater use of technology stems not only from the increased communication speed required between the parties that organize and execute an event, but also from the increasing need to exchange files of all kinds, to allow the execution of services required to make an event run and generate the results desired by its organizers.

■ How gamification and engagement tools can enhance your event

CEIR has conducted research with young professional attendees. Since 2009, they have provided insights on young exhibitor attitudes and preferences about business-to-business exhibitions. The five key findings[2] of their 2015 edition are:

- **Nearly all young exhibitors (98%) find that exhibitions deliver unique value that cannot be fulfilled by other marketing or sales channels.** The most popular aspects refer to ROI, namely the ability to achieve multiple sales and marketing objectives in a compressed period, with face-to-face engagement with customers and prospects top-ranked.

- **For young exhibitors, exhibitions mean business.** More than seven out of ten young exhibitors view the exhibition channel as a medium to accomplish multiple important marketing and sales objectives.

- **For young exhibitors, at the core of the in-booth experience is the product itself and attendee interaction with the product and exhibit booth staff.** Young exhibitors find that situations which feature the product (71%), allow attendees to interact with products (67%) and provide settings that enable booth staff to engage with attendees (66%) are the most effective ways to interact with attendees. A majority also find various digital interactive elements, giveaways and prizes as effective attendee engagement techniques.

- **It is all about face-to-face engagement and interactions.** One-on-one conversations with exhibition personnel, with and without product demonstration, are the number one face-to-face settings of choice.

- **Keep it friendly and inviting!** Emphasis on the importance of exuding a friendly and outgoing approach is uniquely Millennial – and at 77%, it is a top-ranked trait young that exhibitors look for in booth staff.

On the one hand, if young exhibitors have full focus on business generated by creating and maintaining relationships, as noted in the CEIR research, younger attendees require different incentives from those that event organizers were traditionally more accustomed to. For this audience – young and modern – the engagement of all involved in an event is an essential part of the way they do business.

Engagement should be understood by the organizer of the event not only as another element helping to sell tickets for his or her current event, but also as an element that generates greater intimacy with and among its stakeholders, which ensures the success of the current event and strongly stimulates the participation of the public in future events. Thus, engagement should be understood as an essential tool, with applications and reflections throughout the life cycle of each present and future events.

Achieving this multilevel engagement while meeting varied interests and needs is not simple, but some strategies can help at low cost and with high effectiveness. Numerous tools stimulate engagement. Among them are:

- Having a self-service dashboard on the site or event app, enabling attendees to meet other attendees at the event, exchange information and talk to one another and even schedule one to one meetings at the event. Always keep in mind that one to one appointments is one of the greatest advantages of events and therefore should be encouraged to the fullest.

- Offering a platform for displaying presentations, promotional materials and other documents, enabling attendees not only to read, but also to comment on those materials. That gives the opportunity for all parties to collaborate, creating strong ties among all.

- Creating forms of interaction between sponsors and supporters of the event and attendees is a great low cost alternative, but still little explored. The biggest advantage is that it interests both sides, because sponsors and supporters can show their products and services in depth. Furthermore, they can offer promotions and unique gifts of the event, adding more value to both.

- Providing a Q & A (Question and Answer) tool through an app that enables attendees to interact with speakers prior to their presentations and/or in real-time. There can be a mediator to choose the most relevant questions and present them at a panel/dashboard on-site and also through the app, encouraging attendees to submit their questions, concerns and suggestions, which be answered by speakers at the end of their presentations.

- Offering a customizable schedule, where attendees can see all the presentations and exhibitors of the event, and choose those which interests them most, creating their own activity schedule. This schedule can be interconnected with social media, allowing attendees to disclose their interests and interact with the speakers and exhibitors, increasing much more the visibility of the event and of its participants. Additionally, this schedule should be a tool that allows attendees to find other stakeholders with specific interests, enabling one to one appointments to be made.

- Developing specific content of the event, available on the site and apps of the event and in social media. This allows you to show to the local and remote audiences the unique characteristics of each event, facilitating both the engagement of attendees, and the dissemination of the differentials of each event.

- Providing polls and surveys that enable those involved to offer their opinions and suggestions about the event and its participants. These tools can generate engagement, but importantly they can also collect data in real time, which allows corrections and adjustments to the running of the event while it is taking place, and provides important strategic information allowing continuous improvement of future events.

Finally, gamification presents itself as a powerful ally of event organizers as it offers the opportunity for those involved to introduce themselves, and encourage interactivity among all through playful activities. Gamification meets all tactical and strategic needs from event organizers, sponsors, supporters, exhibitors and attendees.

There are numerous applications offering customizable gamification ready for use, but each event can, and should seek to build their own, in order to maximize results. The perfect understanding of the concept of the event, through the needs of exhibitors, and meeting the needs and desires of attendees, will lead to the development of gamification strategies to obtain the best results and ROI for all involved.

When using gamification, always bear in mind three points:

- Fun
- Simplicity
- Rewards

When you put together your gamification strategy to meet these three points, success is virtually bound to happen. It is also important to determine and then pursue your goals that can be, for example:

- Bringing people together in a business environment
- Fostering interactions and networking among stakeholders
- Demonstrating exhibitors' products and services
- Engaging sponsors and supporters along with exhibitors and attendees
- Creating a fun and light atmosphere that facilitates exchanges between all involved

Here are some examples of effective gamification:

- **Rewards** (e.g. gifts, discounts, special offers or points) for performing actions. This facilitates the adhesion of the public to polls and surveys, which allows reaching higher volume of responders and therefore, higher amounts of useful strategic data.

- **Questions from exhibitors**, which generate rewards to answers, provided there is interaction between attendee with the exhibitors themselves. This is a powerful tool for the exhibitor, as it rewards attendees according to the knowledge that they acquire and show on the exhibitor's products and services.

- **Trivia quiz** – featuring complex questions about the event itself and its theme. Therefore, if attendees want to receive rewards, they have to search on the event, its sponsors, supporters and exhibitors.

- **Engagement through social media**, rewarding attendees for posting photos, videos and specific content of the event, marked with hashtags that allow indexing of those interactions.

Before getting participants engaged with the brand of the event and sponsors, it is necessary to have clear understanding of the objectives to be achieved and more important than that, a clear identification of participants, profile, needs and desires. From this base, the main measure becomes defining assertively the marketing plan (online and offline), by selecting the channels where those involved are found.

To help understand the importance and the global trend of those channels, Figure 4.1 shows data from a recent study on the digital world: access and growth of Internet devices used and social media use in 240 countries. The key topics of the 2015 Special Report [3] are:

- Mobiles increasingly control the digital world and by 2016, it will help to push Internet use beyond 50% of world's population.

- Mobile web traffic leapt from 2014 to 2015 by 39%.

- Almost 29% of the world's population have active social media accounts and the percentage continues to grow.

- Facebook still dominates global social media. Around 83% of FB users access through mobile devices.

- Messenger services and chat apps continue to have awesome growth patterns.

- Around 38% of all web pages are [through mobile devices and tablets

Thus, the big question to explore now is the boom of mobile devices, which provides anyone with access to and use of the most advanced technologies from portable devices such as smartphones and tablets that over the Internet open an infinite world of practical possibilities.

Therefore, one must bear in mind that events today are no longer organized solely in closed offices and they do not take place only in the event venue. All Internet-based communication technology allows each participant in the organization and execution of an event to work from wherever they may be and when they see fit. This requires communication channels to be also flexible, so as to enjoy all the benefits that technology now provides.

Of course, one should consider that this scenario is unfolding right now, with technology (platforms, programs and apps) constantly evolving. To know how to evaluate the various existing possibilities enables to choose the most appropriate ones for each case or time.

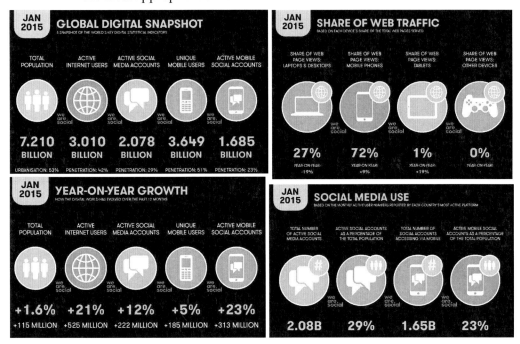

Figure 4. 1: Digital, social and mobile in 2015

Source: http://wearesocial.net/blog/2015/01/digital-social-mobile-worldwide-2015/ 21 Dec 2015. Layout adapted by authors.

■ How to plan and choose the best technology suppliers and other third parties

For the perfect execution of an event of any type, size and focus, one starts from the premise that planning has been done perfectly, paying attention to the needs of the event and the ways to meet them. Studying the previous chapters, you can determine the communication platforms to use in a particular event and how to apply them at each different time in order to meet the specific needs of each participant. In the implementation phase of the event, it is clear how to apply effectively each choice involving technology in the event, to ensure reaching the goals set in the planning phase.

The first thing is to ensure that there is clear communication between all parties, including the main organizers and secondary (if any), hardware and software vendors, and other stakeholders, so that all follow each step, and may influence this dynamic according to their needs and expertise.

Modern communication technologies can be divided into two groups: the free (and more generic) and the paid (and more specialized).

Group 1 – Communication tools based on free use of open technology

Groups on social media can be formed by aggregating the participants in the implementation phase, allowing them to exchange not only messages, but also files (photos, videos, texts) with one another. You can use the more popular social media like Facebook (which allows you to create closed groups, where only authorized members can see the messages and interact with one another), or more specific business-oriented social media such as LinkedIn. It is advisable to check the level of knowledge of the group members regarding different social media in order to determine which one to use. This is so because the effectiveness of using social media as information exchange channel will depend directly upon the ease of its users to exploit all its possibilities.

Co-creation tools on the cloud, such as Dropbox or Google Drive enable users to exchange documents not only online, but also by remote editing, allowing multiple authors to work on the same document, modify and comment on it, until it reaches its final state.

In addition to those file and information sharing tools, we have the more direct media such as Whatsapp, that allow the creation of several groups and instant exchange of messages among participants. It is possible to create different subgroups of participants, under the general umbrella of the event in question. For example, one can have a subgroup consisting solely of organizers, another one of organizers and suppliers, and another one including organizers and promoters, etc.

Group 2 – Closed, paid, highly specialized communication tools

According to the study *Event Management Software Market* from MarketsandMarkets[4],

> With the increase in the number of meetings, incentives, conferences, exhibitions (MICE), event organizers are trying to implement best-in-class technology that can handle the entire event lifecycle from planning to implementation. Thus, event-organizing companies are re-evaluating their systems and processes with a new level of scrutiny. Rapid return on investment is the major factor, which is prompting event organizers to implement event-management technology platforms.

The major forces that have fuelled the growth in this market are the proliferation of smartphones, increase in the meeting spending, social media user platform, integration of solutions and most importantly, cloud platform.

MarketsandMarkets forecasts that the global Event Management Software Market is expected to grow from $5.10 billion in 2014 to $7.78 billion by 2019. This represents an estimated Compound Annual Growth Rate (CAGR) of 8.81% from 2014 to 2019. In the current scenario, North America is expected to be the largest market based on spending and adoption of event management software.

Networking and event engagement

As networking is one of attendees' top needs, an event app offers great opportunities to promote an event before it starts and after it ends (see Chapters 7 and 8).

There is a growing variety of options that can (and should) be used to stimulate networking, such as sharing checking participants list, facilitating appointments, swapping messages, Catchbox (a tossable microphone for audience participation) and so on. You may also use social networking media such as blogs, XML RSS, podcasting, wikis, and other self-publishing media platforms to stimulate and engage your audiences on networking activities related to your events. To create and promote games for attendees is also a great tool.

Nelissen[5] offers a few (but powerful) tips while using apps to improve your results:

- Add speaker rating at the end of each session

- Include surveys to get instant feedback

- Add a 'Concierge' service in the app, where delegates can interact with your staff on schedules, travel arrangement and more.

- Use messaging and 'Meet Me' to allow attendees to message one another in order to get in touch or meet up. The app is a safe way to enable this type of interaction without the need to reveal email address or phone numbers

- Include matchmaking for attendees: let your app suggest other attendees to meet, based on the profile of each individual. For example, match investors with start-ups on a venture forum, based on specific interest domains or industries entered during registration.

McArthur's definition of event engagement is that you should start knowing why attendees are at your event and what their event engagement expectations are. It will help you set up the event´s expectations and to create interactive content that gets attendees' engagement. For him[6],

> *Successful event engagement is the difference between a lively, productive event and a forgettable one. Take some time to identify what attendees will be hoping to get out of your event and exceed their expectations. This will not only leave you with happy attendees, but also keep them coming back for years to come. People want to make connections – with you, your brand and with other attendees. Make it easy on them and make event engagement a critical part of your game plan.*

To engage your message, he suggests that you keep in mind that your event-specific message should be created in each piece of your event communication: "The clearer the event message, the more event engagement you will see." Build the event steps to give the chance for attendees to connect with the members of your world (sponsors, vendors, guest speakers, exhibitors and audience) and to connect to each other. They will feel the organizer really cares about them and it will increase brand loyalty.

■ How technology helps to get subscriptions

The use of technology to generate registrations is another factor to consider in engaging the public with each event. Through the event website, registrations and social media can do various things to engage people, resulting in the sale of tickets for the event. With the appreciation of innovation by business in general, event organizers are in a strong position, as they can use technology both to meet the aspirations of the companies and to create only positive experiences for attendees.

One of the points where technology can help most in organizing events is in the search for registrations. Modern registration systems are much more than mere tools to gather information from attendees and to sell tickets, so choosing the best registration tool is critical in both the planning and the execution phases of current and future events. In order to choose without risk of error there are several steps and features that you should analyze in order to find the tool that best meets your specific needs.

The ideal situation is to have an all-in-one tool that integrates all the steps and process involved in registration. There are currently several tools available in the market. Some points that are mandatory in all-in-one tool are:

- Integration with social media, allowing you to encourage attendees to share and recommend the event to their friends on those social media. You can even create systems of rewards for those referrals, offering discounts for both those who gave the referral as well as to those who responded to it registered for the event. Of course, modern registration tools must contain a data collection system, which will also be useful to allow you to understand the purchasing habits of your attendees, optimizing your offers and sales methods.

- In addition to integration with social media, a registration tool should be able to operate with and combine information from other sales platforms, like your site, email marketing, telemarketing, etc. Another essential integration concerns the agenda of the event, which will make each new registration generate an immediate update on all the communication platforms used. This allows all parts involved in the event to be able to keep track of the progress of registrations, enabling them to plan accordingly.

- Another important point to note is the integration of the registration tool with its financial, tax and audit controls, if any. Seamless integration of these operations enables not only the elimination of a number of possible errors, but also a decrease in the workforce required to operate the system, leading to a large cost reduction.

How to choose the best registration tool

- Ease of use: technology should facilitate the planning and execution of your event. Thus, the tool you choose should have a modern and logical interface, and a stable system supporting it, to ensure that everything works to satisfaction. The ease of tool setup should also be taken into consideration because it is a step that takes time and therefore, and therefore consumes money.

- Focus on quality features, not on quantity: there is no point in having many features you will not use. This not only affects the cost of the tool, but also involves a more complex operation. So choose a tool that has just what you will actually use, and make sure that those features actually work.

- Pay attention to the experience that your tool will deliver to users; after all, they are the ones who will really judge your choice. There is no point in having a tool full of features (even if everything works well) if the end-user experience is not good. At this point, the look and feel of the chosen tool enter into the equation (after all, good looks and usability attest, even prior to use, the quality of what you are offering.)

- Make sure the tool providing company also has a good customer service. The last thing you need is to be without any adequate support at a critical moment.

What should be avoided

- **Fearing new technologies**. Look around you. In your market and in others, everyone is using the latest technological innovations to support their business. Continually test yourself and the new options vendors have to offer – that is the best way to keep updated and make the best choices to meet your specific needs.

- **Underestimating the importance of the chosen tool**. That tool will integrate all the processes involved in registration, so it is essential that it works well, suits all your needs, and that you have all your staff trained to extract maximum potential from it.

- **Underusing your tool**: in order to neither waste money, nor create operating chaos, learn all that your tool can offer. Keep in mind that the registration process is responsible for a large part of your earnings, so keep the focus on maximizing the use of the chosen tool.

- **Choosing by price**: a choice based on low or high price, usually involves either low quality results, or wasting money on unnecessary features. Be clear about your needs and what features are necessary. Search the options available in the market. Only then should you think about saving money in your budget, making sure that all other options serve you well.

Remember that registration plays a key role in the success of an event, so choosing the best tool is essential. Easy and quick setup, usability, pleasant experience to attendees and seamless integration are the points to observe.

Event apps

■ Event app strategy

The best mobile event app strategy has three parts: goal, method and evaluation criteria. Chapter 1 describes some aspects about event and corporate strategy that must be the guide when choosing your event app. The most important thing to have in mind is that the app will improve your event.

To achieve success, your event must have a clear and precise focus. Follow these simple steps (Figure 4.2).

1 **Define your goal**. The event goals will tie back to the corporate goals. The measurable mobile app goals will lead and guide your event to success.

2 **Decide upon the method**: it is how you will achieve your goal and what you will need in order to accomplish it.

3 Evaluation. This is divided into two parts: pre-event (metrics will measure your event app success) and post-event (compare and study data against your evaluation criteria). Find out what can improve your next event strategy

 And so now we've come full circle. The Evaluation stage is where the strategic process begins and ends, and with a mobile app, it is much easier to get the data you need to make smart and informed business decisions for the future.[7]

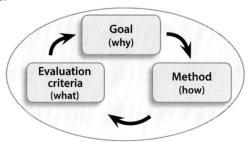

Figure 4. 2: Building your event strategy

Strategies	Advantages	Disadvantages
Develop your own	You can dictate exactly what you want. You'll work closely with developers to make sure it functions the way you wish.	A bespoke app requires many resources (by resources we mean time and money.) As well as upfront costs to get it off the ground, but you will pay to maintain it. As a result, custom developed apps tend to be unsustainable.
Buy an all-in-one software suite	Save time by purchasing from one vendor who sells an events software suite. Simplify your support and billing while buying into a 'one-stop' ecosystem.	All-in-one products often result from acquisitions. While the technology might look okay, there can be problems caused by messy code and disjointed integrations. Since one company is maintaining a fistful of products, it is possible that their offering is a mile wide but only a few inches deep.
Build on a self-service event app platform	Platform-based providers are becoming the norm. Vendors are able to innovate quickly, and their product will grow along with your ongoing relationship. Price scales with usage, so you will get a break the more apps you use. Providers are incentivized to create user-friendly back end interfaces that make app building simpler.	Integrations with other systems are, by definition, not native. Niche features may not be supported or require longer development times. Deciding on an event app building strategy is the first narrowing step. Once you have chosen between custom development, an all-in-one suite, or a platform you can begin to evaluate vendors within that particular space.

Table 4.1: The three strategies to get the event app you want
Source: The event app buyer's guide, Guidebook. 2015. Authors' layout.

Among some of the experts' best strategies for promoting an event app is to start early, promoting it in all pre-event activities, highlighting the advantages and benefits of its use and monitoring adoption rates. For young audiences, it is important to have a focus on social engagement and networking. Promote the event app in all channels and opportunities, on the event website, in emails, at the beginning of every session (opening slides), etc.

■ How to choose an app: features and benefits

Event apps are irreplaceable and fundamental tools for meeting planners because:

> With the increasing professionalism, organizations are adopting new tactics in order to remain ahead in a competitive landscape. Since the emergence of the concept, the event management market has improved in leaps and bounds to overcome the deficiencies and challenges present in its previous counterpart. The latest technologies and software that provides event planners with a dedicated and customized suite of solutions and associated services now rule. Vendors in this market are coming up with complete suites of event lifecycle that includes planning of event, budgeting, registration, ticketing, marketing, and event survey. That software has a predominant role in managing the overall effectiveness and efficiency of events.
>
> Continuously increasing expenditure on meeting and events across the entire industry sector is the foremost factor that is driving the need of this market. Furthermore, mobile apps are regarded as the most promising segment pertaining to future demand of this market.[8]

To achieve exceptional results, the choice of the app and the features available must be based on previously defined goals and be perfectly aligned with the needs of the participants. Each app on the market offers different features, has different levels of approach and differs in the quality of information that is possible to collect and analyze. See more information in Chapter 8.

When evaluating the best app for your event, you should consider some aspects, such as clean design and ease to use (end user and client user); the facility of making simple and instant adjustments; easy, friendly and efficient customer support and good accessibility of content management system (CMS). Ball[9] recommends that after you identify your needs about an app and your attendees' expectations, you must consider the data connections (apps should include and offline option) and the following facts:

- **User experience:** Because of the possibility of downloading hybrid and native apps, many prefer faster, smoother access to information such as speaker bios and agendas. For polling, audience response and survey tools, they also provide a better user experience. If there is no signal when taking surveys, for instance, both hybrid and native apps hold the data and send it when there is a connection.

- **Community involvement:** Developers of hybrid and native apps have made great strides in social interaction by allowing push technology to be used within apps. For example, many developers now embed the use of the device's camera within the app to post pictures more efficiently than web apps.

- **Cost:** While hybrid and web-based apps are typically faster to deploy and less expensive, the newest technology for these options have made it possible to develop apps that offer many of the same experiences as native apps. Therefore, if you do not require advanced programming, it is likely the best way to go. Native apps tend to cost more because they require custom coding of features, use of the device hardware and GPS.

- **Design elements:** The beauty of apps in today's market is that look and feel, branding, menu/navigation, and sponsorship options can all be customized, and they will function similarly no matter the app platforms.

- **Content:** Both static and dynamic content, such as registration, can have customized format for hybrid, web-based and native apps. Attendees' needs and planner recommendations should determine the app content. At a minimum, most audiences expect agenda/speaker information and meeting room maps.

- **Audience demographics:** Knowing your audience is crucial when deciding on what app to deploy. If you are in an industry that relies heavily on tablets or iPads, your audience is probably most familiar with native apps. If this is the case, hybrid apps can be a great option to offer a native app experience without the custom programming cost. In contrast, if your audience is a late adopter to mobile devices, using a browser to view the content is likely to be preferred.

It is also relevant that you check if the event app supports multiple events (this option is often more affordable) and if it is easy to implement and has very good customer support. A good event app has four basic areas (Table 4.1).

Areas	Description
Provide essential event information	It should be a formidable replacement for anything you could create on paper.
	Provide lists of speakers, sponsors and vendors with links and photos.
	Provide additional value beyond what you could do with paper, e.g., daily weather forecast.
	Simplicity and a clear design wins the day.
	It should offer some degree of customization.
	It should be easy to use.
Communicate in real time	The ability to communicate instantly with your audience as a whole and for messaging your attendees as a group. This means a reliable mechanism for sending push notifications and in-app messages is necessary.
Facilitate attendee connections	Most event attendees (75%) have strong interest in networking.
Provide data about the event itself	An event app will cover virtually every aspect of your event.
	Look for a metrics suite that helps you measure the value you offer to your attendees and sponsors. This will provide your sponsors with ROI metrics for overall event and collect both general and individual sessions' feedback.

Table 4.2: The four basic areas and event app

Source: The event app buyer's guide, Guidebook. 2015. Authors' layout.

Even though it does not exhaust the many possibilities, the analysis of the tools available and their use in events is illustrated in **Figure 4.3**. It shows the main options offered by the event and apps for social media in the example of a conference with a parallel exhibition. It is important to consider that it is possible to carry out some of the options in more than one phase. For example: getting profile / bio of the speakers can be performed at any stage and the program of the conference and the schedule and appointment building that can be done before the event starts.

So, create your own basic script, indicating what you want to build into your event, initially for key areas, such as pre-event registration, payment, evaluation, post-event, etc. One should note here that each of them is driven by objectives, needs or features, identified when your event project was started.

From there each area receives further evaluation with the desired approach for each feature. For example, after the attendee signed up, what approaches one should take to promote engagement and encourage his networking with other participants prior to their arrival in person or login as virtual participants? Each one is to be detailed and designed in Event calendar actions to order them in time. If performed with the technology provider, the construction of this planning phase leverages the benefits and advantages that technology can offer. That is, the meeting planner defines music (event type, subject, audience, date, location, objectives, budget), chooses the musicians and instrumentalists (suppliers) and controls the interaction between them (harmonization of aspects of the event the object and choice and coordination of the best options to achieve them).

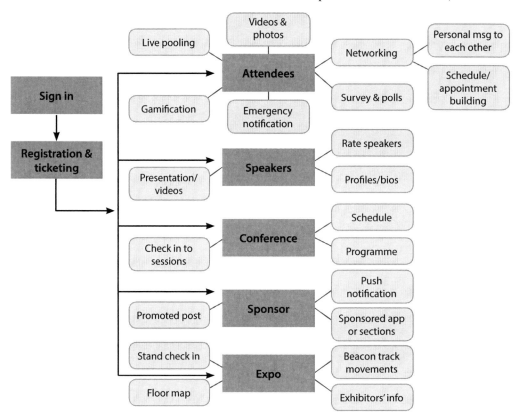

Figure 4. 3: Options and opportunities offered by event apps and social media at events

It is important to remember that the best way to take advantage of an event app is to use it as a two-way communication tool. By creating ways where attendees can express their feelings and opinions, they will be incentivise to engage, help on creation, extend relationship and create a delightful experience among key stakeholders. Everything will be online and in real time and data can be used to enhance this and future events. You can easily drive attendees to live pooling and short session feedback, if they were using the mobile event app for event information and by means of gamification use, as shown earlier in this chapter.

The best event app delivers useful performance dashboards. Doubledutch Industry Survey [10] report named the top type of data requested from management: attendee numbers (91%), speaker feedback from delegates (60%), engagement levels (53%) and time spent at event and brand affinity (35% each). Most debrief reports presented are post-event summary reports

(60%), presentation – e.g., PPT (16%), graphs and graphics and others (7% each). The expected KPIs in an ideal post-event scenario are ROI, sales leads, engagement, client happiness, data collection and testimonials.

The main target is to narrow down the choices based on a few key distinguishing features. Goldberg [11] suggests that you should ask yourself some questions:

- How easy is it to create my app?

- Will it work for my attendees both online and offline?

- Will attendees know how to use it to navigate my event successfully?

- Can I make last-minute changes and publish them immediately?

He also presents some tips:

- **Functions offline and reliability** – some apps are not stored on your device's internal memory and are dependent on an Internet connection. Analyze if such function suits the infrastructure of your event.

- **Personalization** – identify if the app offers White label service and customization of icons and colours

- **Live polling** (a real-time activity where attendees answer questions about their opinion regarding some topics related to the event) – a means to empower the audience and engage them when you ask questions and display them in real time.

- **Multiple editors, enterprise-grade security** – it must allow more members to log into the content management at the same time. The app must make sure that the information in the content management system is safe from abuse and hacking.

- **Session attendance limiting** – the event app must be able to cap and control the number of attendees whenever there is limited space.

- **Drag & drop editing** – it will allow a better and faster app.

- **Free version** – ask for a free version or login to the content management system. That ensures you learn about its use and benefits before your commitment.

- **Costumer service** – be sure the provider will wait on you accordingly.

Table 4.3 presents the most used event apps nowadays (with its most important features and information). On its source website, you will find more infographics that shows the most prominent apps available, their characteristics and price range.

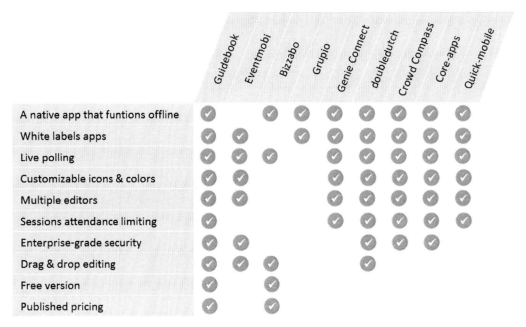

	Guidebook	Eventmobi	Bizzabo	Grupio	Genie Connect	doubledutch	Crowd Compass	Core-apps	Quick-mobile
A native app that funtions offline	✓		✓	✓	✓	✓	✓	✓	✓
White labels apps	✓	✓		✓	✓	✓	✓	✓	✓
Live polling	✓	✓	✓		✓	✓	✓	✓	✓
Customizable icons & colors	✓	✓			✓	✓	✓	✓	✓
Multiple editors	✓	✓			✓	✓	✓	✓	✓
Sessions attendance limiting	✓				✓	✓	✓	✓	✓
Enterprise-grade security	✓	✓				✓	✓	✓	
Drag & drop editing	✓	✓	✓			✓			
Free version	✓			✓					
Published pricing	✓			✓					

Table 4.3: Defining the best event app

Source: guidebook.com/mobile-guides/best-conference-apps-comparison/ Layout adapted by authors

It is clear that event apps are paramount, and every day there are more and more options available in the market, hindering the meeting planner from separating the wheat from the chaff. Thus, it is even more important to have metrics and appropriate references to choose what best suits the needs of your event and the one with the best cost-benefit ratio. It is important to notice that, after defining the features of your event, some of the apps mentioned in it may not appear and/or it is possible to insert new ones. Either because they are not available in your country or in your language, or because they did not receive good ratings according to your parameters. As described earlier for the definition of the basic script, create your own table and references to choose the best event app for your client.

■ Event app cost

Event apps are as diverse as their pricing:

> *Event app prices could be attached to the number of attendees or a specific feature set, depending on the provider. The hallmark of fair pricing, however, is transparency. (...) The best strategy is to think of an app as one piece of your communication budget, as opposed to an add-on. This will help you associate a specific value with the event app relative to total communication costs.*[12]

As shown in Chapter 2, the average cost of an event app is typically around 1.2% of the total event cost, depending on event size. Event app companies say an event app can save costs (82% reduction of paper printing) and increase incoming by attracting more sponsors, selling dynamic ad space and inspiring attendees.

■ Data capture and KPIs

The most common methods of capturing data are exit survey (45.5%) and session feedback (41.5%). Graph 4.1 also shows that attendee arrival and leaving time capture the least data. Meeting planners would like to capture delegate movement and to promote individual engagement activity via an app or event website (26% each).

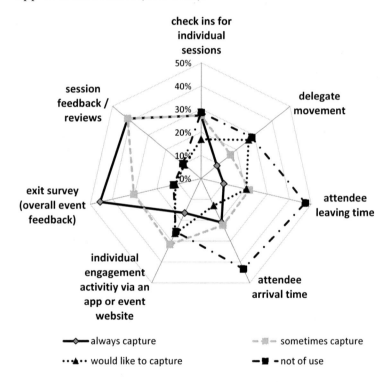

Graph 4.1: Data captured onsite

Source: The event app buyer's guide. Guidebook. 2015.

More than half of organizers use audience pooling as engagement strategy, followed by mobile apps (45.5%). One third of them use a 'second screen', a mobile device used to present real-time content such as extra slides, additional content, videos, social media links, etc. and 22.3% choose gamification.

All surveys pointed to the importance of the insights gained from attendees' data. **Graph 4.2** shows that half of meeting planners measure the number of sessions attended by delegates. The other common KPIs (key performance indicators) measured are session feedback, complaints or queries and sponsor feedback. A quarter of them declared they do not measure aspects of engagement; but a third of them would like to measure it (inter-delegate, during session and interaction with other aspects of the event).

However, only 8.5% of organizers use beacon technology – geo-positioning that allows precise attendee movement monitoring, including metrics as queue times at registration, crowd flow and crowded spots and time spent at stands. It creates great opportunities for sponsors, like targeted pop-up messages.

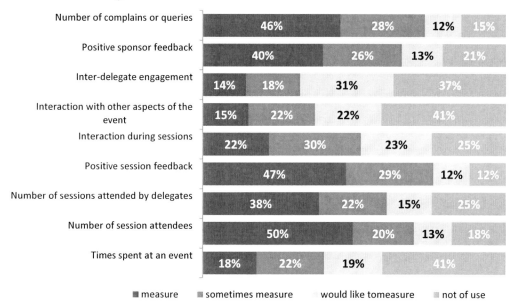

Graph 4.2: KPIs measured in real-time during event

Source: The event app buyer's guide. Guidebook. 2015.

■ Mobile event apps and social media

As noted previously, the Second Screen wave gains strength day after day. Thus, event apps are devised to also surf along that trend, but be sure that the event website, blog and even a native app are all mobile friendly. It is possible to summarize research on motivations of event planners for the use of mobile in events in the need to cut costs and meet the current needs of the participants, who have mobile devices as an essential tool in their personal and professional lives.

Each social media has different uses and applications. Many of these can be found in various chapters. Here are some tips[13] to stimulate the generation of content by participants.

Twitter

Live tweet: Live tweeting blends audience participation with live micro journalism and is usually the main channel of content distribution during your event. Make sure to feed your Twitter account with the following tweets:

- **Tweet insights:** Try to capture the essence of your speakers' talks and tweet the most interesting data they present.

- **Share speakers' quotes:** People have this innate craving for good quotes. Tweet the best quotes from your speakers. They often get loads of re-shares.

- **Tweet with pictures:** Attach pictures to your tweets to increase engagement and reach significantly.

- **Retweet a lot:** Your attendees' tweets are an endless source of powerful insights and they are genuine captures from your event. Show attendees some love and retweet them generously.

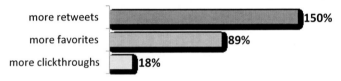

Graph 4.3: Tweets with images get more …
Source: http://www.jeffbullas.com/wp-content/uploads/2015/04/visual-tweets-infographic.jpg

Hashtag

Twitter can offer a great marketing opportunity to promote your event, engage attendees and generate mobile traffic, as show in Chapters 3 and 5. Here are some tips, use and purposes[14] of the mighty hashtag:

Use and purpose

- To make it easier for attendees to find your events and related data.

- To allow tracking the performance on social media

- To increase engagement in Twitter (retweets are typically 40% with a hashtag but only 25% without it) and Instagram (interactions are 80 hashtags per 1,000 followers).

- To keep track of the trends and your competitors

Tips

- A hashtag should be memorable, relevant, unique, distinctive and simple to remember. Make sure it does not create another message or word.

- Use one hashtag to a specific message.

- The call-to-action must be easy, consistent and clear

See more information on hashtags in Chapter 2.

Monitoring social media: importance and uses

It is possible to measure everything on the web. There is such a profusion of data, that it requires strategy to select the information that is relevant. To quote Monteiro[15],

To have an agile performance it is critical to understand the behaviours and issues of interest to consumers. Such understanding, combined with a team that accompanies the data in real time and that is able to seize the opportunities that arise in the generation of content, marketing activities and even to prevent possible crises, is a guarantee of success.

The data collected through social networks represent unique Big Data with consumer information. If analyzed quickly, it can help generate actions with quality and speed, within the time that your customer expects. Besides that information, which can be utilized in real-time and in long-term, these data indicate patterns to predict the behaviour of your audience more accurately.

However, it is necessary to make the Big Data and social networks generate results and become more than just a fad. The main work to be done is to have information available in real time and in a simple way on dashboards, so that the information can be monitored and utilized for all areas of the company in social action, digital and even in offline, especially by Marketing.

There are numerous social media monitoring tools worldwide, with many different focuses and costs. In addition to the monitoring itself, the best ones allow the management of the social media accounts of your company and the delivery of customer service 2.0, i.e. it enables customer service through social media.

The vast majority of these monitoring tools and presence management in social media enable you to define the terms and keywords to observe, allowing you to focus on subjects that interest the event organizers. You can make more general brand monitoring and limit it to specific campaigns and events.

Using those tools is a key differentiator, as they allow you to extract accurately the opinions, desires, needs, suggestions and complaints from the public on the subject or brand monitored.

Similarly, most of them offer customizable and online shareable dashboards, allowing all stakeholders involved in the organization of an event to have immediate access to the results that are obtained and analyzed.

With the use of tags, it is possible to index all the monitored contents, allowing all kinds of data crossing for specific intelligence gathering. For example, it is possible to separate suggestions and complaints by tags, allowing different teams to deal with their focus of action.

The scope of the monitoring can be global, but also localized, including choosing target languages, not only facilitating the operation of local companies, but also companies that have a more comprehensive operation.

Speakers

The speakers are a very important part of any event, as they should attract attendees and sponsors in a large proportion due to their authority on the theme of the event. Because of that, it is important to plan and implement everything regarding speakers and their participation in order to extract all the power they can bring to the event. Bear in mind that it is necessary to take into consideration the differences between on-site or remote or hybrid events due to their impact on the way you present the speakers.

Chapter 3 shows various considerations in hiring speakers (an essential topic to the success of technical-scientific events). Among them, Macedo [16] suggests that you should check the material of the lectures prior to the beginning of the event, in order to make sure that it contains the scope previously briefed to the speakers. He also indicates some actions that can make your performance become special and not merely specific to some points: to encourage them to attend at least part of the event, so that they can understand the audience and better contextualize their content to your specific needs and to other lectures. He also considers it important to involve them, so that at the end of their speech it is possible to interact with fans, answer extra questions, autograph books. During the event, it is time to pay attention to the perfect execution of previously negotiated agreements with the speaker for the dissemination and/or marketing of their courses, books, software or other products. Make sure they are actually engaged in the main reason for their presence, and convey excellent content, rather than just posing for pictures or merchandising products or services.

During the event, the interaction of speakers with participants before, during and after the event can be stimulated and channelled through the event's official media or the speaker's social media, with assistance or facilitation by the event organizers.

Some points are the same, regardless of the typology or type of the event:

- Publicize the name and bios of the speakers before the event, to attract more people

- Make pre-event interviews, written or in video, in order to show what each speaker is going to talk about

- Ask the speakers to invite some special guests from their own lists

- Offer to the speakers the possibility of selling books or other materials they have

- Consider the possibility of simultaneous translation, if needed

- Provide the right equipment for on-site sound and/or remote transmission

- Create a platform that allows attendees (onsite or remote) to interact with the speakers before, during and after the event

- Optionally, hold workshops after the speaker's presentations, in order to optimize your investments and deliver more value to attendees

Communication and publicity

An event must reach the right people, but the organizer should provide the right advertisement. Rocket Fuel's Marketing Research compiled a guide of key insights[17], showing the best design elements on ads for concerts, shows, sporting events, and music services, and music streaming in terms of generating ticket sales:

- The red colour as backgrounds averaged +31% higher conversation rates across all verticals whereas grey backgrounds averaged -8%.

- Showing the artist or star of the featured attraction gets average conversion rates +56% higher than without any artist or star.

- Photos and videos increase attention. The study shows that ads with photos average conversion rates 33% higher than those containing illustrations. Ads with animation get + 98% average conversion rates.

- Those that included pricing averaged conversion rates +213% higher than those that did not include price.

- The best call for action button, with +106% of average conversion, is "Get Ticket"

Two important points to keep in mind in your communication strategy: [18]

1 Communicate only essentials

Keep the invitation brief and simple. Stick to spelling out the Five Ws: who, what, when, where, and why of the event. In addition, do provide a link leading to further information for those interested in digging deeper. Potential attendees need to be able to assess whether or not the event is of interest to them within seconds.

2 Be RSVP friendly

Clearly communicate registration requirements. Make sure that the sign-up process takes less than 30 seconds for a free-to-attend event, or less than two minutes if a registration fee is collected or if there is a choice between individual sessions. Only ask for information you will utilize to improve the attendees' event experience. It is possible to assess any additional information such as demographics during, or after the event.

Some actions and information can help you achieve great results:

- The use and dissemination of an official event hashtag standardizes communication, enhances and facilitates the promotion of the event before, during and after its completion. Ensure that it is published and advertised in all locations and by all possible means (e.g., event materials, projection screens between sessions, and so on)

- Posts – reach potential attendees by publishing quality articles about the event theme on the event website, blog or social medium (see more options in Chapter 3).

- Create and encourage groups in one or more social media.

- Use testimonials of participants of previous editions and speakers

- Hold one or more Webinars, inviting potential attendees to connect and interact with speakers and special guests.

- Use photos and videos – engagement rates in social media are significantly higher when using photos and videos in content: 87% of Facebook pages' engagement happens on posts with photos[19].

Holub's [20] suggestions for using video and photos to create content at your event are simple, but powerful:

- **Video testimonials**: Record on video your attendees and capture their impressions from your event – ask what they have learnt, which speaker inspired them the most, etc.

- **Video thought leaders:** Record thought leaders on video and get their comments on the topics being presented and discussed at your event.

- **Video exhibitors:** Exhibitors are often overlooked at events. Have your exhibitors say on camera how they can or want to help attendees.

- **Share industry predictions:** People love predictions. Ask the key figures in the industry to share their views about upcoming trends in your niche.

- **Share behind-the-scenes video:** Make a video on how your team is setting up or running the event. It gives your event a powerful touch of authenticity and links a human element to your brand.

- **Shoot time-lapse:** Time-lapse videos are surprisingly underused and therefore can have a big WOW factor on viewers. Try to capture the movement of people to magnify the time-lapse effect.

- **Sneak peek photos:** Whet your delegates' appetites by showing a sneak peek of your event being set up, hotel lobbies, surrounding area, etc.

- **Collect selfies:** At events, where people have the chance to meet their 'heroes' and colleagues, they take plenty of selfies. Share them! People love reliving joyful moments.

- **Publish candid photos:** While you often need to wait for a couple of days for the official pictures, you can share attendees' candid captures instantly. You can also encourage more photo sharing by displaying picture tweets on the Twitter walls.

On-site check-in, control access and payments

Technology can help meeting planners to free up time for their staff, e.g., on badge-printing, checking process and payments (to receive and verify payment, issue receipts, handle credit cards, etc.). However, a recent survey found that 44% of events still have manual fee collection. Only one out of 10 meeting planners operates self-check-in by registrants.[21] Most event organizers (79.9%) use pre-printed and handed out badges (Graph 4.4).

Manual registration (e.g., pen/paper and printed forms are used for 46.88% of meeting planners. The most used methods to control access to event sessions are check in delegates when they enter/join session and check that if they are pre-registered for the session (47.32% each).

Scan badges, barcodes or QR codes are the most popular methods of tracking attendees for almost half of meeting planners (48.2%). One third of them do not control or track access (Graph 4.5).

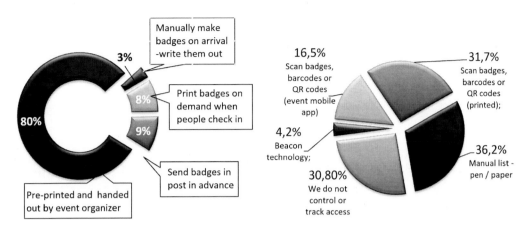

Graph 4.4: (Left) How do you usually manage your badges?

Graph 4.5: (Right) How do you manage the tracking of delegate's entering sessions?

Source: Arrivals to Departures: The Power of on-site technologies. Cvent study

Payments over apps and/or web-based tools can be not only a good way to organize this part of events, but also a way to boost your event visibility over the engagement of the attendees. Several payment tools like Bizzabo Ticket Boost now have features that incentivize attendees to share your event with their social networks. When an attendee registers, they receive a dedicated, shareable, unique discount code that not only lets them provide a sweet discount to their networks, but the attendee sharing the code gets money back on their already-purchased ticket with each ticket purchased through their code.

You may also take some simple actions to get better results:

- Use the advantages of the greater control over online sales, as you will always have real time information which allows you to provide discounts, offers and advantages depending on your results at each moment

- Offer as many forms of payment as you can: that makes it easier for your customers to choose which one best suits their needs, thus gaining better sales

- You may also use sweepstakes over social media channels to boost your visibility and engagement rates among the attendees.

Globo is Brazil's largest television network and the second largest commercial television in the world. Box 4.1 shows one of the live events projects that the brand carries out regularly in order to get closer to its consumers. The portrayed edition of the 'Art on the Street' project took place in December 2015 in São Paulo, Brazil's largest city.

With services and products that include registration and badging, acess control, meeting schedule mobile apps and match making, NFC interactive USB sticks, gamification, touch points and metric reporting, Poken is a full service technology company. Founded in 2007 in Switzerland, it is specialized in management and engagement. Nowdays, Poken networks of partners and resellers are in over 40 countries. Box 4.2 shows the gamification and engagement during The Boy Scouts of America (BSA) in United States.

Box 4.1: Art in the street

Alexandre Mutran

Multifaceted cultural project

With 96 million viewers every day, Globo is an audience leader and the largest producer of content in Latin America. Aiming to be closer to its audience and promote culture off-screen as well as on , it develops and supports initiatives that allow and encourage dialogue with communities. Each one of them is defined in accordance with the profile of the public and the local communication objectives, depicted on the project with activities related to culture, entertainment, sustainability, urban mobility, gastronomy, and street sports.

Differentiated and diversified programs

During the 20-day duration of the 'Art in the Street' in the edition held in Christmas 2015, 120,000 people attended more than 100 free Christmas-themed presentations. Held in 40 different locations in Greater São Paulo, each one lasted 20-60 minutes.

4

The activities were performed by amateur artists and professionals from various styles such as theater, circus, poetry, hip-hop, rock, pop, groove, jazz, 'repente' (improvisation style popular mainly in the Northeast), poetry, opera, Brazilian music, and orchestras, among others, hired especially to bring art and culture to more democratic places: the subway and train stations and bus terminals of the city.

That edition featured the award-winning Orchestra of the Teatro São Pedro (Orthesp), Batalha da Leste (Battle of the East Zone), cultural competition of rhymes and music releases, and the Metro Security Guards Band, consisting of 10 employees of the Metro security staff of São Paulo.

The cultural diversity was also present in several other multi-artistic presentations, such as the mix of juggling and improvisations on the saxophone while the artist balanced on a unicycle, or in funny stories about Christmas told by a clown, and a rap battle that brought together several MCs from across the city.

Promotion and repercussion

Special care was given to the promotion, carried out by a campaign on TV and the Internet, inviting people to activities and encouraging them to lear about the program. To foster the viewers' interest and reverberate the initiative, reports throughout the period of the initiative were shown during local television news, exhibiting the performances and the interaction of the attending audience. During the 30 days of the promotion, press coverage was extensive:

"Make a change through a tale" – Poetry Live

around 75 articles on the 'Art in the Street' project were published or broadcast on the radio, TV, in magazines, newspapers and on website (average of 2 per day).

An interactive website listed the dates, locations and artists, as well as a map with the locations of the performances. Social networks also received intense content sharing consisting of photos and videos. There were over 15,000 interactions on Globo official posts alone, not counting posts made by the public.

Alexandre Mutran is São Paulo Regional Communications Manager for Rede Globo and a professor for post-graduate courses at ESPM (Escola Superior de Propaganda e Marketing). He has wide experience in marketing and communications, having worked in several major agencies including Tudo, Africa, and Dentsu.

Box 4.2: Poken – Gamification for engagement!

The Boy Scouts of America (BSA) is one of the United States' largest and most storied values-based, civic organizations. It convened more than 15,000 promising young leaders for its National Order of the Arrow Conference (NOAC) on its 2015 edition. Audience participation and motivation was a challenge for NOAC organizers. They wanted to break participants out of their shells and get them to connect with others from other parts of the country or attend event programming.

The challenge

At earlier events, they attempted to increase interactions by deploying a smartphone and QR code-based gamification platform. It was an instant disaster: some kids did not have smartphones, while others did not have the latest software or lacked a functional camera (a prerequisite for QR codes).

The results

In total, there were 6.6 million Poken interactions over the course of five days. In 2012, NOAC counted just 90,000 interactions. External vendors also got to share in the fun: they received more than 44,000 qualified leads during the conference, as the Poken devices doubled as lead generation tools for suppliers. And this was just the beginning. After the conference ended, Poken delivered data and analytics about the event to the NOAC organizers. These rich insights will help the BSA make future events even more successful.

The solution

In 2015, they adopted Poken's turnkey solution, which combined interactive USB devices, interactive touch points, touch devices, mobile app, and a customized gamification platform with no learning curve or external connections.

Randy Cline, Deputy Conference Chairman describes the beginning of a great experience: "During check-in, each Scout received a Poken. At the orientation event that evening, we dimmed the lights of the arena and instructed each Scout to activate the device, turn to his neighbour, and touch his Poken to theirs. In seconds, the entire arena was glowing with 15,000 green lights. It was breath taking — the kids immediately understood how to use Poken interactive USB."

Attendees intuitively understand the instant feedback they receive from Poken's signature green glow. In the months before NOAC, the Boy Scouts worked with Poken's development team to create an interactive game called Spark, in which Scouts earned points or badges for completing activities, connecting with other conference.

Interactive touch points were stationed throughout the campus, along with public leader boards that Scouts could use to track their own progress and compete against their friends. The result? A transformed NOAC with astronomical participant engagement that vastly exceeded all estimates. MSU's campus, in the midst of its yearly summer slumber, sprang to life with the buzz of 15,000 Scouts racing to and from climbing walls, ropes courses, sporting events, and seminars, and connecting with new friends using Poken's touch devices.

Poken's Mobile app was the perfect compliment to the gamified event experience. Through the app, attendees could check their progress and profile, as well as access further information such as times and places of activities.

Relevant data for the next event

After the closing ceremonies, NOAC's leadership staff reviewed statistics from the event and walked away with a trove of information they can use to plan better events and forge stronger connections with members. "There's a ton of demographic info about what kids did, what they liked, and what they didn't like, that we'll be able to use for years after the conference," said Mike Hoffman, Conference Chairman. By deploying Poken, NOAC saw interaction and participation with its event that it had not even imagined was possible. The touch devices acted as the Scouts' key to unlock the conference, which they used with resounding enthusiasm.

Chapter summary

The role of technology has changed the ways of communication between people and in events. The use of event apps and social media offer extraordinary gains to events.

Social media can extend the value of your event, connect and engage attendees prior to, during and after your event. The extensive use of technology not only saves time, but also cuts the money invested. The more you use technology to automate some of your processes, the more you can increase your profitability and generate a much better experience for all the people involved, which also increases your revenue and overall results.

You should consider engagement as an essential element for the success of the event today; it is possible to obtain it through numerous options offered by the event app and social media.

To choose the most suitable event app to meet event needs, follow the simple steps below to define the basic parameters.

Practical guide to the chapter

Here is the roadmap of the essential steps described in the chapter, for practical application in your daily activities:

Item	Description
Engaging participants	Having a self-service dashboard on the site or event app that allows exchange of information, contacts and scheduling meetings among attendees.
	Offering participants a rich online platform of event materials with specific content of the event and a customizable schedule.
	Providing a Q & A tool to interact with speakers during presentations.
	Creating forms of interaction of participants with sponsors
	Providing polls and surveys to obtain opinions and suggestions about the event.
	Developing and conducting a gamification strategy that includes fun, simplicity and rewards.
	Applying the hashtag of the event in all materials, making it visible to encourage its use.
Best use of the subscription and ticketing tool	Integrating with social media and financial, tax and audit controls. Operations must have fast, modern and user-friendly interface.

Choosing the best event app strategy	Identify attendees' expectations about your event app and consider the user experience, community involvement, cost, design element, content and audience demographics. Define: **Why** you need it **How** your goal will be achieved and **which** feature should be taken to accomplish it **What** your mobile strategy is. This is divided into two parts: pre-event (metrics will measure your event app success) and post-event (compare and study data against your evaluation criteria). Check if the app has these four basic areas: provide essential event information, communicate in real time, facilitate attendee connections and provide data about the event itself.
Monitoring social media of the event	It is possible to measure everything on the web. The definition of what will be measured demands strategy to generate quality and agility
Importance of photos and videos	The use of photos and videos to create content at your event increases attention and sharing.

For further reading, questions for reflection and additional materials please go to the book's page at the publisher's website:

www.goodfellowpublishers.com/technologyandevents

4

Notes

1   McTiffin, Gareth. How cultural venues are adapting with technology. http://www.eventmagazine.co.uk/blog-cultural-venues-adapting-technology/venues/article/1364816. [07 Jan 2016]

2   2015 Young Professional Exhibitor Needs and Preferences Study. The Center for Exhibition Industry Research (CEIR). Available at www.ceir.org/landmark-study-young-professional-exhibitor-preferences. [14 May 2015]

3   Kemp, Simon. Digital, Social & Mobile Worldwide in 2015 Report. wearesocial. net/blog/2015/01/digital-social-mobile-worldwide-2015. [21/12/15]

4   www.marketsandmarkets.com/PressReleases/event-management-software.asp. [21 Dec 2015

5   Nelissen, Niko. *The event app blue book.* 2015 edition. etouches | TapCrowd.

6   McArthur, J. Maximize your event engagement and make a lasting impression. http://guidebook.com/mobile-guides/maximize-event-engagement. [26/10/15]

7   How to create a result-driven event app. Quickmobile. 2015

8   Event Management Software Market by Software Type, & by Organization Size - Global Forecast to 2019. http://www.prnewswire.co.uk/news-releases/global-event-management-software-event-registration-venue-management-marketing-planning-analytics-ticketing-market---forecast-to-2019-280029192.html. [15/12/15]

9   Ball, Corbin. App aptitude: choosing the nest app for your conference or event. www.corbinball.com/mobile/index.cfm?fuseaction=cor_av&artID=9078. [20/12/15]

10 *Events: How mobile engagement data creates new opportunities*. Doubledutch.

11 Goldberg, Alex. What are the best conference apps and event apps out there? Available at http://guidebook.com/mobile-guides/best-conference-apps-comparison. [19 Dec 2015]

12 *The event app buyer's guide*. Guidebook. 2015.

13 blog.socialtables.com/2015/02/23/20-creative-ideas-content-creation-live-events. [12 May 2015]

14 Schumacher, Stefan. Hashing out the almighty #hashtag. http://blog.surepayroll. com/hashing-out-the-almighty-hashtag. [10 Jan 2016]

15 Monteiro, Diego. Redes Sociais e Big Data: se não gerar resultados, não adianta. www.mundodomarketing.com.br/artigos/diego-monteiro/33645/redes-sociais-e-big-data-se-nao-gerar-resultados-nao-adianta.html?utm_source=akna&utm_medium=email&utm_campaign=news+29.05. [29 May 2015]

16 www.dicaevento.com/artigos/como-definir-um-bom-palestrante-para-seu-evento [15 Jul 2015]

17 *The Definitive Guide to Creative Optimization*. Rock Fuel, 2015. p 22. Available at http://info.rocketfuel.com/rs/rocketfuel/images/RocketFuel_Guide_To_Creative_Optimization.pdf

18 Holub, Juraj. 20 Creative Ideas for Content Creation at Live Events, blog. socialtables.com/2013/04/30/event-guide-how-to-turn-attendees-into-happy-guests-part-1. [20 May 2015]

19 Ervin, Brittney. 10 social media stats you might not know (but should). Available at http://www.business2community.com/social-media/10-social-media-stats-you-might-not-know-but-should-01245250#aziwpBW1L2vFiWXF.97 [8 Jun 2015]

20 blog.socialtables.com/2015/02/23/20-creative-ideas-content-creation-live-events. [03 Jan 2016]

21 Arrivals to Departures: The Power of on-site technologies. Cvent. Available at http://s3.amazonaws.com/wavecast-production/wavecast-platform/sites/245/2016/01/PoL-Arrivals-to-departures.pdf. [03 Jan 2016]

Section III

The event

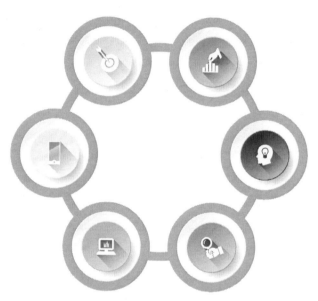

After the project definition and the selection of the most appropriate technology, this section shows how to implement and use it during the event.

Chapter 5 – Attendee, Sponsor and Client

How the use of technology in your event allows:

- A better understanding of the needs of the attendee
- Prompt reactions to the ongoing event through monitoring attendees
- Expanding the possibilities of networking and information exchange
- Great feedback about the impact and relevance of the event
- Engagement and connections with attendees, sponsors, organizers and suppliers
- Attendees to interact and have a voice
- Gathering and handling data from the attendees

Chapter 6 – Suppliers and Promotion

- The main changes in consumer profiles today
- The characteristics of the Millennials and how their impact upon events
- How to enhance the results of events, by promoting engagement

5 Participants, Sponsors and Clients

"As events become more immersive experiences, technology has inevitably heightened the expectation of event attendees. "

Garreth McTiffin

Introduction

This chapter explains the main changes in the profile of those consumers and provides information concerning the key strategies that can be adopted in order to maximize the results of your event, with consumers as the main reference in your choices, increasing engagement, satisfaction and maximizing results of events.

Learning Objectives

After reading this chapter you will have learned:

■ The main changes in consumer profile today

■ The characteristics of the Millennials and how they are impacting events

■ How to enhance the results of events, by promoting the engagement of the participants.

This chapter has been written with the special collaboration of Professor Isaíra Ma. G de Oliveira.

During the meeting sessions, while the speaker is delivering content, younger people use the 'second screen' to look things up and push things out. According to Hamilton[1], organizers must welcome devices in the meeting room, encourage attendees to use event social media platforms and download complementary content alongside their event apps.

From the digital media and the so-called Web 2.0, the focus has shifted to consumers, who have the power to communicate their tastes and desires to companies in a direct way. Those consumers also give, in exchange for benefits or perceived benefits, to companies with which they are willing to maintain relationships, their profile, tastes, hygiene habits, eating habits, sports, and even their favorite places. However, one has to bear in mind that an exchange is expected, as in any relationship. Therefore, be prepared to offer something in exchange for the information you need and your intelligence gathering strategy will bear fruit, allowing an increased interaction with your stakeholders.

Regardless of the type of event, participant satisfaction is the best and most important metric to evaluate the success of your event. The substantial changes in the behaviour of stakeholders, described in Chapters 1, 2 and 4, have transformed the event industry, constantly challenging organizers to offer ever more creative and engaging events, by increasing use of mobile devices, and meeting the demand for customization of services and enhancement of interactivity and sustainability.

As will be explained in this chapter, the specific characteristics of the profile of current consumers, the so-called Millennials, strongly demand the use of digital and online tools to meet their needs.

As smartphones and tablets are personal devices, the best event app should customizable and designed to handle the most important items, such as agenda, schedule, and events attended. While using social technology to support events, a meeting planner will extend their value and use before, during, and after the events:

- **Before the event**, participants can learn about the program and interact with others who are attending, creating from the beginning a networking platform for the attendees. Presenters can conduct polls to help refine their content or gather data to use at the conference.

- **At the event**, they can share their experiences with friends and colleagues who are not attending, as well as look for exhibitors' locations within the event, their representatives and speakers, promo and tech materials, etc.

- **After the event**, they can keep building relationships and continue the learning process[2].

In addition to social media, we highlight the events apps, which are:

Pieces of software downloaded from an app store and installed on a mobile device such as a smartphone, tablet or smart watch, used within the context of a physical event with the intention of providing up-to-date information, enabling interaction and increasing engagement for all stakeholders involved.[3]

By using the available technology, event apps must stimulate interaction and networking to connect and engage the audience, deliver up-to-date information, bring added value, get more insight and dramatically increase the ROI for attendees, sponsors, speakers, exhibitors, event suppliers, and meeting planners by capturing relevant data and up-to-date information at all times.

If the event apps are integrated with the event management software, you will have a state-of-the-art situation. It will allow meeting planners to manage every aspect of the event in real time, including the event content, needs of attendees, speakers and sponsors (lists, login, check in and out, certification, etc.), as well as accounting and financial issues (invoices, receipts, payments, revenues, etc.)

Here is a brief checklist on event apps, for different groups using them:

Attendees:

- Keeping track of their whereabouts, control of arrivals, access and sessions attended, keeping the audience engaged with live polling; surveys to capture valuable feedback; stimulating networking, etc.

- Making sure there is no double bookings

- Strategizing the scope of each message and timing of those involved

- Agenda of the event; venue information, speaker bios, attendance list, provision of speaker slides for download, sharing pictures from the event, sending push notifications

Sponsors:

- Presenting their business image

- Conveying marketing speech

- Offering promotions and/or special offers

- Engaging and starting relationship with target audience

- Capturing BI (business intelligence) data for later usage

Speakers:

- Sharing photos and background information

- Including an outline of their presentations before the event

Event suppliers:

- Ability to find individual exhibitors, points of interest (info booth, toilets, bar, workshop rooms) and meeting points

- Interacting with event venue managers for technical info and details

- Keeping track of venue facilities

Meeting planners:

- Detailed checklist with content and features

- Shareable chronogram of activities

- Communication platform among all involved in the organization of the event

Some of the many challenges that cultural producers face daily can be found in Box 5.1.

Consumer behaviour

Much has been said about the new consumer facing thousands of new technologies that are emerging all the time, especially in the event industry. However, is it possible that the behaviour of event consumers has changed and is no longer the same?

On the one hand, it is so because consumer power has apparently increased (in the way consumers make decisions, participate and purchase more actively). This is reflected in the attitude of companies that strive to meet their expectations through customization of relationships or of their products and services – an approach which is quite evident in the event industry.

As the role of intermediary between services and consumers has all but disappeared, today's businesses are faced with the challenge of relating directly with this new consumer, who has a different profile from former consumers. With the advent of new technologies, ways of communication have been changing constantly. The essence of the Internet is to offer greater interactivity and connection among its users. Mobile technologies (such as tablets, smartphones, net books, etc.) have not only enabled consumers to operate from any location, at any time, but also allowed them to establish multilateral communication in real time.

The new technological and communication tools for offering solutions or streamlining some processes have more visible impact when related to companies and their consumers, directly affecting their trade relations.

5

This new scenario values digital marketing as an essential corporate tool, demanding that event organizers understand the key differences between traditional and digital marketing. It also places greater demands on the main traditional components and concepts of marketing (research, market analysis, promotion, etc.). The digital aspect is rich in terms of details, combining customer information and integration across various communication platforms (such as social media, e-commerce, mobile, video, search engines, content portals, vertical channels, and so on), much more intensely and effectively than by using traditional means. Moreover, it also gives a communication structure and measurement and evaluation tools that are much more sophisticated and comprehensive (see Chapter 7), allowing the selection, implementation and monitoring of KPIs (Key Performance Indicators).

Box 5.1: Technology in shows

Isaíra Oliveira

From the days of old Vaudeville Theaters (since 1870) to the great spectacles created for Brazilian casinos (which had their golden age in the 1930s), producers and artists have always sought to present the best and the most sophisticated special effects to their public. In open spaces, at the time, for example, the great visual spectacle was the famous fireworks and some visual tricks.

Since then, the need for those producers has remained the same, namely to always present innovative shows, where the interaction with the public enables both artists and viewers to have a unique experience. Therefore, many of them had to incorporate other technologies to keep their fans, whether through the CDs and DVDs, websites, YouTube, computer systems such as P2P (peer-to-peer, technology aimed at mass sharing of music and movies) or even investment in major stage structures among other new developments that appear daily in the digital age.

Today, in any big show, there are big screens with high resolution placed in strategic places. Everything goes to enable a closer relationship with the public.

 An example of this is U2, the rock band. Since 1992, they have popularized the screens and other special effects. Even after 20 years, they have brought more innovation and more closeness to the public, with the "360° Tour," where they used a four-legged structure, and a series of ramps, nicknamed "The claw". Besides that, they used innovative sound and LED screens systems, putting up an innovative show because of the use of a stage with more than one million pieces, 150,000 machined pieces and 30,000 cables. Furthermore, they also used screens that had 500,000 pixels and 320,000 fasteners, and effects that can alter the distance between the band and their fans.

However, technology has helped not only the viewers, who felt a great closeness with their idols, but also the musicians, and the sound and light technicians. For example, there is now specialized software, such as the "spectrum analyzers" which are capable of measuring the acoustic capacity of the concert hall. Such advances enabled different set-ups in terms of effect programming and sound equalization in each show, in a faster and more practical way. Everything can be easily recorded, complete with reprogramming of the set list, in real time.

A producer has to think of many aspects, including the most basic – power supply and safety. Three tips for these aspects: The first tip is to visit the venue of the presentation beforehand, as no technology resists a power outage, for example. The second is to be aware of the capacity of generators, power supply, cable thickness, as each of these items could compromise a performance through charge leaks or even electric shocks. As a final tip, check the electronic turnstiles and bracelets, and always work with qualified professionals who excel at the safety of the artists, the public and the staff.

Today, in show venues, viewers can also record their favourite shows and share content in real time using high-quality mobile phones with the latest technology.

Choose the best way to use such technology and value the relationships built with your fans. Because whether using technology or not, artists will always depend on the warmth of people.

Isaíra Ma. Garcia de Oliveira is a professor, researcher, author and cultural producer, with a post-doctorate in art and communication.

According to Brandão[4], technology has provided a more direct approach between products and consumers, taking into account those aspects individually. Therefore, the events sector should prepare for further customization of those new experiences for this new type of consumers. On the other hand, it demands that companies seek better understanding of their consumers in order to provide better products and services, in a more personalized and direct way. How can this be done in the event industry?

According to Terra[5], consumers have been participating more and more in the production of content in the media and business, where they start to get together in communities, and become the most important part in decision-making processes in a company. Our view is that technology has empowered consumers in an unprecedented and irreversible way, making their use of technology more than just a differentiation, but something mandatory in order to succeed in any business, notably the organization of events.

The Millennial generation

The current challenge for companies is to understand how purchases will take place, how the new services will be developed and customized, and how those new consumers will participate in the development and improvement of services offered by companies. A Nielsen study[6] shows the size of the age ranges of the US population and defines the various classifications of the generations from the past century as follows:

- Greatest Generation (1901-24) and Silent Generation (1925-45) – 12%

- Baby Boomers (1946-64) – 24%

- Generation X (1965-76) – 16%

- Millennials/Gen Y (1977-95) – 24%

    - ☐ Older Millennials (1977-86)

    - ☐ Younger Millennials (1987-95)

- Generation Z (1995-Present) – 24%

For Nielsen[7], Millennials are considered the Social Generation or the founders of the social media movement, constantly connected with their social circle online and via mobile (see Figure 5.1). That is why they prefer to live in dense, urban villages. Other relevant aspects about Millennials:

1   **They are social** – For them, what makes their generation unique and their identity is 'Technology use' and, very important to the event organizer, 'Music/Pop culture' (11%). They are heavier internet users than the Boomers (using mobile devices and social media 24/7) and expect authentic experience and a direct, personal and customized experience when interacting via social media with brands.

2   **They care** – Social impact caused by a brand has appeal to this generation when they make purchases. They desire authenticity in the goods and can spend more on products and services from companies that invest in social betterment. Share your Social Responsibility Efforts and social issues to develop a meaningful relationship with them.

3   **Respect their authenticity, creativity and diversity** – To be engaged and to become brand ambassadors, Millennials are interested in customization and individuality. As their online behaviour is based on sharing, they expect participation, collaboration and co-creation. They demand a two-way personalized conversation while using social media, post customer-submitted images and behind-the scenes videos.

4 Relate to them – Celebrity endorsement or relatable characters/ themes on messages deeply impact upon Millennials. Event sponsorship of their favourite music artists are much appreciated (they are bound to try the sponsor's product or service), especially if the celebrity is social and engaged with their fans. As endorsements by influencers and music artists are very well received by Young Millennials (24%) and Older Millennials (26%), find one who mirrors your company values.

5 Give them first-hand and amazing experience – They want unique and sharable experiences.

6 Keep it simple – Websites must be intuitive, simple, clean and with easy to find information.

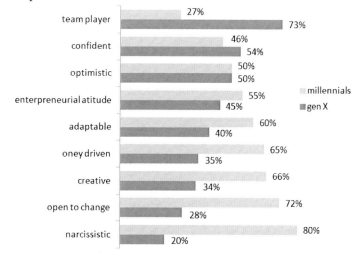

Market size
76,6 Million
Millennials are the largest generation (surpassing baby boomers)

Purchasing power
1.68 Trillion

60,000 Average household income

Figure 5.1: Inside the Millennial mind – Market size

Source: www.cebglobal.com/exbd/marketing-communications/ iconoculture/millenials/millennial-mind-infographic/index.page. Layout adapted by authors

5

We can extract the keywords of this approach by Nielsen almost like a guide to the use of modern technologies. Graph 5.1 shows the qualities each generation are more likely to possess: Millennials' work values and the huge differences from Gen X. When carrying out planning, implementation or management of an event, one should question, in relation to the public, whether the event is social, caring, authentic, creative, diverse, related, simple, and provides great experience. If all these describe your event, you will be able to reap the best results.

Graph 5.1: Millennials' work values

Source: http://www.kpcb. com/internet-trends page 13

team player 27% / 73%
confident 46% / 54%
optimistic 50% / 50%
enterpreneurial atitude 55% / 45%
adaptable 60% / 40%
oney driven 65% / 35%
creative 66% / 34%
open to change 72% / 28%
narcissistic 80% / 20%

millennials
gen X

Events are valued as platforms for content and networking. However, event planners must adapt their programs and content according to their own motivation and that of the new generations. Among them, stand out the Millennials (those born between 1980 and 2000), who will represent 46% of the workforce by 2020, against 16% of Generation X (those born between 1965 and 1980).

However, although technology is a remarkable and essential issue for the Millennials, they desire and find much value in personal and face-to-face interactions. Meetings Nets[8] describes key elements necessary at those events that have a component of the Millennials.

- **Variety in session formats**: The challenge is to find a way to use in-room technology to keep Millennials engaged and learning, since they use the 'second screen' even while content is being delivered. Planners must get comfortable with this situation and welcome the use of devices in the event room. They must encourage attendees to access complementary content and to use social media platforms to get "fluid conversations based on what attendees bring up."

- For this generation, **organizational hierarchy is not a barrier** to the flow of information. The event will create value for them if Millennials could personally interact with the leadership or participate in a question-and-answer format with them. For this restless generation, a seductive format that offers optimal results is breaking up a 60/75 minute session into 15-minute ones featuring different formats, including a small-group reflection and discussion. Another option is to get at least one segment into meeting sessions that use hands-on and creative, interactive and collaborative activities (without technology), like sticky notes, flip chart, and so on.

Faced with this new reality, organizations have to understand that today's consumers are proactive. They create stories, participate actively in digital media, comment on their experiences, take pictures, post them and enjoy them, almost instantly, any issue or placement of their interest, from wherever they may be. In other words, today's consumers recount their experiences with an event at the same moment they are consuming that service. It can happen at several points: during the online application process; during the course of an event; soon after the end of an event; and even at the time to get their certificate of participation. It can also take place while they are trying out specific devices, or any other interactive experience provided by those new tools. Those consumers will take pictures, post them, and make their comments immediately and simultaneously with the event. Therefore, companies must be very aware of those movements and attitudes of those new consumers and participants of events in order to correct any errors that may appear in a more noticeable way.

In this sense, monitoring social media (a topic explored in Chapters 3 and 4) allows us to take a deeper look into the reactions of the public and use that information to improve the experience of the target audiences even more, to build or strengthen a relationship with them. Moreover, we can systematically learn what works best in each event, in order to correct their possible failures and better exploit their strengths.

The influence of social media

It is undeniable that experiences in person and from a distance are quite different, although the distance between them is becoming increasingly small and more tenuous. However, access also becomes important. With so many changes, the contribution of social media has changed consumer behaviour quite a lot, as consumers have become more active and participatory.

With the expansion of broadband, information technology increasingly stimulated interactive media by also facilitating the production and dissemination of UGC (User-Generated Content). One example is the boom in websites, blogs, Facebook profiles, Twitter, portals, and other social networks. A study by Nielsen shows that Facebook access by mobile is a top app for Millennials, followed by Instagram and Twitter (the audience and time spent are unique). As they are the music lovers too, YouTube and Pandora Radio are among top 10 favourites.

For Natal and Viana[9], the fact that those new consumers are approaching businesses via social networks causes a transformation in both parts. On the one hand, producers prepare more targeted strategies directly influencing consumers, who in turn are the inspiration for companies, contributing their opinions and experiences, to create new goods and services and improve existing ones.

Kotler[10] says there are three stages that make up the consumer's process of collaboration in the research and development of products and services through digital media. The first phase is the creation of a platform, so that products can be customized; the second phase consists of the personalization or customization of this platform by consumers, according to their individual tastes and characteristics; finally, the last phase involves feedback – when companies ask consumers to give opinions on the web, so improvements can be developed. The feedback obtained allows companies to identify needs of customers with greater accuracy, and these in turn receive increasingly customized products and services. For companies, that adds greater value to the brand as far as the public is concerned. The new consumers have mobility, 24-hour access to information and use digital media as a practical tool to interact with companies and other users.

5

In the search for strategic feedback, monitoring social media plays a very important role. It allows us to observe the natural and subjective reactions of the public towards a brand, product or service placed on the market, by bringing statistics that allow the extraction of insights, which companies can use to create tactics and strategies to markedly improve the presence and relevance of the brand to the target audience.

The new consumers place less value on mass advertising and give greater value to the opinions of friends and other connected consumers. They have realized that the hierarchy in relationships with brands has changed. Now they (the consumers) are the main players.

The Millennials seek their rights and demand merchandise and services that meet their personal or collective needs through social media. According to Kotler, the advancement of technology influences the attitude of consumers, who understand how to relate to brands, to express themselves and collaborate with other consumers. This new era, known as 'Participation Age' or 'Collaborative Age', finds in consumers (especially in the Millennials) the so-called 'prosumers' (producers + consumers), that is, those consumers also create events and products.

Montardo and Araújo[11] claim that social networks allow for a constant exchange of information horizontally. In other words, engagement means visibility. Digital media have greatly increased consumer power in the corporate world. As interactive channels with easy handling and immediate use at any time and place, social media have facilitated the distribution or communication of written, sound or visual works in various ways and on multiple platforms. Companies must understand that those new tools should be used in their communication strategies of brands and services with their potential consumers. Through online resources, new virtual spaces to meet customers can be developed, enabling internal structural changes in both the way to communicate, as well as in the ways of planning and logistics of their products and services.

Social networks can create powerful relationships between consumers and brands, since they enable sharing information and experiences (both good and bad), regarding any product or service. Of course, all of this applies directly to events that (in addition to their role of disseminators of technical business knowledge) find much of their value in generating networking between the various players involved. Just like in all other areas of business, in organizing events, the intersection between business content and the relationship between the parties is generating greater value.

To fulfill its goals, events need to create a social strategy that feed into and is a relevant part of the event planning. You will provide value to attendees and using social media will be a great extension of your event.

Experts suggest that the initials steps are to define the objectives and to keep them simple. Then, to determine the interests, preferences and capabilities of your audience and survey which social media platforms they use and are interested in (content must be customized for each one) and how they use them. Crowdsourcing can be a great opportunity to spread news and to get great insights for your event: create a venue online where content about your event will be shared among selected participants. It can be at LinkedIn, Facebook, Twitter, Instagram or many other social media platforms. This will encourage networking between your event and your public, as well as among the participants. The best option is to do it before, during and after the event. For example, create an event hashtag where attendees can share their experiences. Please bear in mind that in order to empower consumers, social media must give valuable information to attendees. Listen to them and answer them, too.

Crowdshaping and customization

For Smith[12], the information gathered by crowdsourcing bulky data (crowdshaping) will revolutionize the event industry. It will allow organizers to create personalized attendee experiences at an event, to make adjustments in real time to better accommodate the demands of attendees, to have better control of crowd flow and revamp travel and safety procedures (for example, in reacting to food allergies or getting instant notification if there were not enough busses in rotation):

> The marriage of technology and attendee-centric event planning strategies is creating types of experiences that engage event participants in revolutionary new ways. Two attendees do not necessarily have to have the same experience at an event. Collecting data enables planners to make adjustments regarding everything, on and off the site, quickly and efficiently. Crowdshaping has given planners the ability to have safer spaces, more interactive experiences, and happier attendees.

> Happy attendees are repeat attendees, and repeat attendees are often ambassadors and champions of your brand. The collection of big data in real time is a phenomenon called Crowdshaping. A relatively unassertive process, Crowdshaping harnesses the newest and latest technology trends to detect everything from an attendee's location to their heart beat rate.

Most planners are overwhelmed by the massive amount of data, and the challenge is to figure out how to analyze and protect that data.

5

Engagement and feedback

A mobile event app can produce a 33% increase in attendees' engagement[13]: by offering alternative ways to engage with one another, voting during the attendance, asking questions of speakers; sharing photos; gamification, etc.

How will event organizers be able to use those tools in the service of their events, so that they meet the participants' needs for fast and accurate answers? How to use those same tools to enhance the value of their partners and sponsors in relation to their potential customers? Faced with these questions, we need to understand what this type of approach with consumers can provide to businesses.

While there is this convergence, it is necessary to be prepared to receive praise, but also criticism, which will happen quickly and dynamically. As this closeness gives consumers the same distance between your company or event and all other competitors by a mere click, it is mandatory to be even more prepared to meet the needs of those consumers. Thus, we can see that agility in the exchange of online information creates other values, where the relationship with consumers, who are your event participants, is paramount. Here the monitoring of social media is also essential, as this allows you to see the opinions and feelings of the public posted in social media, in real-time, with all the advantages that come with it.

That power, controlled by consumers, instantly influences your event. Once the event and its consumption occur simultaneously, the chances of becoming rapidly a success or failure leverage up. So, if there are failures, the dissatisfied consumers may be instantly visible. The more consumers are exposed, the more status they seem to have. Therefore, it is up to companies to appropriate such data, interpret it and create new products and services that can meet those demands. A powerful strategy based on the monitoring of social media is to capture messages from the public about the event and share them in real time on screens or monitors in the event: this is known as creating a 'social media wall'. The perception of power that goes to the public, who see their opinions publicly shared, makes a strong link between this same audience, the event organizers and brands of the sponsors, creating a relationship that can be strengthened over time, with advantages for all parties involved. Here are two recent cases of success in the use of social media walls.

- Microsoft Social Balloon in 2015 was a unique social media wall at The Mobile World Congress. A giant air balloon displayed in real time the social happenings from the congress and the show floor[14].

- The Wells Fargo Championship is a professional golf tournament of the Professional Golfers Association of America – PGA Tour[15]. The naming rights belong to Wells Fargo, an American Multinational banking and financial services holding company. During the 4-day tournament in the 2015 edition, a 2 by 4 set of large screens activated social content to interact with fans, with styled social content and a voting app.

Those new tools allow the end of the dividing line between information producers and information receivers. Therefore, social media are characterized not only by interactivity, but also by collectivity, where the participation of all types of users – whether they are individuals, groups or organizations – make it possible to think of changes in buying and selling relationships of products and services.

Terra[16] says that today it is the consumers who have the power, since they determine what content, products or services they want. This is the age of customization, where companies will focus on facilitating access to their products and services through new digital tools, with the choice based on the prior identification of the preferences and desires of consumers.

■ Ask the participants

Despite the increasingly globalized world, people want items specially customized to their different needs: ask your customers what they want and how they want the experience to unfold, as the big challenge for companies today is to maintain a healthy relationship with this new type of consumer, offering an increasingly personalized experience.

Those who care to listen more carefully to consumers today are bound to realize that more participatory consumers volunteer valuable information to businesses. They suggest innovation for products and services, participate in research and development of new products and services and allow businesses to take these to market in successfully – and without the need for large investments. Moreover, people can carry out and present the results of their personal research to businesses at no cost.

Geolocation devices and apps diversify participants' options to meet their needs by allowing them to be identified when approaching a specific location and, for example, receive notification on their mobile devices on news or other information of their particular interest (such as offers, discount coupons, and so on). For trade fairs and exhibitions, geolocation provides numerous essential details to organizers. For example, to learn about the flow of visitors in detail and on time, enabling them to address any bottlenecks in specific areas of the event and optimize services immediately.

Rock in Rio is one of the largest entertainment events in the world. Created in 1985, it has already had successful editions held in Brazil, Portugal, Spain and the United States. The festival is an outstanding communication platform where the brands of the sponsors can interact with participants before, during and after the event. In the 2015 edition in Rio de Janeiro, the search engine for Facebook friends had the geolocation display their location and facilitate the meeting. The event program could be customized for the full list of the various line-up of concerts arranged in alphabetical as well as chronological order, by date and place. "What's hot", another application resource, exhibited the leading artists of the event, based on the popularity of the attractions.

Of the time spent in gatherings and meetings 37% is used to view presentations, but 39% of respondents said they had fallen asleep at some point, though, 85% say they remember the questions that were asked[17]. In order to turn an event into a more immersive experience and allow participants, speakers and organizers to increase interaction and networking, smartphone and tablets can be used during the event in various ways, such as:

- Asking questions
- Downloading presentations and taking notes directly on the slides for later review
- Getting real-time feedback
- Interacting through social media
- Evaluating the event
- Providing event evaluation tools to organizers.

■ Gamification

The concept of gamification is to create games or game-like activities to encourage attendee behaviours that help in reaching the meeting's objectives (networking, content, engagement, marketing and engagement with sponsors) using an event app or a social-media platform. For Meeting Nets, the four basic rules for creating an effective game are "establishing desired goals, developing clear rules for attendees, having a feedback system, and making participation voluntarily." They also recommend that "even with games that have the goal of collective accomplishment rather than personal competition — an important goal to socially responsible and civic-minded Millennials — the use of technology to monitor progress and drive behavior is central to success."[18] As this generation prefers experiences to tangible items and material possessions, a special individual award and recognition for them could be, for example, a private roundtable discussion with one of the keynote speakers.

The 2015 edition of Rock in Rio made available an app that offered the full experience to its users. It was produced by Oi (a Brazilian mobile operator and one of the sponsors of the event). In addition to providing all the festival information, it allowed interaction with social networks of the event, connection with other users, customized schedule of the attractions, gave provided transportation tips and included several games.[19]

These new channels of communication provide a source of low cost and great opportunity for businesses. They also create new relationship opportunities with the intermediate public, who at first were not the main target. An example of this is the fact that, in a matter of seconds, consumers can access events, trips, products, tips or companies that provide the same products or equivalent ones.

■ Predictive sales

Dimantas[20] argues that this new consumer attitude has forced companies to rethink their strategies and the way they relate to and communicate with their customers, because they promote more interaction with them and develop service techniques increasingly personalized and differentiated. They are seeking ways to constantly be present with their customers and even anticipate their needs.

For that purpose, they use the knowledge gained from the collection and analysis of consumer information, such as purchase history and individual preferences. Predictive sales can generate satisfaction and memorable experiences for consumers by offering products based on the observation of their prior consumption habits. By being present at various locations where active or prospects customers are, long before their actual presence at the event, it promotes the engagement and seduction, extending the point of brand performance. Digital platforms and traditional media are relevant channels to make such contact with the brand of the event.

In its third participation as sponsor of the Rock in Rio, SKY (a cable TV subscription company) set up a booth with three floors facing the stage known as 'World', guitar-shaped in allusion to the festival brand. It also created another platform – SKYrock, to strengthen its participation in the festival, featuring exclusive content about music and artists in their official channels in the official networks. In the 'Graphic History', infographics would show the stories of the bands, with biographies and curiosities, and in 'Picto Music' the highlight was the songs of artists. SKY also created coverage of the brand on Instagram and Facebook, allowing participants to follow the action backstage at the festival, and see the stage and all activities in the company's booth[21] in real time.

By understanding that consumers add value to their organizations and that those are sources of valuable information, companies now have a significantly competitive advantage over their competitors.

Mobile marketing

Among the main stakeholder behaviour changes in the events market, stimulated by technology and reported in Chapter 2, are the increasing use of mobile devices, the demand for personalization of services and the appreciation of individuality, interactivity and sustainability. According to a Nielsen study[22], technology is a key component of their lives: about 92% of Millennials own a smartphone, against 76% of Baby Boomers. As three out of every four have a smartphone and 83% say they sleep with them on, mobile devices have become a very efficient way to reach them.

Thus, among the various tools that appear every day on the web, arises mobile marketing, a segment used together with relationship marketing, where marketing actions are forwarded to mobile consumers. The importance of mobile devices as an channel of communication with customers has already been shown in previous chapters. They offer promotions and relationship marketing in terms of new services, among other possibilities. Those devices have as their main objective to promote targeted and interactive actions with consumers in real time and on a segmented basis. Therefore, the events industry has to make use of those tools, more and more, to keep their consumers well informed at all times about what is happening or how they may benefit from their programming, among other services, given the specific features of each event.

Mobile apps and social media – The ideal means of communications to attendees is now migrating from emails and website to event apps for mobile devices for both logistical and strategic elements of their events. Those apps should have a multifaceted functionality that would help start meaningful conversations before and after the live event takes places, see session schedules, get feedback surveys during and after events, allow them to register for events, extend the life of meeting content and better engage stakeholders, and so on. 'Community managers' or content curators are very important, as they keep conversations going and guide them in the right directions.

As Millennials are so attuned to social media, it makes sense for events to develop a way to be present there. However, it has to be done through a well-defined strategy that encourages attendees to use them for meetings-related posts. Organic growth will happen if planners focus on those platforms that are relevant to their audience.

Millennials love to know that they are being listened to and that they are part of the conversation during events, so show posts from attendees, speakers and content curators on large LCD panels display. Such strategy has already been presented in this chapter (see *Engagement and Feedback*)

New mobile technologies provide greater convenience to consumers, reducing the communication barriers with organizations. Thus, among other facilities, consumers no longer actually need to go to shops, or banks, or queue in order to buy tickets for shows, obtain certificates or sign up for events. A single device can carry out all those and many other activities. Every second, thousands of people are keen to position themselves online positively or negatively on any subject or theme. Direct collaboration by users in content generation only confirms their power, as they demand more direct and personalized experiences from companies. Companies that offer solutions from a certain interest or topic, now have prominent positions in relation to their competitors. Figure 5.2 shows the future of mobile application development.

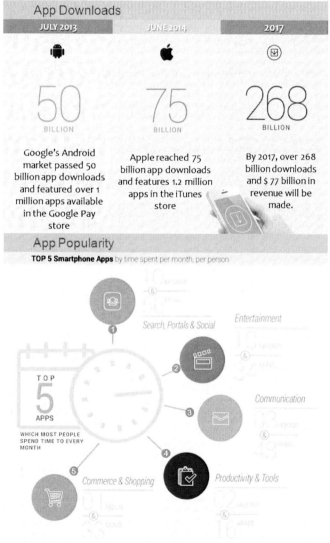

Figure 5.2: The future of mobile application development

Source: http://businessdegrees.uab. edu/resources/infographic/the-future-of-mobile-application/

Nowadays, social media is indeed a valuable marketing asset for any event. However, before designing their social media campaign, it is vital that organizers analyze very carefully their target audience's characteristics and preferences; the most active social media platform, what content they like the most, whether videos and images are shared and the intensity of topics posted. Then, it is necessary to check out the unique aspects of each social media platforms and choose the best options for your audience. Experts unanimously agree that first step is to choose the most relevant social media to the public. Bear in mind that success is also linked to their correct use.

Visual Web

Millennials love their smartphone cameras: 47% uses the camera/video daily and 76% post on social media.[23] The ubiquity of mobile phone cameras and the rise of photo-sharing websites have changed how companies and consumers use the web: a social media phenomenon has arisen, called the visual web. If your target is focused on the Millennial market, visually driven platforms are the ideal way to connect with them.

According to e-Marketer, "one out of every three Americans watches videos on their mobile phones, along with 100 million people who watch them on tablets. With their audiences consuming content across devices, content creators must be ready to deliver on mobile— and to target and track viewers across devices." Visual Web Roundup report[24] estimates that, in 2015, "107.1 million people in the US will watch videos on their mobile phones on at least a monthly basis. That is 13.8% over 2014, and amounts to one-third of the total US population. Watching videos on mobile phones is more common than using them to listen to music. Nearly as many people will watch videos on tablets."

According to their report, nine out of 10 brand marketers think visual elements were important to their marketing functions (69.2% considered it very important). More than nine out of 10 watch digital videos monthly and the US Millennials video consumption habits are more pronounced than other age groups.

Top types of visual content into marketing programs were custom video and photography. Graph 5.2 shows that US companies will continue to use Twitter for marketing purposes (just 1.4% point between 2015 and 2017). However, after Instagram opened up advertising to all businesses, marketer usage will grow rapidly: from 32.3% in 2015, it is expected to jump to 48.8% in 2016 and by 2017, 70.7% of the US companies with 100 employees or more will use Instagram. This report also shows that Instagram will bring US$ 595 million in mobile and revenues worldwide in 2015. By 2017, it should reach

US$ 2.81 billion. E-Marketer estimates that US Instagram users will rise by 20.9%, or 43.1% of social network users (three in 10 internet users, nearly one-quarter of the population). By 2019, its audience is likely to reach 111.6 million (55.8% of social networkers or over four out of every ten Internet users). Other chapters show how viewing videos increases sharing and visualization of information posted on the web, especially through mobile devices.

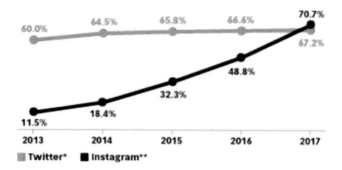

Graph 5.2: US companies using Twitter and Instagram for marketing, 2013-17, percentage of total
Source: Visual Web Roundup report, eMarketer. Oct, 2015.

5

The Rock in Rio Hunt presented cards with photo challenges, and "Caçada Oi" (Oi Hunt) stimulated visitation to various parts of the festival and awards through QR codes scattered throughout the City of Rock. Both could be shared on social networks. Transport information of special lines leading up to the event venue was placed in a simplified map.

Since its launch, Twitter has been a cultural phenomenon providing its users with brief information shared rapidly. According to Kent[25], this platform "allows people to connect with other users (both near and far) and spark relationships based on mutually shared interests, fostering a sense of belonging or acceptance by others. Gaining followers, likes or re-tweets can bolster a person's feelings of social acceptance, validation, and eventually, their self-esteem – even if those interactions exist only in the virtual world." She says, "Using a social network like Twitter fulfills various basic psychological needs, including companionship, acceptance and human connection."

If you choose Twitter as one of your event digital channels, Patel[26] suggests that you must have in mind the following:

- Images perform better than videos – users tweet images 361% more than tweet videos. To maximize your branding efforts, use creative images with humour.

- Texts perform better than images – tweets with links get 86% more retweets and if you keep it under 100 characters, it will get 17% more engagement. Texts with how-to or list-bases articles get 3 times as many retweets than any other content.

- Questions outperform quotes – questions get 1,050% more replies. Consider asking attendees a question, if you want to start a conversation.

During the first weekend of the 2015 Brazilian edition in Rio de Janeiro, the Rock in Rio event generated more than 1.7 million tweets between the 3 AM Friday and Monday (September 18 to 21, 2015). The first day of the festival generated 886,000 tweets. The band Queen occupied the top of the list of the largest TPM peaks (Tweets per Minute), with highlight to their songs "We Are the Champions", "We will rock you" and "Love of my life".[27]

ROI, ROE, and sponsorship

The rate of return on investment, known by the acronym ROI, is a metric used to measure income from a given amount of resources. ROI is calculated by the ratio between the net profit achieved and the investment made within a given period.

Originally used in finance, ROI is one of the many performance indicators to evaluate the value for money regarding investments. This rate has been used mainly to evaluate investments in Internet advertising.

In this case, in order to calculate ROI, we can subtract the gain from the investment from the amount spent on investments and divide the result again by the amount spent on investments. Thus, we have the formula:

$$ROI = \frac{(Total\ Revenue - Total\ Investments)}{Total\ Investments}$$

The rate of return on investments can also be set as a percentage. In this case, the ROI can be calculated by dividing the gain from the investment by the amount spent on investment, multiplying the quotient by 100. Check out the formula:

$$ROI\ (\%) = \frac{Profit \times 100}{Investments}$$

Through this methodology, it is also possible to measure the net income for a business. In this case, simply replace the gain obtained in the above formulas above by net income. Before making the calculation, it is important to take into account all the variables relating to the business, which may affect net income, such as freight, overall operating costs, etc.

For a 3-day conference for 400 attendees (with two coffee breaks per person/day), meeting planners can spend from $24 to $42 (average price of $4,000 per event). In addition, an event app can cost from $10 per person[28], as shown on Graph 5.3. While related to ROI, apps will grant a greater value than coffee costs.

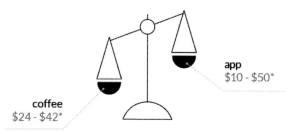

Graph 5.3: Mobile app x coffee expenses (per person)
Source: QuickMobile_Summer_Surveys_2014

There is a growing demand for demonstrating the ROI from previous events to clients and sponsors. Such measurement of results is obtained by defining and tracking Key Performance Indicator metrics – KPIs. It can be accomplished through specific data from before, during and after an event.

To Nellissen[29], "a great event app provides the user with the right information at the right time". Moreover, the three most important parties for whom the event app must add value are attendees, sponsors/exhibitors, and organizers. The essential features an event app should have are general, venue and contact information, news and social feeds; exhibitors catalog, interactive floor plan, sessions and speakers, attendee list, surveys, and slide sharing.

Actions to engage, facilitate and control access, besides identifying, implementing and monitor the main results of the event should be concentrated on them. He suggests some data aspects, such as a starting point to understand your event performance, weighed for importance from app usage (number of app downloads, number of times the app was used, QR codes scanned, bookmarked items, etc.), interaction enabled (number of push notification sent, messages between attendees, percentage of live voting participation, etc.) and feedback from attendees (session and speaker rating results, overall event rating, survey results, and so on).

ROE

ROE (Return on Engagement) is another metric that is being used more widely. For Kurt[30], good brands will focus on an always-on strategy (i.e, message and conversation distribution, 24/7 interaction). The process is simple: brands are publishers of content that build communities of interest around them. Those communities consume the content and engage with it, which leads to brand interest, love and sales. The reason why the goal should shift to a long-term one and move the focus from ROI to ROE is that:

> ...bigger communities, stronger loyalty, an unbreakable bond with the brand, and a desire of consumers/users/fans to refer the brand to others. ROI (as we all know) says something about how you invest your money, and what you get back mostly in economic terms (in media terms, e.g., how much free media it generated). On the other hand, **ROE aims at what you get back in brand strength:** to what extend has your content captivated your consumer, and has it resulted in brand equity, in making the brand stronger? Key 'return' components are:

- *Was there 'participation' (Comments, Shares, and Likes)?*

- *Did it confirm 'Authority'?*

- *Did it generate 'Influence'?*

- *Did it generate 'positive sentiment'?*

Here are a few thoughts on where to get started:

- *Define what you want to get out of ROE*

- *Set up continuous tracking online, on different platforms aiming at the content>equity relation*

- *Work in continuous, repetitive intervals (since you cannot survey 24/7, nor every single piece of content), e.g., every 25 hours <I'm taking an odd number so you would rotate time>*

    1 *a sample of your engaged user group can be surveyed to capture equity and even consumption intent*

    2 *then it can be cross-validated with another survey with a control group of 'non-consumers of the content'*

    3 *If you do that repeatedly over a period of time, patterns are likely to occur*

    4 *Put a few other research elements in the blender, shake it all up and my guess is it will spit out interesting facts*

In Figure 5.3, Murphy describes four categories of ROE. As it can be seen there, the more the public interacts with your contents over social media, the bigger your ROE. From single spectators in the first group on the left, those who simply engage are those who contribute less to your ROE. The second group shows the people who have a little more degree of interaction, starting to contribute in some way to your contents. The third group is the one where people really start interacting with you in a closer way, becoming some sort of "light advocates." Then, the fourth group congregates those real advocates, who bring their own contents to share through your social media channels, beginning to act as co-authors of your messages.

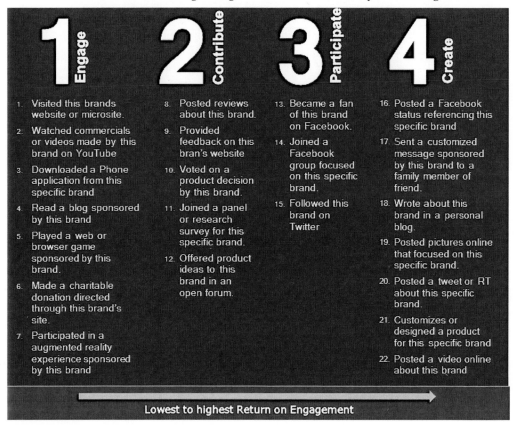

1. Visited this brands website or microsite.
2. Watched commercials or videos made by this brand on YouTube
3. Downloaded a Phone application from this specific brand
4. Read a blog sponsored by this brand
5. Played a web or browser game sponsored by this brand.
6. Made a charitable donation directed through this brand's site.
7. Participated in a augmented reality experience sponsored by this brand

8. Posted reviews about this brand.
9. Provided feedback on this bran's website
10. Voted on a product decision by this brand.
11. Joined a panel or research survey for this specific brand.
12. Offered product ideas to this brand in an open forum.

13. Became a fan of this brand on Facebook.
14. Joined a Facebook group focused on this specific brand.
15. Followed this brand on Twitter

16. Posted a Facebook status referencing this specific brand
17. Sent a customized message sponsored by this brand to a family member of friend.
18. Wrote about this brand in a personal blog.
19. Posted pictures online that focused on this specific brand.
20. Posted a tweet or RT about this specific brand.
21. Customizes or designed a product for this specific brand
22. Posted a video online about this brand

Lowest to highest Return on Engagement

Figure 5.3: ROE of social media actions

Source: http://pt.slideshare.net/brandonmurphy/the-true-value-of-social-media-4267498

■ Attendees

Nellissen also says, "60% of top-performing companies engage attendees before, during and after an event with two-way communication and engagement tactics". For him, an event app must have some features and allow attendees to personalize at least some of them: note, profile, check-in, favourites, personal agenda, agenda, messages and inbox, QR-code scanner, people around it, etc. In-app surveys must be short, easy to complete, with multiple-choice questions and a few open questions.

Holub[31] suggests using content to increase and maximize ROI for attendees:

■ Crowdsourcing and live polling – As shown before, Millennials wants to be part of the presentations and interact with the speakers.

By allowing attendees to create and shape the event content with real-time questions and live polls through smartphones and second-screen technologies, events will get higher engagement and more efficient information learning.

■ Sharing content updates – The online audience is almost unlimited. Live streaming and live-blogging are powerful tools to boost the number of participants, to stream the content and to provide real-time updates.

■ Twitter – Event #hashtag: must be short, unique and memorable. Incite competitions among attendees to boost the number of set tweets and display them on the screens during the event.

■ Sponsors / exhibitors

Data acquisition and supply of differentiated visibility to sponsors can be maximized by using several technology resources. The market already has several events apps options that offer interesting features that can help meeting planners a lot. The best event apps are able to get real-time data from the event floor and reporting must be available at any time. Among the features, stand out the ways of enabling visibility, brand value, effective communication and revenue opportunities to your sponsors and exhibitors, silently measuring traffic and tracking for event insight:

■ Link to sponsor website

■ Priority and precedence of sponsors in the list of exhibitors (premium or top listing)

■ Scan a barcode or QR code on the badge of booth visitors and list all leads captured, customized for each exhibitors

■ Sponsored push notification

■ Banners ads, etc.

■ Organizers

The key is the app's overall event performance. Nellissen[32] suggests some possibilities to promote your event app:

■ Add a section promoting it in the registration confirmation email

■ Include your app in newsletters and other email updates that you send out before the event

■ Promote your app on your event website

■ Show a pop-up to mobile visitors on your event website (pop-up message: "install the app" or "continue to website")

- Promote the app at the entrance of your event with banners or even a promotional team to welcome delegates and assist them in installing the app

- Add a standard slide at the beginning of certain sessions to urge people to install the app for upcoming interactions (voting, Q&A, rating)

- Add a standard slide at the end of each speaker session to ask for session rating in the app

- Consider providing certain information exclusively through the app. Many high-stake conferences ban paper and the app is the only place to find the schedule and stay up-to-date.

As everyone can see, the right use of apps and their perfect promotion amongst the event attendees is fundamental to obtain the best value for your investment. Once you decide to use apps, just go for it, using them in as many areas as possible and integrating them with your organization procedures. Show their features to all attendees and other people involved in the event to extract as much intelligence from them as you can to optimize their usage.

Chapter summary

5

Holub summarizes the theme of this chapter perfectly when he says that "The dynamic of events will keep on changing: from passive reception to active engagement. Attendees will become participants, as event organizers will continue providing audiences with event tech tools for active participation. As a result, participants will be co-creating their own event experience."[33]

Millennials are considered the Social Generation or the founders of the social media movement; they are constantly connected with their social circle via online and mobile devices. They demand a two-way personalized conversation while using social media and their social networks and their circle of friends is powerful. They greatly appreciate celebrity endorsement and event sponsorship of their favourite music artists.

The characteristics of new consumers mean that social media are effective tools for meeting their needs. Mobile Marketing is a form of relationship marketing, where marketing activities are forwarded to mobile consumers. Mobile Marketers have as their main objective to promote targeted and interactive actions towards their consumers in real time and on a segmented basis.

The ubiquity of mobile phone cameras and the rise of photo-sharing websites have changed how companies and consumers use the web: the so-called visual web. More than nine out of every ten users watch digital videos at least once a month and the US Millennials' video consumption habits are more pronounced than other age groups.

Events companies should pay attention to new ways consumers find the information they need and be present in each one that they (companies) deem relevant to the event.

To fulfill its goals, the event needs to create a social strategy that feeds into and is a relevant part of the event planning. You will add value to attendees, and using social media will be a great extension of your event. Experts suggest that the initial steps are to define objectives and to keep them simple. Then, to determine the interests, preferences and capabilities of your audience and to survey which social media platforms they use and how, and which ones they are interested in (content must be customized for each one).

Crowdsourcing can be a great opportunity to spread out news and to get great insights for your event: create an online venue where content about your event will be shared to selected participants. It can be at LinkedIn, Facebook, Twitter, Instagram or any other social media platforms. This will also encourage networking with them and your event and among them. The best option is to do it before, during and after the event. For example, create an event hashtag where attendees can share their experiences. Please have in mind that to empower consumers, social media must give valuable information to attendees; listen to them and provide answers, too.

Practical guide to the chapter

Here is the roadmap of the essential steps described in the chapter, for practical application in your daily activities:

Item	Description
Research and deeply understand the behavior of your public	Through web research on your database, using polls and surveys, and using social media monitoring, you will be able to figure out the average behaviour profile of your audience and the specifics of each different group, as well.
Consider that each group of people demands specific approaches.	Attendees, sponsors, speakers, suppliers, planners: everyone in those groups requires different approaches and actions.
Pay attention to the Millennials	This audience has its own characteristics that must be observed and taken care of. Always bear in mind that they demand real interactive experiences and that they like to be part of the game. The most important online behaviour of the Millennials is about sharing. They also demand a unique online and offline user-experience.
Pay attention to social media	The way people interact with one another and towards your business on social media must be thoroughly understood, as those channels are gaining more importance over time. You have to know as much as you can in terms of tools and strategies in order to raise your bar.
ROI and ROE are paramount	Get to learn or update your knowledge about ROI and start studying ROE as fast as you can. Those metrics are essential to determine your results throughout time.
Engagement & feedback & Visual Web	By listening more carefully to consumers, and interacting with them, more active participation is bound to bring in valuable information to the event. If your target is focused on the Millennial market, visually-driven platform are the ideal ways to connect with them.

5

For further reading, questions for reflection and additional materials please go to the book's page at the publisher's website:

www.goodfellowpublishers.com/technologyandevents

Notes

1 http://meetingsnet.com/site-files/meetingsnet.com/files/uploads/2014/10/Meeting sNetsMillennialSecrets_2014a.pdf. [24/11/15]

2 Edwards, L. 5 Steps to a More Connected Meeting http://meetingsnet.com/social-media/5-steps-more-connected-meeting. [13/11/15]

3 Nelissen, Niko. The event app blue book. 2015 edition. etouches|TapCrowd

4 Brandão, V. Comunicação e Marketing na era digital: a internet como mídia e canal de vendas. Minas Gerais, PUC. Available at http://portcom.intercom.org.br/pdfs63367481050614301224660314786789274330 pdf.

5   Terra, Carolina Frazon. **Usuário-Mídia**: o quinto poder. Um estudo sobre as influências do internauta na comunicação organizacional. São Paulo, Abracorp 2009.

6   Nielsen Pop-Facts, 2013

7   www.nielsen.com/content/dam/corporate/us/en/reports-downloads/2014%20 Reports/nielsen-millennial-report-feb-2014.pdf. [13/11/15]

8   http://meetingsnet.com/site- files/meetingsnet.com/files/uploads/2014/10/Meeting sNetsMillennialSecrets_2014a.pdf. [19/05/15]

9   Natal, G. Comunicação e Construção de Perfis de Consumo e Identidades na Internet: a Marca Mary Jane. Dissertação de mestrado (Comunicação e Linguagens). Curitiba, Programa de Pós-graduação em Comunicação e Linguagens da Universidade Tuiuti do Paraná, 2009.

10 Kotler, Philip; Kartajaya, Hermawan and Setiawan, Iwan. *Marketing 3.0: As forças que estão redefinindo o novo marketing centrado no ser humano.* Elsevier, Rio de Janeiro, 2010.

11 Montardo, Sandra; Araujo, Willian. *Performance e práticas de consumo online: ciberativismo em site de redes sociais.* Revista FAMECOS, V. 20 n.2, pages 472-494, Rio Grande do Sul, May/August, 2013.

12 Smith, Bethany. 4 Ways Big Data is Driving the Events Industry. Feb, 2015, blog. socialtables.com

13 Mobile Apps for Events: Now it's Personal. Available at http://ww2.frost.com/ files/4214/2537/6832/Mobile_Apps_for_Events-Now_Its_Personal.pdf

14 https://blogs.microsoft.com/firehose/2015/03/02/balloon-displays-real-time-social-action-at-mobile-world-congress. [20 Jan 2016]

15 Kimbrel, Anne. 10 Creative Social Media Walls http://www.postano.com/blog/10-creative-social-wall. [20 Jan 2016]

16 Terra, Carolina Frazon. *Usuário-Mídia: o quinto poder. Um estudo sobre as influências do internauta na comunicação organizacional.* São Paulo, Abracorp 2009. p.5

17 http://www.bizbash.com/next-slide-please-unleashing-the-power-of-the-presentation/houston/story/30365?utm_source=Twitter&utm_ medium=BizBashLive&utm_content=Lintelus1&utm_ campaign=ContentMarketing#.VUZKZflVikq. [20 Dec 2015]

18 pt.slideshare.net/confgeneva/meetings-netsmillennialsecrets-2014a. [27 Dec 2015]

19 http://www.mundodomarketing.com.br/ultimas-noticias/34127/rock-in-rio-desenvolve-aplicativo-para-celular-em-parceria-com-a-oi.html and http://www. mundodomarketing.com.br/ultimas-noticias/34170/sky-no-rock-in-rio.html. [07/08/15]

20 Dimantas, Hernani. Comunidades virtuais: heterodoxia informacional. In: Perez, Clotilde; Barbosa, Ivan Santo (eds.), *Hiperpublicidade: atividades e tendências.* V.2, São Paulo: Thompson Learning, 2008. p 389

21 http://www.mundodomarketing.com.br/ultimas-noticias/34127/rock-in-rio-desenvolve-aplicativo-para-celular-em-parceria-com-a-oi.html 07/08/15 11:14 | http://www.mundodomarketing.com.br/ultimas-noticias/34170/sky-no-rock-in-rio.html. [07/08/15]

22 http://www.nielsen.com/us/en/insights/news/2015/millennials-at-the-mall-what-factors-drive-young-consumers-retail-decisions.html. [13/11/15]

23 Dimantas, Hernani. Comunidades virtuais: heterodoxia informacional. In: Perez, Clotilde; Barbosa, Ivan Santo (eds.), *Hiperpublicidade: atividades e tendências*. V.2, São Paulo: Thompson Learning, 2008. p 389

24 http://www.nielsen.com/us/en/insights/news/2015/millennials-at-the-mall-what-factors-drive-young-consumers-retail-decisions.html. [13/11/15]

25 http://www.elearners.com/online-degrees/psychology/psychology-of-twitter. [Oct 10, 2015]

26 https://www.quicksprout.com/2014/03/05/what-type-of-content-gets-shared-the-most-on-twitter. [25/11/15]

27 http://www.adnews.com.br/internet/rock-in-rio-gera-mais-de-1-7-milhao-de-tweets-no-primeiro-final-de-semana. [21/09/15]

28 QuickMobile_Summer_Surveys_2014

29 Nelissen, Niko. The event app blue book. 2015 edition. etouches|TapCrowd.

30 Kurt. From ROI to ROE. Return On Engagement Is The New Thing, 2013. http://www.redhotmarketingblender.com/2013/04/from-roi-to-roe-return-on-engagement-is-the-new-thing/

30 http://blog.socialtables.com/2015/03/24/how-to-use-content-to-maximize-roi-for-attendees-at-your-event. [09/05/15]

31 Nelissen, Niko. *The event app blue book. 2015 edition.* etouches|TapCrowd.

32 Holub, Juraj. Research "30 experts predict the event trends that will shape your 2015" Eventbrite. 2015.

6 Promotion and Dissemination

*"Content isn't limited to describing the value of some other product.
It can deliver value intrinsically."*

Carlos Abler

Introduction

Excellent promotion and dissemination of an event is essential to its success as a business. In the increasingly interconnected and fast world that technology provides us, to know all the possibilities and know how to apply them from planning to execution is more than an option: it is a crucial condition for greater profitability in all kinds of events.

Learning objectives

- Knowing the newest techniques of promotion and dissemination of any type of events, using currently available technology.

- Understanding how to insert those technologies into the planning of the event, how to apply them in the course of it, and how to get from this not only an effective communication, but also capturing intelligence in the form of data that allows the continuous improvement of the promotion and dissemination processes of your events.

The theme of this book is the efficient and effective use of the Internet by event organizers as a means of communication, integration and engagement with all the event's stakeholders. Therefore, it is essential to talk about marketing and digital media. For Gabriel[1], the expression "digital marketing" becomes meaningless even if all platforms and technologies used are digital, since

> *"To be digital" is neither a speciality nor the purpose of marketing. When we refer to mobile marketing, search marketing, social media marketing or relationship marketing, we refer to all the strategic actions of those modalities focused on specific mobile, search, social media, and relationships. Thus, digital marketing does not exist: there is marketing, and strategic planning will determine the platforms or technologies to be used – digital or not. (...) It is very important to note that digital (with its technologies and platforms) does not fix bad marketing, and it may even make it worse. Digital leverages the reach of marketing, both for good and for bad, and adds value to well done marketing, enriching it. (...)*

> *We are coming to a time in which interactivity and experience are the key aspects to the success of marketing strategies. Digital is the platform that gives full vent to interactivity, but not necessarily good experience. Managing to provide consumers/users with good experience involves marketing strategies that go far beyond technology itself and depend on a thorough understanding of the target audience. Furthermore, technology does not stop, and we have new technological possibilities that affect the marketing environment and simultaneously expand the arsenal of strategic tools all the time. Thus, understanding this complex changing scenario and the technologies available at every moment is a valuable competitive advantage for companies.*

Therefore, in the same way that we use the term 'virtual customer' to define the actions of individuals as they navigate the virtual environment, the terms 'marketing in the digital world' or 'digital marketing' will be used to facilitate communication with readers on the subject, and refer to marketing actions within the virtual environment.

The virtual world can host the full range of marketing features, concepts and strategies, but it is dominated by consumers and the almost unrestricted measurability and synchronicity (targetting behaviour) that the virtual environment provides. The lack of control that meeting planners, suppliers and sponsors have over the comments that people make about events is also a key factor. This arises from the inherent characteristics of the Internet, as explained in Chapter 2 and of the new consumer, in Chapter 5.

The starting point to get a better understanding of the marketing context in the digital world is to acknowledge that it is a huge and dispersed market, completely different from the restrictions of the offline world. Therefore, to have a winning corporate strategy, one must understand the rules of the digital world to achieve assertiveness and appropriate responses in business decisions.

What real and virtual consumers have in common is the fact that both have needs, desires, and values, and they seek to be with their peers, people who have similar tastes. Both require engagement and high quality engaging experiences. What differentiates them is the strength of the individuality of virtual consumers, as well as the ease of finding and relating to the communities with which they identify themselves. Meeting planners, suppliers and sponsors should understand that dynamic to perform their activities in and for the event.

According to Torres[2], the behaviour model of consumers on the Internet shows that they perform four basic activities: relationship, information, communication and fun. The search for information and the need to relate highlight the importance of content marketing and strategies to value relationships, detailed later in this chapter. His approach presents seven marketing strategies focused on digital consumer behaviour, with tactical actions (activities to perform) and operational actions (technologies to use in order to implement them). They are presented in Table 6.1. The digital strategies may originate from various digital technologies and platforms.

Gabriel[3] also highlights other platforms and virtual technologies, such as hot sites, profiles, mixed reality (augmented reality, virtual reality – Second Life, etc), mobile technologies (RFID, mobile tagging, Bluetooth, etc.), games and digital entertainment, and emerging technologies (voice interface, web TV, podcasting and immersive video.)

As virtual consumers enter into various environments, and as these are dynamically integrated, the planning of each of those actions must be in an integrated manner. To exemplify such integration and interrelationship, Torres[4] uses the figure of a spider web (Figure 6.1), in which each strategy forms a thread, but it is the whole that allows us to obtain consistent results-controlled monitoring. That is, it is possible to obtain synergy and efficiency with the interaction and coordination between the tactical and operational actions, constantly controlled and validated by continuous monitoring. This increases the amplitude of each action and its impact on the others. The analogy with the spider and web marketing is also in its construction: first build up the main threads to interconnect them, then move out from the centre in a spiral.

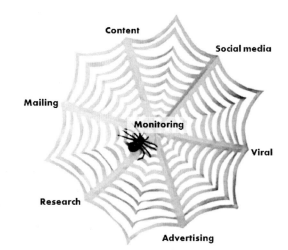

Figure 6.1: Broad view of marketing on Internet

Source: Torres, Claudio. A bíblia do marketing digital. São Paulo: Novatec, 2009 p 71. Layout adapted by authors. Cobweb at http://babbledabbledo.com/

This chapter will detail just some of the digital marketing strategies described in Table 6.1.

Marketing strategy	Digital Marketing Strategy	Tactical and Operational actions	Technologies and platforms used
Corporate communication Public relations	Content marketing	Content generation Search marketing	Blogs SEO/SEM
Relationship marketing	Marketing on social media	Actions on social networks Actions with bloggers	Twitter, Facebook, YouTube, Linkedin, etc.
Direct Marketing	E-mail marketing	Newsletter Promotion Launching	E-mail SMS
Advertising and marketing Guerrilla marketing	Viral marketing	Video Posting Animations and music Widget posting	Social networks YouTube Viral widgets
Advertising and marketing Branding	Online advertising	Banners Podcast and videocast Widgets Online Games	Sites and blogs Social networks Google AdWorks
Market research / Branding Monitoring	Online search	Searches and clipping Brand monitoring Media monitoring	Google Social nedia Clipping

Table 6.1: Marketing and Internet

Source: Torres, Claudio. A bíblia do marketing digital. São Paulo: Novatec, 2009 p 69 to 71. Layout adapted by authors.

Effectiveness in dissemination and attracting sponsors

To get data to define and structure the dissemination is the strategy recommended by experts. At events, it is possible to obtain this data with information gathered from participants while the event is taking place, as well as the information obtained and stored from previous editions, in order to raise the ROI.

New technology has brought major changes that are shaping the events market behaviour. Key amongst these is the growing importance to events of project definition based on an intelligence strategy obtained by cross-comparing accurate information on the needs and interests of participants and sponsors.

From the goals, it is possible to identify where and how to obtain information. The increasing use of social media by events for promotion and dissemination facilitates the collection and analysis of data, as well as the metrics and the behaviour of participants for each action, since the social media offer their native tools for measurement of results. Among other advantages, it also leverages investments in communication. An intelligent and effective strategy also relates to the form of dissemination and the approach to participants and sponsors:

> More than that, those social networks allow you to expand your audience from sponsored postings that can be tailored according to specific audience profiles. Obviously, it is essential that you already have in mind what your target should be. Therefore, observe the audience that you have built organically, review their profiles and cross compare this information with the target lists for the sponsored posting of the social network of your choice. Thus, your investment is likely to become more effective. (...)

> Information about the participants may be useful in attracting sponsorship, and that is precisely an excellent reason to get them. Consider being able to sell your event to one of your possible sponsors as follows: "thirty-five percent of the participants of the event are in leadership positions in the advertising and marketing segments of the business, being interested in acquiring software that can automate processes of their companies. By sponsoring my event, you will have the opportunity to get in touch with each one of them.

> Identifying the specific needs of each of your sponsors and using the data to meet those needs can make your offer irresistible. Therefore, it is essential not only to capture useful data, but also to be able to extract different insights from different perspectives and customer profiles. Only that way

you can reach your target accurately. For many of your sponsors, maybe more important than knowing who the participants of your event are, is being aware of what they want. If the desire of your sponsor aligns with the desire of your participant, you will have the best sales argument in your hand.[5]

Figure 6.3 identifies the metrics most commonly used by CMOs (Chief Marketing Officers) to measure social marketing merits. Noteworthy are site traffic, conversion, and number of members.

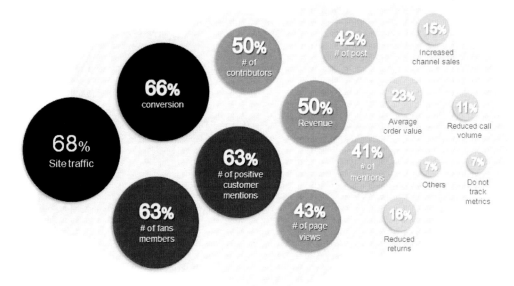

Figure 6.2: Metrics used by CMOs to measure social media marketing activities

Source: http://www.business2community.com/social-media/interesting-infographics-measure-roi-social-media-0885502#YoQxKculHZSQ8a3c.97 27 Dec 2015

6

Content marketing and research

What makes this important is that the digital consumer seeks information above all. Content on websites, blogs and search engines are noteworthy, to the detriment of ads, and in social media content plays an important role in the capture, retention and engagement of the public.

> *Your best content engine: your clients!*
>
> *Roane Neuwuirth*

Therefore, what stands out as key is posting relevant content to draw the attention of consumers to the website and blog of the event, as well as to your social media channels. This turns the search engines into key elements of content marketing, which requires greater attention to the structure of the site and the blog. It demands careful choice of keywords to increase your visibility and positioning, and facilitate scanning the site and blog by search engines.

In terms of content marketing there are several factors that should be taken into consideration by your staff or by the suppliers who will be handling it for you. For Torres they are the following:

- **Improvement of the relationship with clients** – enables companies to engage with clients throughout the buying cycle. This reduces the likelihood of impacts by competitors or clients abandoning the purchase at a point in the decision process.

- **Increased engagement with the brand** – Research claims that consumers do not want to relate to brands that only seek to talk about their products and influence customers to buy them. That is the reason why content marketing seeks to build a relationship of trust that goes far beyond sales: it participates in many moments in the life of consumers, helping them to solve their problems of everyday life (...)

- **To increase brand visibility** – If you are not well positioned in online environments where your audience circulates (Google result pages, Facebook, advertising space on websites and blogs, and so on) someone else will be positioned in your place. (...)

- **Create brand evangelists** – Building a relationship of trust makes even those who are not part of the target audience of a company to become a disseminator of the brand. A single person can recommend your products or services to dozens of buyers, even though he or she never actually becomes a customer. (...)

- **Inform and nurture prospects of the brand with relevant content** – Nurturing the public with high-quality content is not possible without a well-structured strategy. Multiple channels can participate in this nutrition: SEO, social networking, email marketing, landing pages and many others.

- **Increase sales (including upselling and cross-selling)** – People remember companies that were with them when needed (...) Everything that can motivate closing a sale can be considered content marketing: texts about the product or service, videos, images, infographics, e-books, reviews, customer testimonials, success cases, technical information, delivery information, exchange and return policy, etc.

■ Working on after-sales – Completion of a sale is just the beginning. Studies show that almost 70% of revenue of a business comes from repeat customers. This should not be news: those who already know your business are more likely to buy expensive items, more frequently, or recommend you to a friend. What relationship do you have with those people? By what strategies? Which channels? (...)[6]

Thus, it is possible to define content marketing applied to events as the marketing actions that are used to create and share relevant, valuable and consistent content, as a strategy to attract, educate, involve and engage participants. It also has the objective of generating positive brand awareness of the event and/or their sponsors with the active or prospective participants, creating loyalty, improving the relationship between them, and increasing sales. Content marketing applies through SEM in tactical actions and SEO in operational actions.

Although 'social media content' was the top marketing tactic usage (Graph 6.1), the biggest increase was 'illustrations/photos' (from 69% in 2015 to 76% in 2016). The most effective tactics (Graph 6.2) has been in person-event, 75% in 2016 and 69% in the previous year. But the biggest jump was infographics (50% last year vs 58% in 2016).

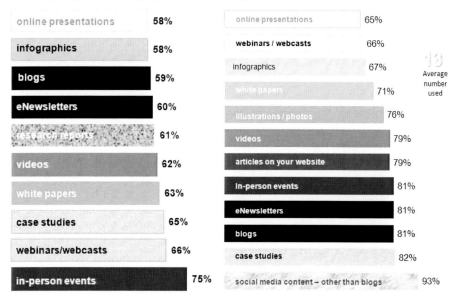

Graph 6.1: (Left) Effectiveness rating for B2B tactics

Graph 6.2: (Right) Content marketing for B2B tactics usage

Source: 2016 B2B content marketing benchmarks trends   North America by Content marketing Institute and MarketingProfs

A well-crafted content strategy can bring many benefits to the brands of the event and its sponsors:

- **Brand awareness**: People know your brand better (after all you have your own audience). Currently, 93% of purchases start with online research in search engines. Classic advertising campaigns such as Google Adwords, Facebook Ads, Twitter Ads and others are effective in generating audience, but always accompanied by high costs. With content marketing, organically you can reach more people at a reduced cost.

- **Competitive differential**: If your brand produces valuable content for your audience, you generate consumer preference. Who would you buy a marketing automation solution from – the company that has educated you about how it works and how to use a certain technology to your advantage or from a company just trying to sell the service to you?

- **Dramatic cost reduction**: By producing content, you are producing a piece that will be accessible to customers and potential clients for life. The investment in production of that piece happens once only, which makes the gains disproportionate when compared to traditional advertising.

- **Creating a scalable and measurable channel that generates leads and sales**: A successful content strategy aims to create a digital asset for your company that constantly brings new business. Content is essential for generation of lead, nutrition and doing business.[7]

For B2C content marketers, sales were the top organizational goal for 83% (Graph 6.3) and for 85% on metrics (Graph 6.5). Graph 6.4 shows that 85% of companies interviewed declare that "lead generation" is the most important goal on B2B marketing content. Brand awareness was a top goal over the previous five years. Graph 6.6 points "sales lead quality" as the most important metrics (lead quality, sales and higher conversion rates). 88% of B2B respondents said they used content marketing, against 76% of B2C respondents.

A survey by localSEOedinburgh revealed some of the most important aspects of that marketing strategy in the digital world in the UK. 73% of respondents prefer online branded content to printed. Most of them use social media (93%) and increased use of video in content creation (77% of them). Brand awareness is the goal for 84% of British marketers.

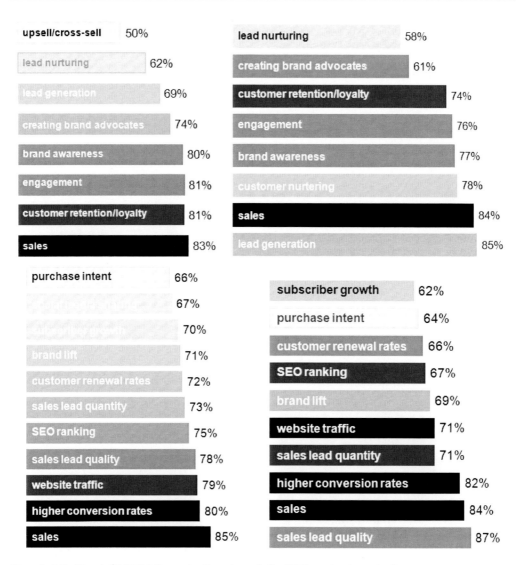

Graph 6.3: (Top left) 2016 Organizational goals for B2C content marketing

Graph 6.4: (Top right) 2016 Organizational goals for B2B content marketing

Graph 6.5: (Bottom left) Metrics that B2C content marketers use

Graph 6.6: (Bottom right) Metrics for B2B

Source: 2016 B2B content marketing benchmarks trends in North America by Content marketing Institute and MarketingProfs

As with preparing the event project, the first step in structuring a content marketing campaign is to have clarity in the definition of the target audience profile: characteristics, events, shopping habits, socio-demographic data, decision process to choose and sign up for events, etc. For Jones[8], it also extends in order to understand:

- Who exactly is using or viewing your content

- How people perceive your content and your brand

- What people expected from your content, and whether it met (or exceeded) their expectations

- What people intended to do when visiting or using your content

- Decisions people made as a result of engaging with your content

- Offline behaviors people took as a result of your content

According to her, to get a complete picture of content effectiveness for branding and marketing, you will need to know what the participants think as result of your content:

An effective survey should not try to measure future behaviour. Instead, it should measure characteristics, perceptions, preferences, and possible reports of current and past behavior. Specifically for content marketing, surveys can measure:

- Roles, demographics, and preferences of your users or audience (audience analysis)

- Perceptions, expectations, and impressions of your content and your brand

- Impact of your content on decision-making

- Impact of your content on offline behavior when no other method to understand offline behavior is available

The knowledge of participants and prospects guides and helps the next step, the production of content, which defines:

- What formats should be used (videos, blog posts, posts on social media, presentations, infographics, spreadsheets, testimonials, eBooks, whitepaper, webinars, etc.)

- How the production and periodic updating of content should be carried out (internally or by specialized supplier)

- What distribution channels should be used for postings (email marketing, own or external blogs, forums, social networks, etc.)

- What metrics to use in order to measure results?

Get to know the market behaviour in your country better. That knowledge helps in Step 3: developing and coordinating the activities calendar, which organizes and guides the production and dissemination of content in a given period, also optimizing the effectiveness of the activities of the suppliers involved. Setting the calendar should be based on previously agreed metrics (e.g., number of leads, visitors, and so on.) The fourth step is the dissemination and promotion of content through defined channels and formats, measuring results as you obtain them. The next step is a possible course correction during the period covered by the calendar.

Graphs 6.7 to 6.9 show more about the content marketing in 2016. The respondents said the social media content is the top marketing tactic usage for B2B (93%) and B2C (90%), whereas the social media platform usage is different: for B2B content marketer pointed to Linkedin and Facebook for B2C (94% for both).

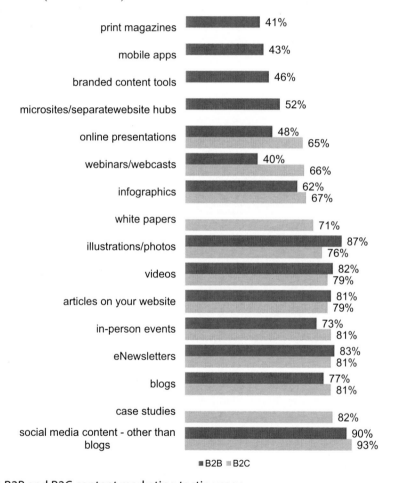

Graph 6.7: B2B and B2C content marketing tactic usage

Source: 2016 B2B and B2C Content Marketing Trends – North America Content Marketing Institute/ MarketingProfs

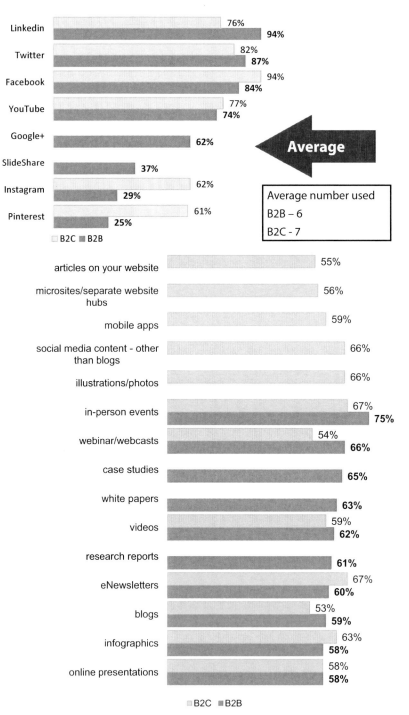

Graph 6.8: (Top) B2B and B2C content marketing, social media platform usage
Graph 6.9: (Bottom) B2B and B2C content creation & distribution

Source: 2016 B2B and B2C Content Marketing Trends – North America Content Marketing Institute/
MarketingProfs

The effectiveness rating of tactics for B2B in 2016 was In-person Events (75%), the same result for the last six years (69% in 2015). However, the biggest increase was infographics (50% last year vs. 58% in 2016). For B2C, as in the previous year, eNewsletters, in-person events and illustration/photos were the most effective tactics. The greatest increase, +21%, was also for infographics (42% last year).

Marketing in social media

For Kawasaki[9] "the biggest daily challenge of social media is finding enough content to share." He defines that "Facebook is for people. Twitter is for perspective. Google+ is for passion. LinkedIn is for pimping. "

As already discussed elsewhere in this book, especially in Chapter 3, social media monitoring is a special tool with regard to promotions. It has exceptional value that can (and should) be used at all stages of an event. Some points to highlight about monitoring in respect of its value for suppliers and in the dissemination and promotion of the event:

- It allows you to observe the big picture of your industry, from your competitors to the perception of the public about the type and typology of your event.

- It allows you to observe public reaction to your communications about your event in real time.

- You can extract information and interesting insights into the use of products and services from their suppliers, and you can optimize the application of those products and services, according to the perception of the public itself that makes use of them.

- It measures in detail the results of your investments in media, both online and offline, allowing adjustments to your media plan.

- It captures changes in your public's behavior. It can help you even in the running of the event, adapting your actions, reinforcing what works and fixing what is not giving good results. Over the past two years, digital media usage has grown overall by 49%, with mobile apps having grown 90% and contributing to 77% of the total Increase in time spent. Mobile browsing is also seeing very strong growth at 53% and even desktop use is still rising (Graph 6.10).

Although desktop usage is not declining in total engagement, it is losing share to mobile – which now accounts for 62% of digital media time spent. In addition, mobile apps on their own now drive the majority of digital media time spent, at 54%.

6

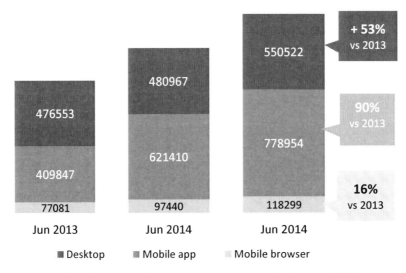

Graph 6.10: Growth in digital media time spent – per total minutes (MM)

Source: 2015 US Mobile app report. Available at http://www.comscore.com/Insights/Presentations-and-Whitepapers/2015/The-2015-US-Mobile-App-Report

Every component is contributing to the massive growth in digital time spent over the past two years. However, the smartphone app has been the biggest driver. It has accounted for two-thirds of all growth in digital media engagement during that timeframe.

It is clear that apps are increasing their importance over the time, which is something to take into account when planning the event through all the steps, to get the best results (Graph 6.11):

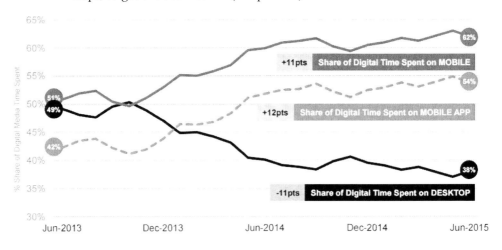

Graph 6.11: Share of digital media time spent by platform

Source: 2015 US Mobile app report. Available at http://www.comscore.com/Insights/Presentations-and-Whitepapers/2015/The-2015-US-Mobile-App-Report 21 Dec 2015

Since Millennials are heavier app users, it makes sense that they also would be more inclined to go out and discover new apps from a variety of methods. This age group is a great target for app advertising, and are likely a big driver of the growth in app install ads.

Push notifications can often be the lifeblood of an app – a crucial method to keep its users actively engaged and not abandon it over time. Nevertheless, it can also backfire, appear intrusive and ultimately annoy users. Smartphone users are split, as to whether they get utility from this feature.[10] (Graph 6.12)

Graph 6.12: How often do you agree to an app's request to allow push notifications?

Source: 2015 US Mobile app report. Available at http://www.comscore.com/Insights/Presentations-and-Whitepapers/2015/The-2015-US-Mobile-App-Report

Leite[11] points to the transformation of mobile devices, which went from simple tools to a style and way of life. He highlights some ways that, according to IBM, reinforce engagement by mobile:

- **Social networks** – More than 80% of Twitter users access the site using a mobile device, and 91% of young people aged 18-29 years old who have a smartphone connect to social networks. Among people over 50, the rate is not negligible: 55%. Therefore, it became unreasonable to think that the presence of media without considering mobile access or devise a mobile strategy and disregard the social networks.

  For social content to be appropriate and shareable on smartphones and tablets, it must respect the brevity that those sites require. Images and graphs must also work on smaller screens. Again, the channel must be integrated into data capture tools and user behavior analysis. It should also integrate with other contact points. Social networks can have, for example, SMS and calls options to download the app.

  It is important to allow login through social networks in other social channels, reducing the time spent by users with registration.

6

■ **Location** – The actions of this kind base on the physical location of the users and their preferences. The data generated based on geographic location of the users throughout the day and month can provide valuable insights, too. Offers and sending content reach a new level with this tactic, as they reach the recipients when they position themselves strategically. Some companies are already using beacons and similar tools to trigger messages at the exact moment a prospect or a client goes through a door or hallway. That movement represents a true convergence of the virtual and real worlds.

A challenge is to overcome people's fears about privacy invasion. Hence, it is important that brands explain exactly the benefits that customers will have if they authorize receiving targeted messages based on their geographic location. In addition, to avoid annoying users, it is necessary to consider setting limits to the amount of content sent to an individual during a specific period.

Mailing

For Gustavo[12], 50-80% of the purchase process happens before the company has the chance to talk to the buyer. Together with the growth in the use of social networks, mobiles and especially the acceptance of e-mails, there are many advantages in integrating email marketing with social networks. He suggests some steps to follow to optimize your marketing:

1 Add an opt-in form on your Facebook page

2 Use the News Feed on Facebook and Twitter – newsletters articles are great posts, as well as their regular promotions.

3 Promote your social campaigns in your emails.

4 Re-post popular social content in e-mails – on Pinterest, add the most popular pins to your wall and that of your followers. On Twitter, watch out for tweets that generate retweets and favorites. Follow comments on Twitter hashtags or Twitter-party campaigns.

5 Add your social networks icons where people can see – test to find out where the best position is.

6 Promote your social networks in your emails – add the icons of your social networks on blogs and communities.

7 Promote your content in your emails and posts – identify the best content format for your business (videos, content blogs, postcasts, whitepapers, webinars, guides "how to" and testimonials/case studies) and publish them.

8 Create fun/funny emails that people will want to share.

9 Invite unsubscribers to follow you on social media – add a link to social networks in the registration confirmation page or on the subscription management page.

Advertising

In the US, for the second year, the most used paid advertising methods to promote/distribute content for B2B is SEM - search engine marketing – (66%). Graph 6.13 also shows that over 2015, the use of all methods has increased, but promoted posts increased the most (42% last year vs. 52% this year). For B2C, the promoted post has the greatest effectiveness rating increase (from 59% last year vs. 76% this year). It was followed by social ads (14% increase from 2015) and SEM (13% increase).

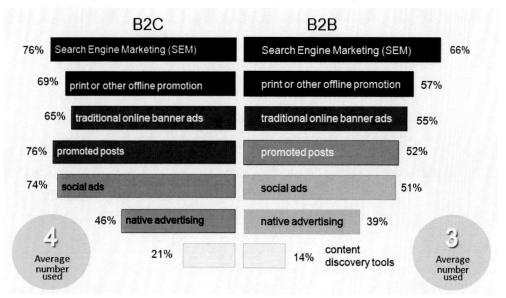

Graph 6.13: B2C and B2B paid advertising usage

Source: 2016 B2B and B2C Content Marketing Trends – North America Content Marketing Institute/ MarketingProfs

Viral

The use of viral marketing, although somewhat complex and with no guarantees of results, can be a strong element of increasing the impact and reach of your messages. That happens because of the fact that when people find your content so good that they decide to share it with their network of contacts, those people is not only increasing the visibility of that content, thet are also giving their tacit endorsement to that material.

It is very difficult to predict what kind of content can be viral, but you can get clues about that by studying your previously published content and checking which had higher share rates. With this, you can gain insight into what issues, approach, and types of message (text, photos, videos, and mix between them) achieved better results earlier. It is reasonable to assume that what worked well before will keep working well.

Once this has been established or inferred, content types tend to be shared most, set up a personal "handbook" with tips of what to use in order to try to generate content most likely to become viral.

Testing is a golden rule. Test each hypothesis that has been built from the observation of previous results. If you found out that videos work well, test posting the same content in video format as well as in text format, then observe share rates of each. As it is the same content, varying only in its presentation, the results obtained will confirm your hypothesis, and you can apply a particular rule in your future content posts.

The essence and reasons for the success of an event app lie in the optimization of the results of the events that it can offer. Box 6.1 describes some steps for choosing events apps. Moreover, it details the results obtained by the implementation of the mobLee platform in two events.

Box 6.1: Enhancing the experience

What an event app can do for you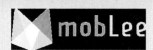

The development of processes results in the continuous evolution of the product itself and is obtained through the understanding of the roles, the alignment of expectations, the demands of each party and the balance between them. Similarly, identification of increasingly more accurate customer profiles in the customization of products and services and changes in evaluation metrics imposed by technology (which can measure a multitude of aspects that were once unthinkable) have transformed the relationships between people as well as with companies.

In addition, the event duration has to be perennial – it has long been extended beyond the time of face-to-face interaction. All this is largely due to the growing importance of the use of mobile phones, driven by the use of apps for those devices, including specific event apps. For that segment, such specific software potentiate the two most important aspects for participants: networking and content. Data gathering is now very simple, and companies gain relevance when their value proposition is in providing intelligence to converting data into useful and practical insights.

Choosing the best app

The market has several options available that offer great results to organizers' needs. Among the actions to develop when choosing the most suitable event app, planning is an essential part for the successful implementation. Therefore, the following topics are essential:

1. Prior to selection, organizers must map the problems and needs of the event, in addition to knowing the potential of the app as a communication channel and which features offered are suited to the needs in the three phases of the event.

2. After the selection, they must choose their internal team and define tasks for each member.

3. To strengthen the partnership between organizers and the supporting team of the business app provider.

4. To align expectations of organizers and sponsors for the construction of a set of actions that can achieve the goals.

Messaging

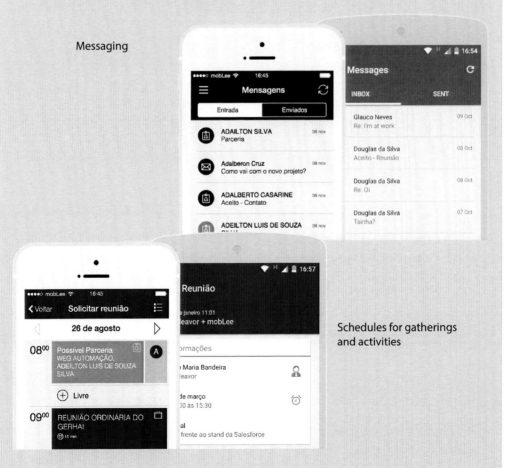

Schedules for gatherings and activities

Maximizing deployment and use

1. After the initial setup and selection of resources (menu, icons, images, languages, and so on), content (programming, speakers, sponsors, etc.) are inserted and social media of the event are synchronized to the app.

2. With the availability of the app for download, all content inserted is dynamic and can be updated and modified quickly.

3. The use of the app is encouraged by consistent campaign to disseminate the benefits and applications.

4. The communication plan is designed with different actions at each stage of the event, promoting notifications to encourage the meshing of participants. Engagement and network through the app depend on the features and resources available. The creation of a community and interaction among users by the app can be made through messages, content uploading, likes and comments on others' posts and questions submitted to speakers.

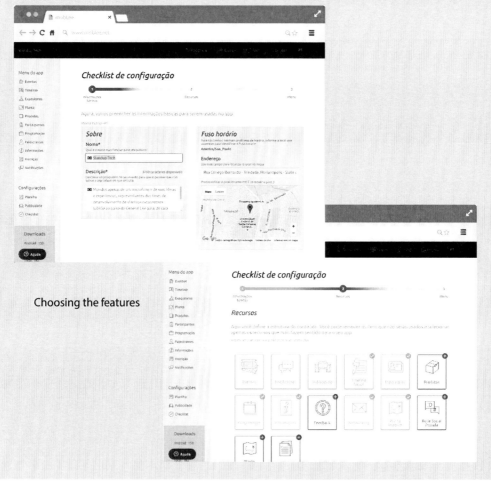

Choosing the features

Other application screens

Levering results

mobLee is one of the most popular mobile platforms for events in Latin America. It offers many integrated features for various types of events. Below are two solutions and some of the results achieved by customers.

Concrete Show, the largest event of civil construction segment of South America (and the 2nd largest in the world) has more than 300 exhibitors and about 30,000 participants (mostly engineers and partners of the concrete production chain). From the 2014 edition on, the event has included the sale of the event app as an advertising space, generating revenue from marketing solutions. The interactive event plan has offered systemic view of the physical space and of exhibitors, enabling to trace roots to all booths automatically. Moreover, it has marked the ones already visited and those yet to visit. The reduction by 32% in the number of printed materials, the increase in revenues and the improvement of the experience of the participants were some of the results obtained.

The event denominated Millennium Hepatology is a continuing medical education event focused on issues related to liver disease and is in has in the interaction among 1,000 participants a matter of great importance. Among the benefits generated by the use of the event app are the centralization of information and resources on a single platform, and the ease and speed of any changes.

Technology can be a partner and the main engine of amazing transformations in your event! Seek to learn more and more about the possibilities!

6

Chapter summary

The currently available and the upcoming technologies allow much more effectiveness in the promotion and dissemination of all types of events.

You should study the correct use of those technologies continuously, in order to be certain of applying the most effective tools and processes available at every moment.

The use of modern technologies in the promotion and dissemination of events has an impact not only on the profitability of a given event, but also on the subsequent events of the same organizer.

As well as the obvious immediate benefits, applied technology also allows capturing data and information on the participants of events, and this intelligence can be used in other areas of the organization of events.

Practical guide to the chapter

Here is the roadmap of the essential steps described in the chapter, for practical application in your daily activities:

Steps	Description
Identify the objectives to be achieved	The objectives will guide the collection of data and metrics to inform the decision at the next step.
Set the digital marketing strategy	Choose the tools: content marketing, social media marketing; e-mail marketing; viral marketing, online advertising and monitoring
	Specify in detail the actions for each strategic tool
	Implement, execute and monitor every action performed

For further reading, questions for reflection and additional materials please go to the book's page at the publisher's website:

www.goodfellowpublishers.com/technologyandevents

Notes

1   Gabriel, Martha. (2010) *Marketing na era digital*. São Paulo: Novatec. pp 105-109.

2   Torres, Claudio. (2009). *A bíblia do marketing digital*. São Paulo: Novatec, pp 66-70.

3   Gabriel, Martha. (2010). *Marketing na era digital*. São Paulo: Novatec. p 107

4   Torres, Claudio. (2009). *A bíblia do marketing digital*. São Paulo: Novatec p 71

5   Convertendo informações sobre os participantes do seu evento em ROI, http://blog.moblee.com.br/2015/04/convertendo-informacoes-sobre-os-participantes-do-seu-evento-em-roi. [18 Mar 2016]

6   Torres, Claudio. (2009). A bíblia do marketing digital. São Paulo : Novatec p 71

7   Marketing de conteúdo para resultados. Rockcontent | Resultados Digitais. http://rockcontent.com/marketing-de-conteudo. [16 Dec 2015]

8   http://contentmarketinginstitute.com/2013/12/surveys-help-create-effective-content-marketing. [15 Jan 05 2015]

9   http://pt.slideshare.net/AyeshaAmbreen/10-times-guy-kawasaki-proved-that-he-knows-social-media-better-than-anyone-else/13-Thank_you . [05/01/15]

10 The 2015 US Mobile App report - http://pt.slideshare.net/VictorKongCisneros/the-2015-us-mobile-app-report-by-comscore. [18 Nov 2015]

11 5 ferramentas e táticas para o engajamento mobile, segundo a IBM. https://www.mundodomarketing.com.br/reportagens/digital/35908/5-ferramentas-e-taticas-para-o-engajamento-mobile-segundo-a-ibm.html?utm_source=akna&utm_medium=email&utm_campaign=news+05.04.16. [20 Mar 2016]

12 http://pt.slideshare.net/mediaeducation/como-realmente-integrar-email-marketing-e-redes-sociais-ber-golalves?qid=98c4f8eb-a887-4cf4-bbc6-6712d1ca58dc&v=qf1&b=&from_search=39. [27 Nov 2015]

6

Section IV

Extending the Residual Effect of the Event

The two chapters of this section show that when the event comes to its end, there is much more work to do.

Chapter 7 – Closing and Evaluation:

- The key data from the event and how to translate it into intelligence
- The benefits of Business Intelligence (BI)
- How to keep the attendees in touch with each other and with your company after the event
- How technologies can stretch the organizational and economic life cycle of events
- Measuring ROI and ROE of the event through BI
- How to build up and reinforce relationships throughout and after the event
- Why building lasting relations before the event will improve your business

Chapter 8 – When the Event Ends:

- Considering and nurturing two kinds of relationships: from your company to its attendees, and the public among itself
- Technology is as an efficient tool for improving the next event.

7 Post-event or Another Pre-event?

"Being well today does not mean it will continue being well tomorrow. However, the comfort of the current success blurs the vision of future challenges!"

Walter Longo

Introduction

Perhaps the most significant sign of change that the application of technology in organizing events has brought is the evolution of the post-event phase. As the title of the chapter goes, is this stage post-event or is it the beginning of a new event?

If previously the post-event limited itself to some research, building a relationship via e-mail or phone bank and later sending invitations for future events, nowadays it is almost possible to call a post-event "continuity of the event for its upcoming editions or other related events through continued relationships with its participants."

In this chapter, we are going to deal with all the necessary actions for both the closing of the event as well as the attitudes that allow either the survival of the event (if it is unique), or its continuity through future editions in the case of a series of events.

Learning objectives

■ Understanding that an event, should not end on the date of its official closure.

■ Studying how one can plan and conduct the event in order to extend its life.

■ Determining procedures and tools required to generate continuity to the event after its official end.

■ Providing the participants of an event with the possibility of continued interaction, bringing exponential and long-term gains to all.

The general scenario of technology applied to event organization has been undergoing a strong and continuous development, especially in recent years, and this trend is likely to accelerate exponentially in the near future. With the increasing and deeper use of the Internet, the possible uses of technology are virtually endless, as the public lives and works increasingly immersed in that universe.

Consequently, the events industry turns more and more to technology through companies specializing in supplying products and services that use mobile apps, social media, live streaming and many other new applications. It is necessary to understand that this does not only give us a new way of thinking about business events, but also a path event organizers have to follow and explore, in order to not lose ground to their competitors and even to their public. One must regard technology not as something for the distant future, but as a current and essential condition in this business segment.

The adoption of available and future technologies must be a central focus of all event organizers or those connected to that industry in some way. All recent surveys point to an accelerated adoption of those new technologies, which clearly indicates that it is no longer about using them as a differential, but as a fundamental part of the business.

Among the clearest and already well established benefits of using available technologies are:

- Economies of scale,
- Operational efficiency,
- Engagement with the public,
- Creation of new models of interaction,
- New forms of communication and dissemination and
- New types of event.

However, it is important to point out that new benefits arise every day from clever and creative use of technology in the form of new applications and uses. It is up to each company or professional operating in that area to continuously research the technological tools available and, through their experience and creativity, to develop new uses and applications that suit their needs.

One of the most important gains for the events industry by the use of technology in planning and organizing events is the ability to capture, store, manage, study and extract intelligence from behavioral data from all involved in events.

The thorough understanding and use of the information embedded in the data will produce a gain in terms of the attractiveness, assertiveness and profitability of future events. It creates a continuous cycle of benefits that will influence decisively the competitiveness of future events, whether by a particular organizer, an entity or other groups and associations that use events as a tool for business, marketing, communication and/or relationship with their audiences.

This data is not only obtained at a particular moment in the life cycle of an event, but rather a continuous action, planned and implemented in the pre-event phase, managed in the cross-event, and finished precisely in the post-event, so that the cycle perpetuates itself indefinitely in future events.

Hence, the provocative title of this chapter. The question "post-event or another pre-event?" has only one answer: that the post-event phase of a certain event ideally binds itself to the pre-event phase of another. It represents an ongoing and virtuous cycle where data extracted and intelligence generated in a given period permit better immediate tactical actions and support the strategic decisions of the future steps. (See Box 7.1)

Box 7.1: After the event

Taylor Tomita

As an event comes to its end, a very common mistake made by attendees is that they disregard the event completely, but maintain the relationships built during the event. Yes, the event experience can be quite overwhelming, but it is important to understand that what you do after the event can open enormous opportunities for yourself and your business. It is vital to follow up with the contacts you had gained during the event.

Following up with the other businesses who participated, the individuals with who you had communicated, and the event coordinators can be a surely fine opportunity to inform them that you truly care about the conversations you had. This leads to promising relationships for a business, because the event already ignited the spark; the business just needs to keep the fire going.

Following up

Thanks to technology, the task of following up has become incredibly quick and accessible to individuals throughout the world. Tools like email and social media give businesses hope when it comes to relationship building.

When it comes to following up with contacts after an event, one good rule of thumb to have is to give them three or four days to recuperate before reaching out. This allows the individual to get back home and settle in before being flooded with emails, phone calls, and social media requests. No matter how you are reaching out to a contact, it is of high importance to keep the following three points in mind:

■ **Be quick** – When reaching out to a contact, it is important to make it as concise as possible. Chances are, this individual will also be taking time to reach out to their newfound contacts, and may not have time to read a wordy email.

■ **Be personal** – This rule should always be at the front of your mind when reaching out to event prospects. This allows the individual to know that you actually care about building a relationship with them, and shows them that you are not just another business trying to make a sale.

■ **Be specific** – It is important to include as much information about yourself as possible when outreaching event prospects. If you are lucky, they will remember who you are, but it is always good to be sure. Simply mentioning the conversation that had taken place between the two of you can immediately refresh that individuals mind.

The end can be just a great beginning

The ending of an event is just the start of many fruitful relationships for your business. Following up with and maintaining the relationships prospected will ensure that you have gotten the most out of attending, and ensure that people will know you during the next year's conference.

Tomita is a creative writer, musician and enthusiast of all aspects of marketing and social media.

The measurement and evaluation of the data must be continuous, throughout the duration of the event and beyond. Of course, depending on the event type, the size of its audience or its duration, the amount of data to process and analyze can be huge. There are numerous big data tools available, but their use is still new and challenging for most professionals. Therefore, here is a tip: use your common sense to decide which part of the captured data can allow you to extract that information which is most important to your situation.

Finally, always bear in mind that the collection and use of data to obtain insights, and the tactical and strategic use of information should not be static, unchanging. Always think about possible new ways to capture data, in order to obtain further insights on the behavior of your audiences, and test new ways to segment and analyze your data.

It is often possible to extract different and relevant information from the same database, by simply changing the portion of the evaluated data or the method of analysis. If we consider that the data is a "responses bank", different questions can bring different results. Therefore, test, try, and do not be afraid to innovate, because if environment into which people come is the same at any given time and place, those who offer the public something different – a richer, targeted and profitable experience – will be bound to have the advantage. It is possible precisely by the extraction of behavioral data to gain the intelligence needed to design the actions that will move this audience.

Data measurement is continuously growing. It is a trend getting stronger every day, as shown by Event Track 2015:

Measurement is on the rise

A continuation of a long-term trend shows in the data below: today 79% of brands are measuring their event and experiential programs. This is up from 78% last year and 71% in the 2013 study. (Graph 7.1)

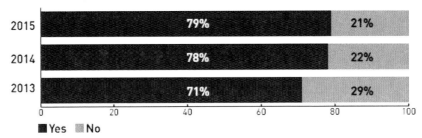

Graph 7.1: Measurement is on the rise

Source: Event Track 2015, the fourth annual edition of Event Marketing Institute and Mosaic EventTrack among Fortune 1000

■   Top three criteria used to measure events and experiences

The top measurement factors and criteria according to the survey of brands are total attendance, Facebook and social media activity, and the number of leads. (Graph 7.2)

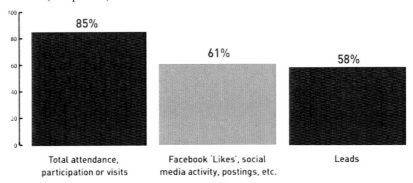

Graph 7. 2: Top three criteria used to measure events and experiences

Source: Event Track 2015, the fourth annual edition of Event Marketing Institute and Mosaic EventTrack among Fortune 1000

■ ROI generated

Events and experiences provide a significant ROI. The survey asked specifically the expectation of ROI from the events. 48% of brands expected a ROI ranging from 3:1 to 5:1 and 29% indicated their return to be over 10:1. 12% say ROI should be 20:1 or higher. *(Graph 7.3)*

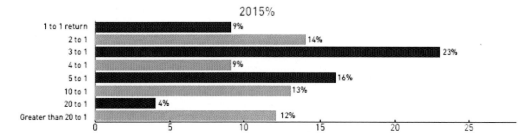

2015%

1 to 1 return	9%
2 to 1	14%
3 to 1	23%
4 to 1	9%
5 to 1	16%
10 to 1	13%
20 to 1	4%
Greater than 20 to 1	12%

Graph 7.3: ROI Generated

Source: Event Track 2015, the fourth annual edition of Event Marketing Institute and Mosaic EventTrack among Fortune 1000

The Event Track 2015 report also shows comparative annual review 2012-2015 among the criteria used to measure the events and experiences (Table 7.1). The top criteria are full attendance, Facebook activities and leads. The consistent annual growth of 11 of the 13 factors presented highlights the equal rise in the importance of measuring to both organizers and customers.

As seen earlier in this chapter, being fully aware through the stages of an event of the possibilities for data capture and management, and determining which are really important, allow organizers, at any time, to find out if data capture is taking place in a satisfactory way. In addition, it is possible to use the data to make intermediate behavioral assessments, which allows you to make tactical corrections in various parts of the event.

It is important to say that in addition to more 'traditional' uses of behavioral information that is collected, analyzed and transformed into tactical actions during the event, it is also possible and desirable to seek innovation. You can try different actions, communications or interactions with your public and immediately assess their responses. More and more technology facilitates obtaining information through specific tests. It is important to keep in mind that in a world where behavioral and market transformations are happening with increased speed, to work solely on the empirical knowledge accumulated through time will most certainly distort the answers, increasingly distancing the results from the proposed actions. Hence, the importance of conducting experiments, even if small and specific, both to test hypotheses and to test different responses to similar actions applied in a different way.

7

Criteria	2012	2013	2014	2015
Total attendance or participation	74%	83%	80%	85%
Facebook 'Likes', social media activity, posting, etc.	45%	37%	57%	61%
Leads	62%	67%	64%	58%
Post-event sales	46%	49%	66%	57%
Public relation, press coverage	56%	54%	59%	47%
Website traffic	41%	50%	46%	47%
Gross sales related to the event	49%	54%	32%	47%
On-site sales	31%	29%	41%	44%
Time spent at experience	31%	25%	34%	44%
Other online activity and postings	29%	26%	30%	44%
Retail shelf lifts	Na	na	9%	18%
Gross profit related to the event	24%	30%	32%	na
Other metrics	11%	5%	9%	5%

Table 7. 1: Criteria used to measure activities at events

Source: Event Track 2015, the fourth annual edition of Event Marketing Institute and Mosaic EventTrack among Fortune 1000

The use of the behavioral data takes place during the events, allowing tactical corrections. However, it is only after the event, with the dedication of more time and resources, and observing the behavioral scenario of the event as a whole, that we can actually extract the deepest strategic knowledge from such data, and apply it in an organized and structured way in future events. That behavioral data apply to everyone involved in the event, including:

- Attendees,
- Sponsors,
- Supporters,
- Strategic partners,
- Suppliers and
- Media.

There are several ways to obtain that data (as noted elsewhere in this book):

- Data collected by apps
- Access information to the event website
- Return and marketing mail return rates
- Online or in-person research results
- Information collected points of access or passage
- CRM Information
- Reactions and opinions on speakers

Based on what has already been described in this chapter, you can direct how to apply this knowledge to the situation in your events, extracting from the data the information, insights and intelligence that will allow continuous improvement of the results of your efforts. Through the use of mobile apps, data capture can occur during all phases of an event, such as at enrollment, registration or arrival, or when checking into sessions and exhibitors' stands, by observing messages and networking among attendees and the videos and photos that they upload, by movement-tracking beacons, polling, surveys, interaction with speakers (interests, profiles, presentations, rates, questions) and post-event feedback. See Table 4.3 for more details.

Apps extend the residual effect of the event

We can see that we may have both a very high volume of data and a great many different sources. The processing of such data for the thorough extraction of their strategic intelligence is a matter for skilled BI (Business Intelligence) experts. The best decisions come from the best information[1]:

With the increased use of technology also comes increased understanding of attendees through analytics. Collecting this passive data is critical because there is often a gap between what people say and what they actually do. Event apps and website analytics offer the ability for event planners to understand what people actually care about, making it easier to answer questions such as:

- Which sessions were the most viewed on the app and website?

- What content is the most popular?

- During which session did attendees become most engaged?

- Did people find the sponsors relevant?

- Did people engage with location-based alerts?

There are two ways to deal with such demand:

1   By forming and maintaining your own team of business and of BI experts. Such a team should include at least one analyst focusing on the extraction and processing of data, and another one directed to the reading and analysis.

2   By hiring a specialized company. This can be brought in as a consultancy right at the beginning to help plan and implement each action of organizing the event in order to facilitate the uptake of the significant data.

Whatever your choice for the BI management, the work needs to be organized along the following lines:

1   Align the data processing with the initial planning of the event, to check your short, medium and long-term goals. The KPIs established and indicated in the initial planning of the event determined many of those goals. Compliance is essential for the proper evaluation of the data obtained.

2   Cluster the data according to the tactical and strategic variables that the initial planning anticipated and consider the different data sources:

■ Commercial focus
  □ Immediate sales
  □ Future sales
  □ Continued sales

■ Focus on relationship
  □ External relationships (attendees)
  □ Internal relationships (sponsors, supporters, suppliers, etc.)

■ Temporal focus of the event
  □ Survival, where the event is a single one
  □ Continuity, in the case of a series of events

3   Other strategic needs

■ **Data extraction and processing**, noting the importance that will be given to each type of information, according to the way it was sorted in the clusters above. It is essential to understand each extracted data group well, in order to focus on the important variables and discard what is unimportant, so that the analysis of the data at a later stage happens without reading deviations. It is important to note that it is possible to allocate some types of data to more than one cluster, to meet different strategic needs. In such cases, processing the variables of each data can also vary according to the different clusters that contains that data.

■ **Analysis of the data already processed with a focus on the assumptions of the initial planning**. Understanding the behavior of the public in the event will take place from the comparison of certain variables in the previous phases of extraction and processing. It is possible for graphs and tables to demonstrate the behavioral patterns present at that time, according to the needs and/ or preference of the professional who will conduct the intelligence extraction in the next phase.

- **Extracting intelligence** is the phase that will use the data, their relationships, causes and effects to determine the behavior of the public and understand when this behavior was favorable and when it worked against the needs and possibilities of the event itself. That final phase will also consider other conditioning factors of the event that may have affected the behavior of the participants, such as the external influences that can affect the numbers visiting the event, or internal influences, such as infrastructure difficulties. Correlating the information that the data present with the reality experienced by the public of an event is an exercise that will be subjective to some extent, but it is necessary to avoid misinterpretation of the cold numbers drawn from the data without considering external variables.

Research[2] conducted by MPI (Meeting Professionals International), with event organizers, shows the most cited event data uses for the decision-making process of future events:

- **Metrics**. Usage. Ease of use. Value to the event. Ease of integration. Attendee engagement. Content satisfaction. Costs. Attendance. Attendee demographics. Successes. Failures. Room pickup. Post-event sentiment. Attendee experience. App adoption. Website visits. Downloads. Logins. Open rates. Traffic flow near technology deployment. QR code usage. Social media statistics. Attendance history. Thoughts and feelings. Views. Leads. Registration patterns. Sales and size of virtual audience.

- **Methods**. Reports from specific software companies (Registration. Mobile app. Networking. Member management. CRM, etc.) Attendee surveys. Budget review. Appreciative inquiry meetings. Post-mortems. Comparison of technologies by attendee demographic. Radio frequency identification (RFID). Year-over year graphs. Centralization. Session tracking. Audience response systems and testimonials.

- **Actions**. Build on successes. Change/grow usage of tool or technology. Make history comparisons. Share data with venue. Evaluate speakers. Select session topics based in attendee preferences. Determine ROI. Negotiate with venues. Choose event locations. Analyze trends. Determine areas of improvement. Track lessons learned. Adjust room sizes. Re-evaluate food and beverage selections. Share with sales department. Personalize contact with attendees. Anticipate attendance. Plan Internet bandwidth needs. Select suppliers and allocate future resources.

7

Continued engagement

Engagement with all the stakeholders (from the attendees to sponsors, supporters, partners and suppliers) is a factor that all event organizers should consider more strongly. In addition, they should consider such engagement in a different timeline, that is, consider not only each event, but also all of them together over time.

One of the most important points to observe in building engagement is that the work necessary to establish a relationship with any public does not need to be restricted to only a single event (nor it should be). It is simpler, cheaper and more profitable to nurture a relationship already established so that this lasts for a longer time, than to end it, just to build it again at some future time.

In the final stage of an event comes the opportunity to solidify and strengthen the relationship with the public through a series of simple measures, such as:

- Sharing information about the event that came to an end;

- Inviting the participants to give their opinion about the event

- Allowing and encouraging networking among visitors to the event

- Providing commercial benefits to those who maintain continued relationship with your event, such as loyalty rebates, membership facilities and advantages in future events.

There are several types of actions that can help to create a continued relationship. However, currently three stand out as bringing the best results, while being easy to measure:

1 Stimulate the feeling in your audience that they are special – VIPs. Create special offers and advantages for those who relate to you. Examples of these are gifts, discounts, special offers, promotions in your communication channels, etc. The important thing here is to create a sense of belonging, as those people who feel recognized and valued will become your ambassadors – they will tell their friends and acquaintances about you, spreading your message and events.

2 Use activities in social. Almost everyone today is on social media, so the activities of your event that you promote through social media should certainly bring great results. Always remember that it is important to give your audience the chance not only to interact with you through social media, but also to let them see themselves in your channels. Photos, videos, short interviews – all this creates great engagement, enhancing your actions in social media.

3 Creation of qualified leads through engagement actions. In order to achieve the best results, focus on creating engaging content that has high value to your specific public. Make your message important before, during and after your event, keeping yourself on the radar of your audience all the time. This creates a greater understanding of the value you have to offer, naturally attracting the most appropriate audience to your interests, which of course also reflects in generating more qualified and effective leads.

Tip	Description
Tracking results	Your communication actions in social media will generate visits to a landing page, hot site or event website (and even specific apps – with special offers). Establishing KPIs, tools and metrics for monitoring in the initial planning stages of the event, as well as their possible adaptation and/or correction due to the event dynamics allows the constant and immediate real-time measurement of the actions developed in the pre-, trans- and post-event phases of the event.
Interaction with the brand of the event	The frequency or amount of interaction of the participants with the event on the social media constitutes the metric resulting from the visits mentioned above. The set, frequency and recurrence indicate the most relevant results, creating a series of parameters that will allow the construction of history of actions, and improvement of the communication and interaction performance strategy.
Actions towards followers	We must always follow the attitudes of participants in social media. Sharing messages or conversations move performance and results. Here co-creation manifests itself in a more obvious and important way. Observe, measure and respond to the concerns and needs of the stakeholders involved – this is the key to the successful use of modern communication technologies in organizing events.
Attention to entries	In the digital world, it is possible to measure everything. Watch out for filling registrations and monitoring them. Encourage strongly the public to fill in the registration as they interact with the brand of the event, offering exchange of relevant content, unique possibilities of interaction between the public, gifts and promotions. Interact and innovate routinely. Detailed registrations allow the customization of services and information, enabling event organizers to offer to the public "a unique, special and custom event" almost customized for each participant.
Identify and seduce opinion leaders	Messages and interactions make the organic expansion of the mesh of social networking possible. Evangelizers or ambassadors (powerful partners who deserve special attention, as they influence large number of people) enhance the process. The opposite aspect also makes it possible to identify detractors (those who criticize the event, and understand their complaints), allowing event organizers to take actions to mitigate the potential problems caused by them. That is possible both in groups (according to the type of complaints), and at individual level (with those with greater power of impact or influence exercised on their own network of followers.)

Table 7.2: What is vital to measure on social networks?

Source: Innovation Insider. Layout adapted by authors.

It is essential and critical not to lose connections established during an event. Once participants leave an event, create conditions and give them reasons to stay in touch with you. As seen in Table 7.2, there are several ways to achieve this. However, bear in mind that you should aim to keep it almost personal, making each individual of your audience feel important and unique – the success of continued relationship depends upon it. Above all, never forget that everything can (and should) be measured for further evaluation. To that end, the key is to be clear about what you should see regarding the KPIs established in the planning phase, in order to get the most useful intelligence.

In this sense, social media have a key role as communication and marketing tools, by helping build and maintain relationships with public of events. *Innovation Insider*[3] presents five tips on how to succeed with those initiatives (Table 7.2):

It is possible to extend the event life cycle with after-event content. This also gives greater value to your attendees and helps to convince the audience to come to the next edition. Among the most desired takeaway materials is the slide deck, or speakers' presentation deck. Get prior approval from your speakers and share the decks with your attendees. They also appreciate sharing photos, videos, post at the event website or blogs and other platforms.

■ Acknowledgements

A few days after the end of the event, thank the participants and other stakeholders by email, making this a pleasant experience: we suggest you include photos, send additional material, etc. Moreover, use your communication channels such as your website and social media to thank your audience, both the audience in general and specific people or companies. Especially in social media, thanks made after an event tend to generate great impact, as each person or company officially recognized in its communication channels tend to advertise the fact, for canvassing image gains for themselves, starting from your communication.

It is necessary to collect and analyze information on the evaluation of the event by the stakeholders, generating complete and detailed management reports, as discussed below. There are numerous ways to get ratings; the following are the ones most used at present:

- Polls
- Surveys
- Quizzes

■ Reports

The references and metrics defined when planning are analyzed in detail in a range of sector and global reports, such as:

a) Board - receives general and detailed view of the administrative, sales and finance, addressing:

- Expenses and revenues estimated and actual;
- Participants (expected, confirmed and paying ones, statements, results of satisfaction survey)
- Disclosure – impacts, paid media and spontaneous monitoring of social media, and so on;
- ROI, etc.

b) Sponsors – analyze the impact and results of all actions from the point of view of spomsors, demonstrating mainly:

- Brand exposure
- Translation value
- Creating a relationship with the public
- ROI.

c) Marketing – includes all the marketing gains of the event, such as:

- Number of affected people
- Comparative evolution of public profile
- Increase awareness of the brand of the event organizer
- Event recognition value
- Creation of long-term relationships
- ROE, Return On Engagement
- Creation of new business conditions
- Organizational evolution of the event.

d) Commercial – which analyzes the financial impact of the event:

- Global event billing
- Comparative billing evolution
- ROI, Return Over Investment

As a point of observation and analysis, currently the KPIs most considered by event organizers are, in order of importance:

1 Number of attendees (91%)
2 Speaker feedback from delegates (60%))
3 Engagement levels (53%)
4 Time spent at event (35%)

  5 Brand affinity (35%)

  6 Other (23%)

Many professionals in the area still face problems in establishing a safe and effective method of calculating the ROI for events. However, according to Stevens[4], calculating ROI is easy and it can be truly simple. She suggests that among the objectives of the event, you should set one primary objective and two secondary ones and make them as specific as possible. Below are the most common ones:

- Achieving a ROI
- Building awareness
- Closing sales, signing contracts or generating RFPs
- Conducting market research
- Entering a new market
- Gathering new prospects for the database
- Generating qualified sales leads
- Influencing the press or financial community
- Introducing a new product
- Recruiting, educating, or motivating distribution partners or new employees
- Retaining current customers, penetrating current accounts
- Supporting your industry or community

Measuring ROI

The Holy Grail for many marketers is ROI. However, what is the best way to get at that metric? There are three common approaches to measuring the return on event marketing investments. All of them are useful, but they vary in their complexity.

The most complex approach to event ROI calculates the incremental margin contributed by the event. This method subtracts the incremental event expense from the incremental variable margin generated by the event. Then divide that number by the expense itself, as follows:

ROI = Gross Margin – Event Expense / Event Expense

To convert the event revenue to margin, you subtract out the variable cost of goods sold (COGS) and the direct cost of sales.

In some companies, it can be fairly challenging to identify the COGS and the direct sales costs. In that case, the best approach is to use revenue instead of margin in the equation, as follows:

ROI = Event Revenue – Event Expense / Event Expense

In both of these approaches to ROI, the result appears as a percentage. A zero indicates that the program broke even, and a negative number means a loss on the investment. If you spend $1 million to generate $1.2 million in new margin (or revenue), then you have achieved a 20% ROI.

The third approach is even simpler. For the numerator, use the sales revenue resulting from the event, and in the denominator put the total event expense, meaning all variable costs. The resulting number is in dollars, and represents the number of gross dollars returned for every incremental dollar invested.

About ROE (Return over Engagement), in Chapter 5 we studied this metric in depth. However, it is worth addressing here some main points one more time.

ROE has been gaining importance rapidly, mainly for its ability to bring about benefits through relationships generated and managed through the Internet, through which it is possible to leverage the opinion of the public for the benefit of our business.

Keep in mind that ROE demands the observation of four key points for the correct measurement of the return:

- Does it generate or enhance the participation of all stakeholders?
- Does it confirm its authority on the subject (events, in our case)?
- Does it generate influence for you and your business?
- Does it generate positive feeling regarding you and your business?

Last, but not least, do not forget that ROE demands continuous monitoring of all your online actions for proper measurement and analysis, so it is essential that you keep this monitoring work in constant operation.

Chapter summary

7

The appreciation of the event as an essential tool of corporate strategic planning happens when it becomes relevant part of their relationship with stakeholders. To increase the residual effect of the event and maximize the results, metrics for measurement and evaluation gain strength and importance in the corporate setting.

This chapter describes the importance of the post-event phase, not only from the aspect of measurement of immediate results, but also as a valuable intelligence generator for future improvements. We believe that one should not regard an event as something unique and individual, but as an action in a chain of many others, past and future, and therefore one should pay attention to this aspect, to be able to extract the maximum results from each action, always.

There are many important aspects presented, but the main point is to plan carefully each event, viewing it as a continuous timeline, so that each action connects to the previous and next, maximizing efforts and results.

Practical guide to the chapter

Here is the roadmap of the essential steps described in the chapter, for practical application in your daily activities:

Item	Description
Timing of the event	Position your current event within the set of your previous and subsequent events correctly, so that you can use that learning in the continuous improvement of your business.
Establishing KPIs	You should calculate your actions to generate some return, because it is essential to establish clear and easily measurable KPIs.
Measurement	All your actions should consider the established KPIs, and generate metrics to evaluate their performance (individually and globally), within the event.
Relevance of data	Capture enough data in order to allow the accurate measurement of performance of each action taken.
ROI	All actions must be measurable from the ROI (Return On Investment) standpoint, in order to allow appraisal and improvements in the profitability of the individual event, and of future ones.
ROE	Take Return On Engagement seriously: its importance is central to evaluating the performance of each event.

For further reading, questions for reflection and additional materials please go to the book's page at the publisher's website:

www.goodfellowpublishers.com/technologyandevents

Notes

1 Nesvig, Ben. How Second Screen Technology Is Revolutionizing Events. Available at http://blog.socialtables.com/2015/02/02/second-screen-technology-revolutionizing-events. [09 May 2015]

2 The State of Event Technology Adoption. MPI, 2015. Available at https://www.mpiweb.org/docs/default-source/research-and-reports/technology-adoption-report_v2.pdf?sfvrsn=2. [10 Jan 2016]

3 5 dicas do que é vital medir nas redes sociais. Available at innovationinsider.com.br/5-dicas-do-que-e-vital-medir-nas-redes-sociais/. [27 Oct 2015]

4 https://www.linkedin.com/grp/post/60415-6031204172618092545

8 What's next?

"Meeting planners HAVE to realize their job has transformed.
They've become community organizers."

Sarah Michel

Introduction

Talking about the future of technology in a printed book can be seen as a folly. Something impossible to do, because the speed of change in the virtual world often quickly shoots down any publication or post on this subject. It is essential that the long-term vision of the meeting planner also leads to understanding the current situation, coupled with possible trends.

It is necessary to reiterate here one more time that, given the growth by greater specialization of the professionals involved and the large volume of innovations and changes (synonymous with the virtual world), successful meeting planners must be generalists – conductors of their orchestras, formed by suppliers, to enthrall the audience of listeners (the participants), and please the sponsors. To obtain results and offer experiences that delight and involve, they must know and choose the best musicians and types of instruments to play each song. They will not play any of them, but they are solely responsible for the harmony, development and delivery of the final product that the group.

To be attentive to innovation, updated with the main trends and know the main products, services and market players are among the most valued qualities of this professional in the events market. This chapter will provide an overview of the scenario that now dawns, and present issues and concerns that the event professional should have.

Learning objectives

- Understanding that the future of technology in events points to a people-based approach, where experiences, and the continual reinforcement of relationship are kings.

- Seeing technology as an efficient tool for improving the next event.

To take the generalist approach, you should channel your attention away from the specific tools, apps, products and services available or yet to be launched. They are consequences. Instead, seek the causes, and consider these tools and apps as means to achieve your goals. Try to understand why they are on the market, the reasons and the main benefits that their creators want to pass on to users. In addition, identify clearly what and how they fit into the needs of your event and stakeholders. This way you will achieve sustainable development and significant gains. You will be a step ahead of your competitors and closer to your customers.

Attendees' expectations today go far beyond just getting access to static data. They also demand that event helps to build an interactive experience in social communities. The speed of relationships and business is no longer the same: everything is moving faster than ever and changes take place very quickly.

Technology is everywhere. For McTiffin[1], it…

…has always played a part in the industry by shaping how guests understand and network through events. Today, this technology plays an even bigger role, helping to streamline admission and operational processes as well as helping event organizers to market and interact with their attendees before and after the event.

Technology is becoming a key investment throughout the industry – but it is not just at work, it is part of our daily lives. That is why the crossover to events continues to be so rapid; technology plays an integral part and shapes how guests understand and network through events.

As events become more immersive experiences, technology has inevitably heightened the expectation of event attendees; basics like Wi-Fi, integrated lighting and sound systems are the norm and can be found in most places as part of the venue's offering. Our everyday use of technology, from Twitter and Instagram to event apps and ticket purchasing, makes technology the 'norm' on any event planner's list.

What has changed (and is constantly changing) are the desires, needs and demands to be close and to share experiences with loved ones and like-minded people. The energy, dynamism and agility that the virtual world provides has enabled the voice and wishes of individuals to be recognized and valued at the companies. That has revolutionized the commercial relationship format worldwide, once and for all! Moreover, participants of corporate events are seeking more and more networking, knowledge building, unique experiences and the best way to share it with others.

One thing for sure has not changed – the essence of the structure and dynamics of functioning of the market. After all, each of the companies working with products and services offline or online have as an essential objective to develop their offerings to meet specific consumer needs, thus finding a lucrative market niche.

The very strong growth in the use of smartphones has boosted the take-up of event apps and enabled improvements of efficiency and quality. Thus, the digital connection and interaction between all stakeholders as well as their dependency on these applications grow. The massive amount of data generated is also diverse and can be widely used in events. Despite this, event apps still are used relatively little, but the trend is towards and increasing awareness of their importance by event planners. As well as their use in real time, they will strategically empower the event on several fronts (membership, information hub, communication, measurement, community building, engagement, and so on.)

As 87% of consumers consider that live events are more effective than commercials in helping them to understand a product and service (for EMI/ Mosaic EventTrack 2015), events will continue to be a relevant strategic tool. Thus, if you understand what your active and prospective participants and sponsors of your events want, where they want to get it and why, you will be well equipped to choose how to do it (see Figure 4.1). By doing that, the best suppliers can help you structure and execute what is necessary to exceed the expectations of your target audience. As simple as that! Be open to listen, read and learn more about a variety of issues, and make a habit out of it.

Participants increasingly visual and moved by emotion

The essence and the absolute focus of meeting planners have always been towards the consumer. The difference now is to understand those and other changes in order to provide what they seek from the convergence, impacts and demands of the offline and online worlds. The best and most powerful activity that organizers can have is to focus on the needs and the objectives to be achieved, and only then to find the technology that they can use, and thus find and hire the best provider.

Consumers' emotional involvement in the ownership of material goods is growing more and more, creating a strong impact on the delivery that consumers expect from companies. To Rencher[2]:

> People today have greater affinity with moments than with material goods. Just think of our feeds on Instagram. What is that? Nothing more than people seeking and sharing experiences. That is what brands need to

8

understand. We are no longer in the business of selling products: we are in the business of selling experiences.

To attract attention and engage the participant, the social character of the event and the interaction between the event and the participant becomes increasingly important. To achieve their engagement, events that stand out are those that stimulate and value different forms of networking among participants. Among the face-to-face ones, coffee breaks or networking sessions between lectures are growing in terms of popularity. The event app offers tools that play a key role as continuous networking platforms, covering all stages of the event. The role of the meeting planner in the success of the event is increasing in terms of intelligence and strategy, given the endless combinations of options that can stimulate engagement and networking through apps and social media.

It is already possible to note the growth of animation and motion in content produced for events. It seems that demand for experiential event will continue to grow, inspire and promote music and entertainment for brand experience on events.

Several surveys and studies confirm the increase in consumer appreciation for images, photos and videos, as the testimonial by Newton[3]:

The biggest trend and opportunity we see in the sector is around the creation and use of video as a creative form of communication. Video for business communication has been steadily growing and has been brought to attention by Forbes – among others – whose 2010 Insights report "Video in the C-Suite" found that executives like video a lot."

Social media that use them, like YouTube and Instagram, confirm that trend, as does the observed greater impact of the messages that have videos or photos, to the detriment of those that only have text. In addition, the attraction is greater when the appeal involves emotion and calls for sharing it. In events, it is possible to see that fact in many ways, such as the search for set designs and alluring surroundings, changes in themes, the search for creativity and activities that promote meeting and networking.

Those born in each generation have particular characteristics. Try to understand what those characteristics are. That will bring direct benefits to your event, which should offer services and products tailored to the specific needs of that audience, such as the Millennials or Generation X:

It is all about connection and unique experiences in 2016. For example, pop culture continues to be en vogue and millennials that are entering the industry, are bringing fresh, new advancements for connection that go beyond technology and more towards inclusion and purpose-driven events. However, that also engages and excites event attendees at the push of a button.[4]

Chapter 5 provides a wealth of information that will help you in this task. It is worth mentioning again that participants prefer digital content rather than printed one and among their most significant demands are more interactive and engaging activities. They also want to help in shaping the experience to and at the event.

Micro	Macro
A private social network around one event. Yours.	A social network for everybody
Its purpose is to be hyper relevant to attendees of an event.	Its purpose is to give information from around the world.
Focus on communities; information and conversations are highly relevant only to that community.	The world is their community which drives excessive noise and low local relevancy
When you are part of social community at an event, there is no need to 'friend', 'follow' or 'hashtag'.	Heavily dependent on 'friend', 'follow', 'like' to drive sensibility in online conversations

Figure 8. 1: Micro vs macro event based networks

Source: Patwardhan, Neil. Macro vs Micro Networks. The Rise of Micro Networks in the Events Industry

Micro vs. macro networking

The last few years have shown technology breaking various barriers and stimulating meeting planners to create experiential events and position them as an efficient channel for interaction of companies and their consumers. All signs indicate that this is already a strong trend for the future.

In addition, great experiences between attendees and brands are synonymous of connection, engagement and, importantly, of staying very relevant to each other. So far, the focus is on events-based communities. That is where technology and mobile are working hard together to help everyone the most. For Patwardhan[5], "There is an interesting trend in the world today; humanity is starting to grow weary of the issues above and psychologically reverting back to smaller more intimate communities." Figure 8.1 shows comparison between a micro and macro event based networks.

8

He has a strong argument when the subject is the importance and value of networking, as well as the effectiveness of small groups. After all, the smaller the group, the more likely its members can get stronger and lasting ties. Figure 8.2 shows four relevant aspects that help meeting planners to understand the path to build great networking and meaningful conversations. Technology and event apps are the best tools to allow attendees to stay intimately connected with each other pre, during and post event.

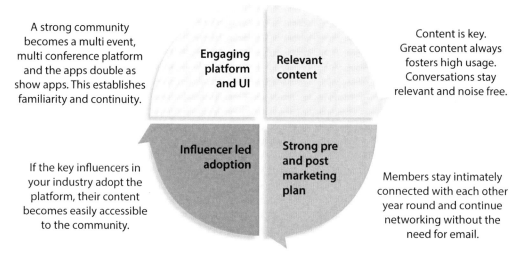

A strong community becomes a multi event, multi conference platform and the apps double as show apps. This establishes familiarity and continuity.

Engaging platform and UI

Relevant content

Content is key. Great content always fosters high usage. Conversations stay relevant and noise free.

If the key influencers in your industry adopt the platform, their content becomes easily accessible to the community.

Influencer led adoption

Strong pre and post marketing plan

Members stay intimately connected with each other year round and continue networking without the need for email.

Figure 8.2: How does a private community become successful?

Source: Patwardhan, Neil. *The Rise of Micro Networks in the Events Industry.* Layout adapted by authors

Second screen, iBeacons, wearables and IoT

As time goes by, apps are becoming more effective than ever which creates new opportunities for event organizers and sponsors. The demand for mobility drives cloud computing, where it is possible to access and share virtual data and resources remotely, enabling innovations like the IoT – Internet of Things, explained below.

With the gathering, storage and processing of data in almost infinite volume, Marketing has to deal with new, increasing, extremely complex and volatile premises and variable. They are difficulties that may also bring advantages, such as reducing costs, improvement in traffic and data security and expediting cooperative working in teams geographically distant from one another. The available wealth of data demands greater professionalism and speed in the definition of metrics and reports that one should use to understand, predict, provide and even exceed the needs and desires of today's consumers.

The technology known as iBeacon allows micro-location of participants via Bluetooth from their smartphones with iBeacon devices installed at the venue of the event. It can obtain information from and transmit it to the organizer and to the participant (two-way communication). Generated in real time, messages, improvements and necessary changes now have agility that was not possible before. This also allows customization and optimization of the user experiences.

More than ever, the second screen will continue to be actively used by Internet users and participants of events for many more years to come. The connectivity gap between the offline and online worlds is becoming narrower through the rapid growth of mobile penetration, which goes far beyond the use of smartphones. The use of the second screen at events increases engagement and interaction in real time, creating endless possibilities for all stakeholders. Moreover, this affects everyone and everything: hardware and software manufacturers, brands, advertisers and consumers.

Technology is and will continue to be the biggest driver for events. Thus, organizers turn their attention to the use of event apps and apps for mobile devices as a successful strategy. There is already congestion in the segment, with lots of options, highlighting the difficulty for meeting planners to know which to choose and how to find the best platform for their events.

In today's complex world, what attracts is simplicity, mobility, practicality, the desire to interact with those who have the same affinity and ease to find what you want quickly. Instead of reading and typing, simply touching the screen can get the answers to the needs. The quest for simplification and flexibility is endless. Experts are already developing voice-operated tools. The Internet of Things, described in Chapter 3, and wearables are revolutionizing the concept of interaction between human beings and computers.

Wearable computing...

> ...*facilitates a new form of human-computer interaction comprising a small body-worn computer (e.g. user-programmable device) that is always on and always ready and accessible. In this regard, the new computational framework differs from that of hand held devices, laptop computers and personal digital assistants (PDAs). The "always ready" capability leads to a new form of synergy between human and computer, characterized by long-term adaptation through the constancy of the user-interface.*

> *A wearable computer is a computer that is subsumed into the personal space of the user, controlled by the user, and has both operational and interactional constancy i.e., is always on and always accessible. Most notably, it is a device always with the user. The user can always enter commands and execute a set of such entered commands, and the user can do so while walking around or doing other activities.*[6]

8

One of the features of a wearable is that it is 'part' of the user's body, and is in constant operation, dispensing with the need to turn it on or off. Some of the most popular applications are Google Glass, smart glasses, which have a small device at the top of one of the lenses and run on Android operating system; smartwatches; wristbands (bracelets that measure the distance travelled and work with an app to track desired goals of physical activity); straps keeping track of heartbeats, etc. Each one of them can bring opportunities for partnerships, business and profits for the event.

One of the advantages that the virtual world provides for businesses is the valuable and abundant amount of information and data on consumer behavior, besides creating new advertising formats and dissemination and customization of contacts. Meeting planners will have the challenge of collecting data, and learning about the best way to analyze them. The demand for deeper data and analytics about attendees' experience will continue to increase.

The migration of the Internet from desktops and notebooks to mobile phones (see more in Chapters 2 and 6) now moves into a new frontier – ubiquitous computing – in which the connection is extended in various ways, such as wearables, automobiles, in refrigerators (control stock and offer online connection for purchases) and other household appliances. Many brands have begun to explore the new opportunities for contact and building relationships with consumers that this new reality offers.

Apps

This whole scenario catapulted apps to the top of the priority list of the events market. However, it also brought difficulties for meeting planners to understand the new dynamics of the market and know how to separate the wheat from the chaff, and to choose suppliers, applications and uses. Among the main event app selection criteria (see Chapter 4) are the features offered, ease of implementation and usability, flexibility, customization possibilities, reliability and technical support.

Most of the growing trends relate to mobile apps use: event app, more use of images and videos, gamification, etc. It is also about wearables, push-notification and IoT, metrics and measurement. The insights of Corbin Ball[7], a renowned even technology expert, for 2016 and years to come, are that:

- Virtual reality (VR) and augmented reality (AR) will grow, especially for product demo, venue inspection, virtual meeting, etc. It also will flourish in second screen technology and mobile engagement tools.

- As the next generation of smartphones, when combined with mobile event apps, can be trackable, this will provide precious data for organizers, that can allow customized marketing content based on participants' needs.

- Images and videos will dominate event social channels.

- Wearables, beacon technology and the Internet of Things will connect people and objects, provide unprecedented convenience and efficiency and transform attendee experience.

Thus, hardware and software continue to refine and introduce new features with the focus on the participant's experience. For that, they will need to evolve to be able to capture and analyze information from participants in volume, quality and scale never seen before and to deliver relevant data, and in real time.

This scenario only reinforces the importance of intelligence and the expertise of meeting planners in the identification and analysis of this information that will enable them to know the audience. Even with the growth of virtual events, Ball believes that face-to-face meetings will remain because:

The opportunities for networking, brainstorming, and relationship building are usually far greater at face-to-face events than online. For an exhibitor, it is often the best way to meet so many qualified buyers in such a short time. For buyers, it is a great chance to meet vendors of interest – all together in one location, categorized and mapped for your choosing. Meetings provide a vastly richer, more targeted, and more focused learning experience than nearly any virtual meeting.

The search for engagement strengthens gamification, found in an increasing number of meetings. It produces many options in terms of ultimate takeaways, a lot of fun and engagement. User experience is getting more sophisticated (with new ways of touch control, voice integration, and so on) and users are demanding applications with new and simpler ways of interfacing, requiring the integration of event app to other platforms, unifying the user experience.

The appreciation of the event app as one of the most valued items at the event is also increasing, due to the high return that sponsors get. The apps that will stand out, will offer full integration with management systems, besides the high quality of the user experience.

8

Sustainability

The consensus among experts is that sustainability is already one of the drivers of several changes in the events market, such as delivery of key event information (calendar bookings + event details) in a paper-free guest experience. Many of the changes affect and stimulate solutions in the event apps and in specific software formats. They also claim that the practice will spread further every year, gaining more fans and intensifying its use among those who have already adopted sustainable practices in their events.

Box 8.1: Giving Day

#GivingTuesday (www.givingtuesday.org) is a global cam-paign initiated in the United States in 2012. It already reaches 80 countries.

The first edition in Brazil happened in 2013 with the name in Portuguese of #diadedoar. The following year, it reached 20 million people in the country, with 400 partners. In 2015, it had more than 1,180 partners. The movement promotes the sustainability of civil society organizations; it encourages solidarity among people, through donations and philanthropy during the period of year-end celebrations.

The campaign stimulates culture and actions such as donating or raising funds for social organizations through the collective effort of individuals, companies and civil society organizations.

To disseminate the idea, it promotes campaigns on social networks and multiplies the message through the media and an interactive website. To Pechlivanis (from Umbigo do Mundo – an important partner in the 2015 campaign): "To carry out a mobilization, we need to bring people together and show the strength that this group has. To bring people together, we must make them aware that they are able to make changes. The truth is that people do not want new discourses. They want practical and reliable solu-tions, especially amid the crisis of values that we are living ".

ABCR (the Brazilian Association of Collecting Resources) is responsible for its organi-zation. The 2015 campaign addressed a wider public. Among the outstanding results obtained, Vergueiro (Executive Officer) highlights: "the communication actions of people who are not part of our network, promoting the date in their own groups (...). We cannot quantify this result. However, we are able to quantify it for the videos, materials, posts by bloggers, with over 500,000 followers, artists with millions of followers, who called attention to the #diadedoar, without a more targeted work aimed at them."

Compared to the previous year, the campaign grew almost seven times on Twitter (131 million impressions), doubled the number of photos posted on Instagram (1.1 million of 'likes') and 430,000 people impacted on Facebook.

Among the actions made, we highlight the online activation carried out by Fundação Amor Horizontal (a foundation that seeks to facilitate links between causes and donors) that promoted the collaboration with several Brazilian celebrities. They posted on social media an outstretched hand containing a painted heart. Technology companies promoted another great action focused on multipliers. The NGO received an award for the most creative campaign. Fifty of them registered.

This campaign achieved the breadth, scope and results by focusing their actions on the use of social media. When these receive intelligent and well-directed strategy, they are powerful digital tools that respond quickly and efficiently.

Sources: http://www.mobilizaconsultoria.com.br/joao-paulo-vergueiro-dia-de-doar-amplia-seu-alcance-e-impacto-no-brasil/

http://www.diadedoar.org.br/

http://www.mobilizaconsultoria.com.br/joao-paulo-vergueiro-dia-de-doar-amplia-seu-alcance-e-impacto-no-brasil

Hybrid events: a new generation of events

Following market developments and new trends will make you aware of new event formats. When receiving invitations or checking event information, analyze them and notice all the details such as event type, format, theme, speakers, sponsors, venue, and suppliers. Create your mental database. Make comparisons. You are bound to come across rich examples in terms of information and to expand your knowledge in various aspects.

The MPI Meeting Outlook 2015[8] report shows a growth trend. Organizers expect a 3.1% growth on virtual events, in comparison to 2.4% for live events. Although only one out of four organizers use hybrid, they expect to increase the use of virtual (59%) and hybrid events (61%). The reasons for the growth are due to the pursuit of simplicity and its cost effectiveness.

Among the innovations that deserve greater attention are hybrid events. Since 2000, Vanneste has been leading the hybrid events scenario, much more on the practical side than on the theory side. The evolution of The FRESH Conference over the years traces a timeline of the evolution on hybrid events and sets a beacon on the future of this exciting event typology (please check the boxes in Chapters 1 and 3). Box 8.2 presents his interesting points of view about the evolution and future of hybrid events.

8

Box 8.2: Evolution and future of hybrid events

Hybrid networking

By Maarten Vanneste

As networking grows in terms of importance in association conferences, we need to look at how we can get together the online and the on-site audience. As a webcast has serious delays that can vary from 5 to 50 seconds depending on your location and device, no dialogue is possible when 100,000 people are watching. In 2015, Skype maximum groups were limited to 10 persons on video and 25 on audio.

From past until today

At FRESH 2013, we introduced three laptops with head-sets on site in Copenhagen. They had different links to Skype, GoToMeeting, and another meeting format. All of them with participants online with (almost) no delay, so a real conversation was possible. On the first day, a few on-site participants were able to chat with the online participants.

On the second day, laptops were transferred to the hall just outside the meeting room. Several on-site partici-pants had a conversation with the online participants. A real hybrid networking happening when an online participant, introduced himself to another online participant and/or an on-site participant. In the same edition, a Skype meeting screen was located next to the stage on a TV screen, allowing all participants to see the faces of those who used video and to know about the online participants.

Also at FRESH 2013, a student walked around with a tablet and a headset during breaks. On-site participants would see online partici-pants and vice versa. If someone was recog-nized, the headset was handed to the on-site participant for a short conversation.

In the next edition, beta-technology was used, allowing up to 30 people to partici-pate in a video call. It became a real break-out room, where people had conversations (without delays!) and when some found out they were from the same city, they could make an appointment to meet.

The future

As with everything in technology, things will get better, faster and less expensive. Networking will move forward, too. Skype and GoTo-meeting facilities will have great improvements. I guess that it will become very easy to join a conference remotely by using your laptop.

The maximum and minimum number of participants can be set by the organizer and the group will be split when it becomes too big and merge into small ones, based on subcategories set by the organizer, and again, by a sub-subcategory if the group is becoming too large again. Then, a conference may start with one main group called FRESH than split into two groups: 'Learning' and 'Networking'. As soon as the networking group becomes bigger, attendees will be asked to choose between staying there or moving to a smaller (Learning, Gamification, and so on).

Technology will help online participants to find other online participants based on their profile (language, location, and so on). The current appointment systems used at tradeshows and conferences, will allow online people to meet on-site people. Robot participants in wheels or on a table will help both online and on-site to feel as close as possible to a real meeting.

The online moderator

From past until today

At FRESH 12, we started with one online moderator that during breaks filled the 'empty' timeslots with interviews of key people for the individual online participants. She was in the back of the room, had one camera close to her and conducted standing interviews. The background of the moderator was the set.

The next year we had a small stage with two stools on the side of the meeting room and several moderators would take turns doing seated interviews, again during breaks. They also could introduce the next speaker, or explain what was going on and how to get involved during discussions. For the following edition, we built a real stage with furniture and its own back wall, light, and a separate video/sound desk with two technicians and a person to 'powder' the faces of interviewees.

A social media moderator sat close to pass on messages to the online moderator. The fourth year had a complete TV studio with a counter, a male and female presenter. The double glass back wall showed the set of the plenary room in the background.

The future

For the online moderator I see possibilities and challenges: The possibilities lie in the less expensive, easier and more reliable ways to make the connection possible. There is no need for the online moderator to be onsite. A limited number of tasks can be done from home… The main question is about the role of the online moderator.

8

■ Does he (or she) really need to create more content for the participants to watch and consume? Like talking or conducting interviews during the breaks.

■ Or should he (or she) focus on the engagement, activation of the online participants. I would like to experiment with the latter! Is learning losing importance in conferences and is networking gaining importance? So how can an online moderator better help people to connect, as they are both online and on-site attendees?

Only sending a tweet or a question in the chat box is not enough. The correct answer is to enable them to find people and to make appointments, to discuss in small groups, etc. If the job was well done, a significant number of online participants will have met new people, enjoy their company and, maybe, even start a future project or business.

The online participant

From past until today

One of the most amazing experiments so far was with the 'double participant' at FRESH 14. Evelien Aernaudts wanted to be at FRESH, but could not because of her very young baby. We used a double robot and during the entire conference, she was present full time (except for a few small 'baby' breaks). The double has a base of two wheels that can drive and turn. On that base stands an extendable pole that holds an iPad at about 1.30M to 1.70m high. Evelien stayed home behind her laptop using a head set. She could drive the double around in Copenhagen from where she was in Belgium.

She could see over her laptop what the camera of the iPad would see. She could hear in her headset everything in front of the iPad microphone. Connected through that 'robot', she was able to see presentations, be present at the breaks, talk to individuals and even be on stage to make a presentation.

More recently at IMEX America 2015, Evelien again was virtually present using a little robot. This time she was representing her company as a group stand. She stood on a high table in a Kubi (a stand that holds an iPad that can turn up, down, left and right). In other words, she could look around. Evelien made about 30 appointments with Hosted buyers and talked to them about the seven innovative devices on the table.

The future

Those two devices are quite recent, but more are being developed as we speak. Things will get less expensive and better, so more of virtual presence supporting robotics will be coming to the market. That will make it easier and funnier for an online attendee to walk around and meet people at a conference without actually being there. However, this will never replace being there in person.

The remote speaker

From past until today

Sometimes it is difficult or expensive to get a speaker at a conference. In some cases, a speaker may decide to stay home for some reason. It is rather simple to get him on the screen for a live but remote presentation. Although a live speaker can be much more engaging on-site than when he (or she) sits behind a webcam.

Remote speaking will therefore never fully replace the real presence. It will add possibilities and create opportunities, but not replace real speakers from a real stage in front of a real audience.

The future

More hybrid meetings will be hub-based and every hub will have its 'local' speakers, and some of them will be allowed to speak plenarily (for all the hub audiences). As technology and production improve, the speaker will feel more and more the influential presence of the audience(s).

Webcasting and recording

From past until today

Is the recording of sessions a form of hybrid? Maybe it is on the edge, but once recording is happening, the step to a webcast becomes pretty simple. Just feed the video and sound into a streaming device or a streaming laptop and for a really affordable price you can now webcast to an unlimited virtual audience. Recording for on-demand viewing creates great value, and if you are able to sell tickets for that content, it can become a new revenue stream.

In the past, webcasting would take a whole lot of equipment and extra lines for bandwidth. Today, webcast has become easier and cheaper as the equipment fits in the palm of your hand. Then, what will come next?

8

The future

Webcasting is now entering the smartphone space. Cameras are now in the hands of the participants. For a while, some will feel compelled to webcast whatever they want, but that will not last. However, as technology evolves, cameras will get inexpensive whereas technology will become more sophisticated. Imagine a conference where every room has five small, Wi-Fi connected and (all day lasting) battery powered mini cameras that, location-based, synchronize into one web stream. They follow the speaker automatically and switch between speaker and slides. The system ecognizes what is on the screen and switches to the slide, as soon as the speaker talks about something that is on the screen.

Or then maybe five parallel streams and the remote participant can walk smoothly from camera position to camera position. As smartphones can stitch pictures together to make a panorama or sphere, this can be done with video too, based on multiple super high definition cameras with a minimal overlap.

The future of hybrid events

It is to be expected that the more people see the possibilities and understand the dynamics of hybrid events, the more it will increase their use to allow for meetings that otherwise would not be possible (see Box 1.1 in Chapter 1). To create new meetings and add more participants is probably the greatest advantage of hybrid events. Hybrid meetings will also be more complex to organize, involve more professionals and will take additional time and extra budget.

However, before things cool down again, they will heat up more. The tools and technology will become more available, bigger, faster, easier and cheaper. Venues will try to build it into every room before they find out that this does not work for everybody, since each client has specific needs. However, as long as there are reasons for people not to come to a conference, remote participation can be an option.

For the FRESH conference, I expect the development of the hub concept in the short run. It will be about connecting several countries with good and dynamic video, voting, and co-creation of systems. In addition, it will have (small) groups following the conference remotely with their own local speakers, some of which will be speaking locally and others plenarily to the FRESH conference and all its pods. An ongoing set of innovations will be shared with participants for them to experience and judge, based on that experience, what, when and how to use hybrid events for their own needs.

The future of meetings will be more hybrid than ever for reasons of cost-saving, ROI increasing, enabling of otherwise impossible meetings, travel bans because of natural and other causes, etc. FRESH conference will be the ultimate platform for experimenting and testing. I look forward to discovering it with you.

Maarten Vanneste is CEO of ABBIT Meeting Innovators, author of Meeting Architecture and founder of the Meeting Design Institute and the FRESH conference

Sponsorship and online advertisements

The event app revolution has affected the way that sponsors relate to events and participants, whether by increasing the possibilities of interaction, or in the time expansion that brands can affect consumers:

> *Sponsors do not deny the importance of a booth at an event, or even the physical exposure of your brand, but it is no longer enough. The digital medium allows sponsors to create activation campaigns for their brands from before the event itself, and when it actually happens they can interact even with those who are not present at the stand. The app in itself is already a highly valuable source of data for the sponsors[9].*

The trend is that the relationship of the participants to the event and brands has also become closer and personalized. The event app can have a key role in this task, when it becomes the main bridge of information between the parties and a strong driver to bring more value to the participant's experience by improving processes and strengthening the message of brands.

The technology enables sponsors to expand the range of options and visibility exponentially, increasing the possibilities and creating new spaces and formats to sponsor in events. Mobile internet advertising has shown strong and consistent growth, changing consumers' way of living and disrupting business models.

The tools for the generation and analysis of data will provide increasingly accurate information to guide investments and actions for both the organizer and the sponsors. In addition, they increase the chances of converting into profit investment made with technology. Advertising forms found in apps for events will continue to increase and vary according to companies. Meeting planners must seek to identify the interests of sponsors and participants and the most appropriate available advertising options for each case. The selected form should be the most appropriate to the profile of participants and most effective for sponsors. Among the options used are virtual storefronts, banners, sponsored ads in the middle of texts or on timelines (native advertising), push notifications (short advertising messages), random ads with advertorials profile, splash screens (displayed screen while charging app) and highlights on the exhibitors' list.

Meeting planners obtain the best results in attracting and retaining sponsors by establishing great partnership relationships, committing to those customers in achieving the expected results.

8

Others, but not less important

EMI/Mosaic EventTrack 2015[10] pointed out the increase in the importance of events in large corporations: 89% of them will integrate events and experiences more closely with wider corporate marketing and branding Initiatives (a rise of 8.5% from 2014).

Nowadays, there is the need to go physically to the conference to listen to experts. Attendees can watch the video at their best time and convenience or participate in a hybrid event. Besides these profound changes, some of the leading experts such as Corbin Ball believe that in person-event will remain. That is why content is much more about triggering interaction and engaging participants between themselves and with sponsors.

Although it is not a trend yet, Hilliard[11]'s opinion on the importance of innovation and creativity in events has all the components to be:

One change I hope to see is more variety within meetings and events. Most conferences I attend are mirror images of each other. No matter how much the word 'innovation' is thrown around, I see very little of it in our industry. I see different room sets, calls for more 'interaction', and uses of technology, but too many of these things end up just being gimmicky rather than meaningful differences. Until meeting and event professionals start focusing on people first and then building meetings and events around their differences and preferences, there will be no true innovation.

This and other chapters in this book show the profound changes caused by technology in the daily life of each one of us. The certainty is that they will continue to happen and permeate everything around us. The good news is that they have already been channeled to bring more intense and memorable meaning to personal and professional relationships.

Chapter summary

Participation in events is different from what it used to be, and the impact, relevance and experience that the participants demand from events have changed. Bevacqua[12]'s thoughts sums up the biggest trend for years to come:

If there was one common theme amongst all this palmistry, it is this: event planners should – and will – get a lot more in tune with attendee experience, use mobile and digital technologies both strategically and tactically in order to deliver more value and more entertainment at their events.

To surprise and attract, the meeting planner seeks innovative, differentiated and compelling solutions for which the technology has offered incredible tools that are constantly being renewed. The great insights and the key component of event marketing will be the data received from the combination of social media and event mobile applications. However, face-to-face events will still offer relationship and network building far greater than online events: "Meetings provide a vastly richer, more targeted, and more focused learning experience than nearly any virtual meeting."[13]

The relationship of the events market professionals with technology moves towards identifying opportunities to improve and strengthen ties between stakeholders. Everything points to the improvement of data management, which is now high in volume and real-time, driven by detecting the micro location of participants by iBeacons installed at the venue of the event. The second screen shows value as well as increasing the importance of and highlighting the need for integration of platforms and the possibilities of mass customization.

Practical guide to the chapter

Here is the roadmap of the essential steps described in the chapter, for practical application in your daily activities:

Item	Description
People-based approach	Everything is determined by the involvement and emotions of participants
Community	Stimulating networking at all stages of the event
Second screen	Identifying and highlighting networking opportunities with participants through the event app and social media
Event app	Choosing the most suitable to the needs of your event
Sustainability	Greening the event is one the most important issues
Hybrid event	Understanding their nature to use them efficiently
Sponsorship and mobile internet advertising	Knowing and using the new formats offered by technology
Micro localization and iBeacon	Studying and choosing the best application of this technology

For further reading, questions for reflection and additional materials please go to the book's page at the publisher's website:

www.goodfellowpublishers.com/technologyandevents

8

Notes

1   McTiffin, Gareth. Technology is an ever-changing landscape. http://engage-magazine.co.uk/blog-technology-is-an-ever-changing-landscape. [07 Jan 2016]

2   'Não podemos vender apenas produtos, temos que vender experiências'. Available at http://www.adnews.com.br/adobesummit/nao-podemos-mais-vender-apenas-produtos-temos-que-vender-experiencias 23 Mar 2016.

3   Newton, Alan. http://www.eventbrite.co.uk/blog/event-trends-2016/#sthash.0ySNLLMh.dpuf [07 Jan 2016]

4   Woodward, Melanie at http://www.eventbrite.co.uk/blog/event-trends-2016/#sthash.hkvNFrHh.dpuf [07 Jan 2016]

5   Patwardhan, Neil. Macro vs Micro Networks. The Rise of Micro Networks in The Events Industry. Available at http://www.corbinball.com/assets/MicroNetworks-Skoop.pdf

6   Mann, Steve. Keynote presented at 1998 International Conference on Wereable Computing – ICWC, Toronto, Canada. Available at http://wearcomp.org/wearcompdef.html.

7   7 Mobile apps predictions for meeting and events in 2016. QuickMobileMobile App Predictions 2016. [05 Jan 2016]

8   MPI Meeting OutlOOk Report 2015 http://www.mpiweb.org/Portal/Research/meetingsoutlook [08 Jan 2016]

9   O que esperar dos aplicativos para eventos em 2016. Relatório anual. Moblee. Available at http://blog.moblee.com.br/2016/01/relatorio-anual-o-que-esperar-dos-aplicativos-para-eventos-em-2016/ [18 Mar 2016]

10 http://www.eventmarketing.com/eventtrack-2015/ [06 Jan 2016]

11 Tyra Hilliard: Mentor, Hero and Educator. Available at http://meetgreen.com/2016/01/hero-tyra-hilliard/ [12 Jan 2016]

12 McTiffin, Gareth. Technology is an ever-changing landscape. http://engage-magazine.co.uk/blog-technology-is-an-ever-changing-landscape/ [06 Jan 2016]

13 Ball, Corbin. Ten Transformative Meeting Technology Trends for 2015. Available at http://www.corbinball.com/article2/35-ten-transformative-meetings-technology-trends-for-2015

Index